D0084269

Working with Qualitative Data

Working with Qualitative Data

William J. Gibson and
Andrew Brown

Los Angeles | London | New Delhi
Singapore | Washington DC

© William J. Gibson and Andrew Brown 2009

First published 2009

Apart from any fair dealing for the purposes of research or private study, or criticism or review, as permitted under the Copyright, Designs and Patents Act, 1988, this publication may be reproduced, stored or transmitted in any form, or by any means, only with the prior permission in writing of the publishers, or in the case of reprographic reproduction, in accordance with the terms of licences issued by the Copyright Licensing Agency. Enquiries concerning reproduction outside those terms should be sent to the publishers.

SAGE Publications Ltd
1 Oliver's Yard
55 City Road
London EC1Y 1SP

SAGE Publications Inc.
2455 Teller Road
Thousand Oaks, California 91320

SAGE Publications India Pvt Ltd
B 1/I 1 Mohan Cooperative Industrial Area
Mathura Road, Post Bag 7
New Delhi 110 044

SAGE Publications Asia-Pacific Pte Ltd
33 Pekin Street #02-01
Far East Square
Singapore 048763

Library of Congress Control Number 2008939442

British Library Cataloguing in Publication data

A catalogue record for this book is available from the British Library

ISBN 978-1-4129-4565-3
ISBN 978-1-4129-4566-0 (pbk)

Typeset by C&M Digitals (P) Ltd, Chennai, India
Printed by CPI Antony Rowe, Chippenham, Wiltshire
Printed on paper from sustainable resources

Mixed Sources
Product group from well-managed forests and other controlled sources
www.fsc.org Cert no. SGS-COC-2953
© 1996 Forest Stewardship Council
FSC

Contents

1 Introduction: qualitative data analysis in context   **1**

Introduction   1
What is qualitative data 'analysis' anyway?   2
Contextualized analysis   6
The notion of 'qualitative' in qualitative data analysis   7
Describing the research process   9
The relationship between theory and analysis   11
Some common areas of concern in relation to theory   12
The structure of the book   13
Recommended further reading   14

2 Theory, grounded theory and analysis   **15**

Introduction: the practice of theory   15
Theoretical concepts   17
Is one theory as good as another?   19
Characterizations of the role of theory   19
Top-down theory   20
    The example of critical discourse analysis   21
    Applying Fairclough's ideas to other empirical domains   22
    The relationship between forms of data and forms of theory   25
    The iterative nature of analysis and research practice   25
Bottom-up theory   26
    Key features of grounded theory   27
    An important criticism of grounded theory   29
Generalized theory practices   30
Concluding remarks   32
Recommended further reading   32

3 Engaging with literature   **33**

Introduction   33
The uses of literature   34
    Concept development   35
    Secondary sources of data   37
    Alternative analyses   37
    Directing theoretical sampling   37
    Validating theory   38
Literature searches   38
    Exploratory and systematic literature searches   38
    Focused literature searches   41
    Conducting literature searches   42
    Combining concepts in literature searches   43

Bibliographic databases 44
Concluding remarks 46
Recommended further reading 46

4 Research design 47

Introduction 47
'Research designs' vs. the research design process 47
Approaching the design of research 48
Research topics, concepts and questions 50
From words to concepts 50
From concepts to questions 51
From research questions to research plans 53
What kind of data is needed to answer a question? 54
A plan for gathering data 55
Triangulation 58
Ethics and research design 60
Ethical considerations in research design and data work 61
Research design and the analysis of data 63
Concluding remarks 64
Recommended further reading 64

5 Using documents in research 65

Introduction 65
Primary and secondary data 66
Choosing and working with documentary sources 67
Combining documentary and other empirical sources 69
Analyzing documents 70
Categorizing documents 72
Two examples of document categorization 72
Forms of documentary data 74
Digital, electronic and online 74
Newspapers 74
Diaries 76
Letters and other forms of communication 79
Photographs and other images 81
Concluding remarks 83
Recommended further reading 83

6 Generating data through questions and observations 84

Introduction 84
Asking questions 86
'Idealized' interview types 86
Interview structures in practice 90
The diverse character of data 92
Modes of interview 93
Interview analysis sheets 95
The organization of the interview setting 97

Contextualizing research 97
Narrative analysis 98
Examples of narrative analysis 98
Methodology and analysis in narrative approaches 99
Observation 100
Levels of structure in observational research 100
Participant and non-participant observation 102
Covert observation 104
Recording observational data 104
Analyzing observational data 106
Concluding remarks 107
Recommended further reading 108

7 Transcribing and representing data 109

Introduction 109
Analysis in transcription 110
Transcription as a guide to data 111
Transcription as analysis 111
Transcription and forms of data 112
Forms of transcription 113
Indexical transcription 114
Timeline transcription 114
Unfocused transcription 116
Focused transcription 120
Technology and transcription 123
Transcription and epistemology 124
Concluding remarks 125
Recommended further reading 125

8 Identifying themes, codes and hypotheses 127

Introduction 127
The concept of 'thematic analysis' 128
Critiques of thematic analysis 129
Distinctive features and resources in thematic analysis 130
Code 130
Coding and data 131
Apriori and empirical codes 132
Why and how do researchers develop codes? 133
Basic coding procedures 135
Creating and managing the code definitions 135
Splitting codes 136
Deleting or discontinuing codes 137
Code properties 137
Keeping a code log 137
Moving beyond individual codes: relational analysis 138
Code family 138
Hypotheses 139

Sub-codes and parent codes   142
Super codes   143
Concluding remarks   143
Recommended further reading   144

9   Images and texts   **145**

Introduction   145
Analyzing images: semiotic analysis   146
Key concepts in 'Saussurian' semiotic analysis   147
Critiques of semiotic forms of analysis   150
Analyzing written texts: rhetorical analysis   151
Key concepts in rhetorical analysis   152
Critiques of rhetorical analysis   157
Other forms of textual analysis   157
Concluding remarks   158
Recommended further reading   159

10   Video and audio data   **160**

Introduction   160
The character of audio and video data   160
When to use audio and video data   162
Analyzing audio and video recordings   162
Ethnomethodology and conversation analysis   163
Conversation analysis and the analysis of audio data   165
Exemplar: the evaluation of the professional practice of
primary school teachers   165
Two basic conversational maxims   167
The organization of topics   168
The process of analysis   169
A critique of conversation analysis   170
Gesture and the contextualization of talk   171
Implications of the analysis of gesture and other modes of
communication   172
Practicalities in the analysis of social interaction through video 173
Concluding remarks   175
Recommended further reading   175

11   Using technology   **176**

Introduction   176
CAQDAS   177
Code and retrieve functions   178
Theory-building functions   180
An example of theory building   180
Technology and collaborative analysis   181
Hypermedia and qualitative analysis   184
Linking different data representations   185
Linking ideas   186

Creating alternative narrative routes   186
Data integration and corpus sharing   186
Concerns and debates in relation to technology and qualitative research   187
The convergence on grounded theory   187
The removal of context   188
Automated coding   189
Concluding remarks   190
Recommended further reading   191

12   Writing and presenting analysis   192

Introduction   192
Presenting analysis   193
Writing   194
Analysis is not analysis until it is written down   194
Research diaries   195
Collaborative writing and critique   195
Presenting different forms of analysis   196
Presenting thematic analysis   196
Presenting ethnographic analysis   198
Presenting discourse analysis   198
Modes of presenting analysis   199
Conferences   200
Journal articles   201
Professional reports   201
Academic theses   202
Some simple rules of thumb about analysis and writing   203
Concluding remarks   204
Recommended further reading   204

13   Concluding remarks   205

Introduction   205
Revisiting 'analysis as situated practice'   205
Approaches to data analysis   207
Analysis and theory   208
Components of data work   209
The nexus of data and topic   211

References   212

Index   219

1

Introduction: qualitative data analysis in context

This chapter discusses the following issues:

- The notion of analysis in qualitative research work
- The nature of qualitative enquiry
- Theory and qualitative enquiry

Introduction

The 'success' of a research project is very much contingent on the analysis of data: on working with data to *achieve something interesting* and perhaps even *important* in relation to the substantive focus of a research project; on successfully relating such findings to an academic or professional field; on being able to *say something* through engagement with the data and using it to reflect not just on the particular setting being explored, but ideally, to create some generalizable or at least 'generally interesting' finding or idea that can be taken forward in other contexts.

In spite of its importance, the analysis of data remains one of the most difficult aspects of social research to discuss. There is something very nebulous about analysis, which somehow seems to evade tight description. Where very detailed descriptions of analysis are given, they tend to be offered in relation to a particular example of analysis – i.e. in relation to some problem or context – or in terms of a particular approach to doing analysis, like grounded theory, or narrative analysis, or phenomenological description. Such very specific accounts of analytic work can be alienating for researchers, who can find it hard to relate their interests to working contexts that are very different from their own, or to ways of doing research with which they are unfamiliar. The problem here is not that exemplifying analysis or showing how particular approaches work is not helpful; they most certainly are. The difficulty is that doing so is not *sufficient*, as in their specificity such descriptions may not demonstrate more generally how analysis in different contexts, with different kinds of data, and drawing on different conceptual languages might proceed. Researchers, particularly new and inexperienced researchers, often want clear guidance on how to work with data, but the complex relation between analysis and context, research topics, theory, the every-day contingencies of doing research, the dispositions of the researcher and so on, mean that analysis resists prescriptive codification, which makes the provision of clear and generalizable guidelines hard to provide.

This book is about the ways in which data analysis relates to, impacts on and develops from the other aspects of social research practice; it is about analysis and data work as a feature of qualitative social research, and the intersection of research *problems*, *specific* approaches *to social research* and research *data*. We do not prescribe a mechanism or template for doing data analysis. Rather, we want to consider the ways that the work that people do with data relates to the other components of social research work. We want to encourage an approach to analysis that is not just about techniques for dealing with data, but is also about thinking through the relation between a particular research setting and problem, and the literary and theoretical context of research. Through this approach, we hope to provide a nuanced picture of the relationship between analysis and social research practice in general.

In this book we will be discussing particular approaches to data analysis, and working through some of the key issues related to data work. We do this not, we hope, in a dogmatic way, but as a means of showing how analysis can work when particular strategies and foci are adopted. We have attempted to address all phases in the research process, from the development of a question or research focus through to the writing and presentation of research. In each phase we have emphasized the processes of working with data, and more specifically an analytic engagement with data.

In addition, we have looked at specific forms of data, such as documents, interviews, observations, video and audio data, and explored some of the general strategies and concerns running through the processes of qualitative data analysis, such as transcription and representation of data and the identification of themes in data. In all cases, we have sought to present and discuss *data work* and *the process of analysis* in the context of specific approaches to research or specific projects.

But we are getting ahead of ourselves… Let's start by thinking a bit more closely about the notion of analysis in relation to qualitative research, as it is from this that our thesis will begin to take a little more definite form.

What is qualitative data 'analysis' anyway?

Data analysis is an aspect of research practice that seems to create significant confusion for those new to, or working outside, qualitative research paradigms. Most areas of research work are quite intuitively grasped – generally speaking, people seem to have little trouble imagining what a literature review might involve, or what research design or writing-up are, and data collection is usually quite unproblematically understood. That is not to say that there is nothing complicated about any of these things, or that people are always right in their assumptions, but at least the general purposes of those activities, and the kinds of things that researchers might get involved in when they engage in them can be understood to some extent, or at the very least, they can be guessed at with some degree of accuracy. Very often, the issue of analysis seems to be quite different, and is seen to be rather mysterious to students, not only in terms of the practices that allegedly comprise it, but also in terms of the general aims behind it.

In the contexts of more quantitative forms of work, analysis is a little easier to conceptualize. We can point to the ways that different statistical tests work, and to some of the mechanisms for organizing data so that those tests can be performed, and that often seems to satisfy as some kind of explanation for what analysis involves. The notion that analysis will produce an explanation of the relationship between variables is also usually regarded as giving some idea as to the purposes of such analysis. In qualitative analysis, though, things are much more murky, and there are few tangible practices that can be discussed as features of work that 'constitute' analysis. It is also often unclear, it seems, what the purposes of analysis are and what the outcomes ought to look like. It is not uncommon for students to express the idea that there is some kind of secret that they haven't been let in on in relation to qualitative analysis – some set of tricks or ways of working that they haven't yet been told about.

In this brief section we would like to work through the notion of analysis in relation to qualitative research as a means of creating some kind of response to this general lack of clarity. We will start by thinking about the general usage of the term 'analysis'. As we note in Chapter 2, many of the terms in social research have some counterpart meaning in non-research discourse, and it may therefore be useful to explore this meaning in order to create a more specific meaning that relates to qualitative social research. The *New Oxford English Dictionary* defines analysis as follows:

> Detailed examination of the elements or structure of something, typically as the basis for discussion or interpretation.

Here, the emphasis is on the exploration of the 'structure' of 'things'. Clearly, what 'elements' or 'structure' might mean depend on what the 'something' refers to; there is nothing specific here whatsoever as an account of what analysis is. The *context* in which the term 'analysis' is used and the '*things*' to which it is directed are crucial to understanding what analysis might refer to. All we get from this definition is something about the examination of structure. Does this idea give us much purchase on the work of social researchers? A researcher may look at the structure of an opinion, of consciousness, of personnel in an organization, of a legal process, of communication, of experiences, of attitudes, of stories, of pictures, and so on. A part of examining structure might involve trying to understand how that structure works. This could entail explicating the **constitutive components**, looking at the **roles** of those various components, or examining the **relationship** between them. It might also call for some element of **evaluation** of the components, which could be in simplistic 'good'/'bad' or 'effective'/'non-effective' terms, but might be in a more complex and exploratory way. It might, though, be more straightforward and simply involve a **description** of those structural elements.

While this definition throws up some ideas, there is nothing tangible here – nothing that we can point to and say 'that is what you do when you do analysis'. How does one do this 'examination of the elements of a structure', and what do we mean by 'structure' anyway? The problem here is, again, the absence of an understanding of a context in which analysis operates or an issue to which analysis is directed. But that is quite a useful step: we can begin to see that particular context and issues are key for gaining a sense of what analysis means.

So what about social researchers? How do they define this notion of analysis in relation to their work with data? Does analysis take on a more certain and definitive shape when used in this domain? Marshall and Rossman define qualitative data analysis in the following way:

> Qualitative data analysis is a search for general statements about relationships and underlying themes. (2006: 154)

The reference to *relationships* and *themes* here implicates an interest in structure, as in the previous more generic definition of analysis. In Marshall and Rossman's view, analysis involves using generalized themes to look at the relationships between components of a data set. Indeed, this kind of thematized comparative work is at the heart of a number of distinct approaches to qualitative data work (see, for example, Miles and Huberman, 1994; Glaser and Strauss, 1999[1967]; Boyatzis, 2008). Now, there are some techniques and procedures that we can point to here. We can describe the ways that codes can be used to categorize data, and the types of operation that researchers might perform in order to interrogate the relationships between their codes. We can discuss the difference between codes that are created prior to the analysis of data, and those that are created from data. We might also think about the ways that computers can be used as a means of facilitating such work. All of this is important, and we will deal with these matters in some detail (particularly in Chapters 8 and 11).

However, although this gives us some idea of what analysis might entail, there is a real problem with thinking of this as *constituting* analysis. To begin with, not all researchers think about analysis in these kinds of ways; this kind of 'thematized analysis', as we describe it, is not, for example, a good way to think about how conversation analysis or critical discourse analysis works. The limitation here is that while it may be broadly appropriate to describe some of what people in these areas do as being concerned with comparing data through themes, this description doesn't tell you much about the nature of the interests that drive the enquiry. Concentrating on the processes of generating a theme, in these quite procedural ways, doesn't explain why the theme is of interest in the first place. This problem is not just limited to disciplines like conversation analysis and critical discourse analysis, though, but is a much more general issue. Analysis is always *about* something or *of* something, and the *thing* that it is 'about' or 'of' is fundamental for understanding how that analysis works. In other words, thinking about analysis in a decontextualized and 'general' way and about 'procedures' to analysis does not really solve the problem of how to explain how analysis works or what it is all about.

Let's look at another definition, this one from Harry Wolcott:

> ...analysis refers quite specifically and narrowly to systematic procedures followed in order to identify essential features and relationships... (1994: 24).

This definition comes from a distinction Wolcott makes between 'description', 'analysis' and 'interpretation', which represent three components of qualitative work. Wolcott does not suggest that these are clear and mutually exclusive categories, but merely that it can be useful to make a distinction between them. **Description** involves producing an account that stays close to the original data. The general aim in producing descriptions is to create a narrative that presents the original data in a motivated way (i.e. that operates as a description for a particular purpose). **Analysis** involves going beyond these largely descriptive iterations and systematically producing an account of 'key factors and relationships among them' (Wolcott, 1994: 10). Again, we see some similarity with the previous discussion of themes and generalized statements here. Finally, **interpretation** involves trying to give sense to the data by creatively producing insights about it. A crucial difference between analysis and interpretation as used by Wolcott is that the former is constrained and conservative, and is bound by the data, while the latter is inventive and creative and less empirically cautious (Wolcott, 1994: 23).

Wolcott describes the relationship between these three elements of qualitative work through the analogy of a see-saw or 'teeter-totter'. Description is the central part of the balance, and analysis and interpretation are the two opposite poles of the stem that balance on it. Researchers rest their analysis and interpretation (as defined above) on their description, and can give more or less emphasis to one or the other by raising or lowering one or other side of the see-saw. Wolcott's description, and the distinction itself, is a very interesting and influential way of demarcating the activity of 'analysis' in the context of qualitative research, as against analysis in any other domain of activity. It draws attention to some of the different features of data work – of ordering or *rendering* data in particular ways; of systematically working through data in a comparative manner; of using the data to 'say something' in a more general way.

Wolcott's work is useful, then, for illustrating how difficult it is to talk about this thing we call 'data work'. These types of distinction and analogy are all attempts to give some slightly more definite shape to these practices, such that novices, outsiders, or those we wish to convince can have a better idea of what this business is all about. Through some clarification and manipulation of language (and we do not mean to imply anything negative by using the idea of 'manipulate'), Wolcott specifies some distinctive enterprises that can be pointed to as 'the business of qualitative analysis'. For all its successes – and it is undoubtedly a very important text – Wolcott's definitions of description, analysis and interpretation as distinctive practices are a little too nebulous for helping people to understand what they might do when they undertake *their* analysis.

But we have a problem then. We have said that analysis is always contextual, and that it is very difficult to talk about in general terms away from the specifics of a setting and problem that *constitute* the analysis. The limitations that we have pointed to in Wolcott and in accounts of thematized analysis are their *generality*. Now, it is clearly impossible to address every empirical setting and conceptual problem, so how are we to talk about analysis in a meaningful way? Other than examples of analysis in practice, what can we use as a means of illustrating how analysis works and, indeed, what analysis is? The Wolcottian and thematic approaches to meta-description of analysis represent one way of doing this, and they work and are useful up to a certain point. In this book, though, we wish to try out another way of talking about analysis, one that involves going 'back to basics', for want of a better expression, and thinking about the ways in which analysis relates to other kinds of social research work. We want to talk about analysis in the context of other social research practices.

Contextualized analysis

But we have still not yet provided a definition of what we mean by analysis in the context of qualitative research. This is because the contexts, problems, questions and issues that constitute analysis are necessary parts of the definition of what analysis is. Any generic definition will be so general as to be of no particular help in defining it, and will likely result in the types of confusion that we have identified. If this is considered too much of a cop-out, then we would like to offer 'using data to deal with some problem, issue or other' as a definition.

A part of what we would like to accomplish with this book is to provide something of an account of how analysis relates to the other practices of social research – what we call *contextualized analysis*. Our definition of analysis is about the relationship between data and conceptual problems, and our aim is to explore this relationship as a feature of all social research work. We are interested in looking at the ways in which researchers use this basic issue of the relationship between 'data' and 'problem' throughout their research as a means to, or *as an aspect of*, undertaking their research work. Our basic thesis is that one way to think about *data analysis* is as one component of a broader analysis of a problem in relation to data. What we hope to shows through this book is that when analysis is considered in this more general way, it becomes clear that the distinction between data work and other types of work is in many ways unhelpful, and is part of the reason why people find qualitative analysis so opaque. The situated approach to analysis helps to show, for example, how research problems are developed through data work; how literature is used to construct research problems and to think about and even work with data; how research plans and designs are produced and worked through in relation to data and the analytic work it is supposed to do; how 'gathering' data through research always involves a simultaneous analysis of that data. When viewed like this, 'data' and 'analysis' becomes much less abstract, and more tightly integrated into research as a whole.

But this may raise a question: there may be nothing different about it *conceptually* and at this general level, but surely there is something distinctive about data work as a *set of practices*? Surely there is something that constitutes data work? Well, the answer is both 'yes' and 'no'. We will show through this book that, in fact, when you reflect on the research process many of the problems that people face when thinking abstractly about data work disappear, as the issues to which analysis is directed become much more visible. However, the practices of dealing with data are different from, say, dealing with literature or planning a research project, and there is a lot to say about the particular things that get done during data work. In addition to working through our approach to contextualized analysis, then, we will also be addressing some key issues related to data work, such as the use of computers in relation to research, the ways that audio and video data can be handled, and the issues of transcription in qualitative enquiry. Given what we have said about the contextual nature of analysis, our discussion of these matters is not in any sense complete. We could not possibly show, for example, how *all* researchers ought to analyse or deal with their video data or what a good transcription should look like. Our discussions should be taken as restricted (how could they be otherwise?), and as offering ideas and illustrations rather than firm and generalizable methods of working.

But what we have said so far does not take account of the fact that when people talk about qualitative data analysis, they often do so in relation to some more or less formal 'approach'. Discourse analysis, thematic analysis, rhetorical analysis, conversation analysis, narrative analysis, critical incident analysis, semiotic analysis, cross case analysis, grounded theory analysis, ethnographic analysis – these are just a few of the terms that are often used when talking about qualitative data work. This extreme diversity, and the wide range of theoretical and disciplinary perspectives that feed into it are another one of the reasons why qualitative analysis is so difficult to address or to make sense of. Wolcott provides a list of more than 50 different distinctive approaches to analysis (1994: 27), many of which could easily take up a book in their own right. It would be impossible for this or any book to provide a thorough guide to this immense body of work. While we will be looking in detail at a number of them, our purpose in doing so is to exemplify the ways that particular forms of analysis direct enquiry and data analysis. In this way we hope to raise people's interests in enquiring about different approaches or modes of analysis, and to encourage an attitude of critical reflection in relation to them. This should not be seen in any way to retract or distract from our arguments about the situated nature of qualitative data work. On the contrary, it is precisely by working with data in *context* that the relevance or otherwise of these diverse perspectives and approaches becomes evident.

We hope that these opening pages have provided some clarity as to our purposes and general approach. But there are a few more issues to clear up before we launch into the more focused discussions of the book's constituent chapters. In particular, we would like to say something about the process of qualitative enquiry in general, and about the role of theory within that process.

The notion of 'qualitative' in qualitative data analysis

Already in this opening chapter we have been implying and occasionally actively using a distinction between 'qualitative' and 'quantitative' research, and qualitative and quantitative data analysis. However, providing definitions to support this well used distinction is a notoriously difficult thing to do (see Snape and Spencer, 2003). A part of the difficulty is that the methodological debates, epistemological positions and research practices to which the distinction pertains are not easily divided into two separate camps, but are areas of discourse that have a complex relation to one another. It is common for the aims of qualitative research to be defined in the following ways:

Examining the construction of meaning
Understanding the details of peoples' lives or frames of reference
Reflecting on the role of the researcher in the generation of data

The practices of qualitative research are often described as being *flexible, iterative, naturalistic,* and as resulting in *thick descriptions* that are *reflexive* about the ways in which research data is constructed. All of these characterizations are appropriate as general descriptors, but they hide significant variations.

As the 'other' in the dichotomy, quantitative research is often described as involving an interest in the correlation between variables, and with the uses of scientific methods and statistical procedures to generalize findings – we have described it that way ourselves earlier on in this chapter. Again, though, such definitions invariably gloss different practices, methodologies and commitments, and oversimplify a complex interplay of ideas and traditions. It is, then, a characteristic of the labels 'qualitative' and 'quantitative' that they perform crude glosses. They divide up the social research community in a way that many researchers would not themselves choose. With this caveat in place, we will invariably, and frequently, make use of the loose distinction implied by these terms.

Box 1.1   Key concepts in qualitative research

Reflexivity is a key issue in social research that refers to the process of reflecting on the role of the researcher in the construction of meaning and, critically, of *data*. The 'reflexive turn' has been particularly visible in ethnographic research, and is exemplified nicely in the writing of Clifford and Marcus (1986) and of Clifford Geertz (1990).

Thick description is a term made famous by Clifford Geertz (1973) and involves the production of rich descriptions that outline the details of the contexts of people's actions and practices so that they become intelligible in their own terms.

The term **naturalism** is particularly difficult to define as it refers to a set of debates about the socially constructed nature of the social world and the implications of these characteristics for social research practice. Lincoln and Guba (1985) provide a very influential paradigm for thinking about these issues that draws attention to the multiplicity of perspectives in social life, their negotiated character, and the requirement for *contextual* explanation and understanding.

Quantitative data is usually thought of as that which can be coded numerically for the purposes of statistical analysis. By this definition, qualitative data can be characterized as 'everything else'. It is common for quantitative research to produce some qualitative data (i.e. things that can't be numerically coded, like descriptions of experiences), and for qualitative research to generate data that can be described numerically and analyzed statistically. Such data forms are often entirely complementary, and illustrate the oversimplicity of the qual/quant distinction. Indeed, the difference is often not actually in the data itself, but in the uses to which it is put (on this point, see Wolcott, 1994: 4). In writing a book about qualitative analysis we are, by implication, focusing on the 'everything else' that is left over from numerical analysis.

In spite of the title, this book is not just aimed at 'qualitative researchers', but is relevant to all forms of social research. Our aim is to explore the relationship between data and research problems in general terms, and to create an orientation to data work as a continuation of this same problematic rather than *just* a matter of searching for data manipulation and organization *techniques*. While the use of statistical tests are a part of what researchers might do when dealing with their numerical data, they are not the beginning and the end of the matter of analysis. Another way to put this would be to say that '*analysis* involves deciding what counts as variables in the first place, on making sense of any relations that may be found between variables, and on relating statistical findings to research questions and concepts'. While our concern is not with numerical data and statistical analysis, the conception of analysis that we develop throughout this book is as relevant to 'quantitative' researchers as it is to 'qualitative' ones.

Describing the research process

A common way to conceptualize and describe social research is as a linear process, where researchers move from a research topic, through various stages of research (literature review, research design, data 'collection', 'data analysis') to the production of a written research report (see Figure 1.1). This conception has a strong resonance with research practices in the physical sciences, where pre-formulated hypotheses are subjected to empirical examination, with the aim of either proving or disproving the theorized relation presented in the hypothesis.

In the social sciences, however, this model is not a very good description of the real-world practices of research. All social research (and not just 'qualitative' research) is iterative in the sense that the 'stages' are best conceptualized as 'forms of work' that

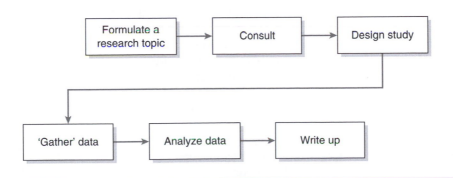

Figure 1.1   A linear model of the workflow in social research

mutually inform each other. If this were to be represented visually, it might look something like the process depicted in Figure 1.2. Researchers can move from analyzing data, to consulting literature, to collecting more data, to designing an alternative approach to data collection, to writing, back to analyzing data, and so on.

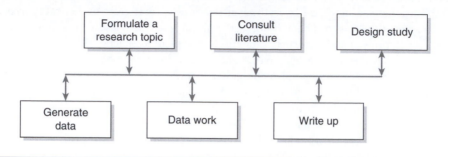

Figure 1.2   A Slightly more realistic depiction of the workflow in social research

But, the movement through the research process is by no means entirely non-linear either. Researchers do start research because they have a topic of enquiry, however vague that may be, and typically begin the process by trying to specify that interest further, usually with reference to existing studies. Similarly, researchers cannot really start collecting data until they have a broad sense of the types of data that they require and the ways they are to be used to address the research topic. Perhaps the best way to think about the research process is as being *orientated towards* the model implied in Figure 1.1, but with an awareness that it will never quite work out like that.

Figure 1.2 also involves some visual *mis*representation of the actual practices of social research. Indeed, it illustrates the problems in using diagrammatic forms to represent complex and difficult-to-codify processes. While researchers may concentrate on one particular aspect of their work more than others at any given time, it is not typically the case that the other aspects are in abeyance while they do so. Researchers usually work on more than one of these aspects of work consecutively (and sometimes all at the same time). This does not mean that there are no phases to research – as we have seen, some practices do logically precede others – but these phases are not as distinct and transparent as is commonly presented. The diagram shown in Figure 1.2 disrupts the conventional representation of research as a linear process of distinct phases. It signals an interaction between, and an interdependency of, elements in the research process, but cannot meaningfully represent or map a process that, in practice, can be realized in a multiplicity of ways.

To depict the research process in this way suggests a question:

Q: If research is not entirely linear, how do researchers know what to do next?

In other words, if there is no clear pattern involved in research work, then how do researchers work their way through the various tasks that they have to do? As we suggested above, the main referent for all research practice is the relationship between *data* and *research topic*. Researchers decide what to do next on the basis of the challenges they are facing in relating these two aspects. This book is directed towards showing how this process works in real-world research situations.

The relationship between theory and analysis

In addition to the types of terminology we introduced earlier (interpretation, themes, description), **theory** is a phrase that is very closely associated with the kinds of things that get done when undertaking analysis. Like analysis, though, there is nothing precise about the term, or particularly generalizable about it as an activity. It is perhaps its lack of clear shape that make it, like analysis, such a difficult topic or area for so many social researchers.

In many instances, researchers work within defined theoretical fields, which are constituted in a range of commitments or interests that are shared by a community of scholars and researchers. This 'general perspective' may be definable as a broad academic discipline (like social psychology or sociology or human geography or philosophy), or some more specific genre within a wider discipline, such as ethnomethodology, or Jungian psychoanalysis, discursive psychology, or phenomenology (although to describe such collective commitments as 'genres' is to imply a subject relation that the members of those communities may not themselves accept). Often, however, such general categories will not be particularly useful descriptors of the very specific theorizations that authors produce and with which they work.

Just like the term 'analysis', 'theory' is so varied in the manner in which it is understood and realized in practice that it is extremely hard to discuss in any generalized sense. We might describe the role of theory as involving:

- Categorizing – creating groupings of particular aspects of the social world
- Describing – providing new ways of characterizing some feature of the social world so as to draw attention to particular characteristics of it
- Comparing – juxtaposing features of the social world
- Interrogating – problematizing the taken-for-granted aspects of data
- Generalizing – moving from particular empirical domains to more general understandings or claims.

But this list is *extremely* partial: theory can act as a tool in analysis, as a means of working with data in some *particular* and *motivated* way. That is to say, theory is an important aspect of analysis and is constituted in the working out of particular problems in specific circumstances and in orientation to defined intellectual commitments and practical obligations. As such, the list provided above can only operate as a very general heuristic device for demonstrating *some* of the ways that analysis might function.

One of the implications of the contextual character of theory is that it is extremely hard to discuss in *decontextualized* terms. The process of theory work as an aspect of analysis makes most sense when it is seen *in action*. In this book, we provide a number of examples of the ways in which theory acts as a motivated move towards data. In some instances these examples are situated within recognizable and defined approaches, and in other instances they are not. These sorts of examples are not arguments for 'how analysis should be done', but are merely exemplifications of how analysis through *those* perspectives and *those* contexts, and in relation to *that kind of data*, might work. The generalizable feature of these examples is that they all involve working with concepts and particular theoretical positions in relation to data. In other words, they represent a working out of theory in the context of real-world data.

Some common areas of concern in relation to theory

'Theory' is a very common area of anxiety for social researchers: three of the most common questions that are often raised in relation to theory are:

- Do I need theory to analyze my data?
- I don't have a theory – how do I get one?
- Do I have to do grounded theory?

There are no simple answers to any of these questions, which all pertain to the relation of theory to data and the role of theory in analysis, but it may be useful to provide some reasonably direct responses to the questions at this point:

Do I need theory to analyze my data? Whether or not theory is *necessary* very much depends on the context of a given research project. Policy-orientated research will often not involve any explicit theoretical work, but there are probably very few examples of qualitative postgraduate work in the social sciences that do not include a strong orientation to, and use of, theory. This answer draws attention to the fact that social research is characterized by a number of *genres*, and that 'what counts as analysis' is genre-specific. While in some instances theory might not be *necessary*, the academic community generally regard it as offering opportunities for more insightful engagement with data. The absence of an explicit reference to, or incorporation of, theory often results in a rather descriptive and impoverished analysis.

I don't have a theory, how do I get one? Theory is developed through research, both in the critical examination of a body of literature and through the close examination of data. However, it is usually better to think about the ways in which very specific *theoretical components* may be used for analyzing data than to worry about the requirement of having 'a theory', which can sound rather daunting.

Do I have to do grounded theory? The term 'grounded theory' is heavily associated with qualitative research, but it is by no means a necessary component of qualitative analysis. The prevalence of the term does lead some people to assume that 'theory work' in qualitative research *is* grounded theory, but this is not the case. In fact, grounded theory is a rather ambiguous term, which can refer to something extremely specific and to nothing much in particular, depending on how it is being used. Where researchers are interested in undertaking grounded theory, it is important to be clear about what *exactly* is meant by the claim.

In this book we address all of the above themes in detail.

The structure of the book

Chapters 2–12 of this book deal with distinctive features of research work. The thread that runs through all of the chapters is the demonstration of the ways in which the orientation to the relationship between data and research topic features as a general issue in social research and the notion of 'analysis' as a general feature of research practice.

Chapter 2 looks at the roles of theory in social research, and demonstrates the various ways in which theoretical concepts can be used in and produced through research. We distinguish between two approaches to theorization – top-down and bottom-up theory – that operate as potentially complementary strategies for developing conceptual resources that enable data to 'speak'. In Chapter 3 we turn our attention to the processes of orientating to the 'discursive spaces' of research and the ways in which an opening-up to, and interrogation of, literature can help researchers to specify and develop particular analytic concerns and interests. Chapter 4 explores the process of design and shows how the concern with generating data in order to deal with a particular research topic functions as a means of creating effective and analytically rich research strategies.

Chapter 5 is the first of two chapters to focus on data *generation* and looks at the ways in which documentary sources can be put to work in research, and the particular analytic roles that they can play. Chapter 6 explores the various practices of, and issues in, interview- and observation-based research, and the processes of using these methods to create topically focused and relevant research materials.

Chapter 7 moves on from this to explore approaches to transcription, and illustrates how such modes of representation – or as we describe it, *re-presentation* – form central tools in the process of data work. Chapter 8 outlines some of the key characteristics of what we describe as 'thematic analysis', and shows how these can be put to work in the schematized coding of various forms of data. Following this, Chapters 9 and 10 look at approaches to analysing images, text, videos and sound. These chapters use examples from semiotics and conversation analysis as a means of demonstrating the potential value of such data forms and of showing how particular concepts and theoretical concerns can be used in data work.

In Chapter 11 we discuss the various roles that computers can play in the analysis process, and explore the ways in which particular packages and strategies of use can impact on the ways that qualitative researchers work with data. Chapter 12 reflects on the ways that researchers can effectively work through their analysis in the context of writing and other presentational media and contexts. The final chapter draws together the key themes that we have discussed in this book.

Recommended further reading

Geertz, C. (1990) *Work and Lives: The Anthropologist as Author*. Stanford, CA: Stanford University Press. In spite of the title, this book has much to offer to all qualitative researchers as it provides an elegant discussion of the implications of the reflexive turn for social science practice.

Lincoln, Y. and Guba, E. (1985) *Naturalistic Inquiry*. London: Sage. This text has become a classic, giving an account of the debates and implications of the notion of 'naturalistic' inquiry in qualitative research.

Silverman, D. (2005) *Doing Qualitative Research: A Practical Handbook* (2nd edn). London: Sage. Silverman is an important author in qualitative research methods. Students usually find Silverman's work very accessible. Like Wolcott, Silverman's work is interesting as it quite clearly comes from a distinctive perspective (interactional sociology), and often exhibits the concerns and interests of this particular approach. See, for example, his descriptions of the use of naturalistic data.

Wolcott, H. (1994) *Transforming Qualitative Data: Descriptions, Analysis and Interpretation*, London: Sage. Wolcott's theorization of analysis provides a very interesting account of the distinctive practices of qualitative data work.

2 Theory, grounded theory and analysis

This chapter discusses the following issues:

- Theory and theorization in social research
- Theory and data analysis
- Top-down theory
- Bottom-up theory
- The intersection of theory and data

Introduction: the practice of theory

We make a distinction between two approaches to theory: 'top-down' and 'bottom-up' theory. Much of the time, researchers use some preformulated theoretical and conceptual schema and commitments to classify, characterize and make sense of the social world – we call this 'top-down' theory. In other instances, researchers describe themselves as *creating theory* through their research, of generating and clarifying concepts through the analysis of data – i.e. 'bottom-up' theory. These terms are not intended to set up a dichotomy of practices, but merely to describe two aspects of research. Social research typically involves *both* of these practices – a specification of theoretical ideas in relation to an existing body of work, and the working out of these ideas in relation to data. We will return to discuss this point in more detail later in this chapter.

Box 2.1   Terms and definitions

Metatheory is the study of theory. George Ritzer (1990) has been influential in the developments of discourse around metatheory as a means of making sense of sociological theory. Ritzer uses the term **meta-data-analysis** to describe the process of aggregating the analyses conducted by other researchers.

(Continued)

(Continued)

Grand theory refers to broad-ranging theoretical systems that are developed to give accounts of very generalized social practices or forms of social organization. A distinctive aspect of grand theory is that it is not just about a specific, localized, empirical domain or setting, but about the creation of theoretical accounts for understanding more general practices.

Top-down theory – theoretical components that are specified prior to empirical work and are put to use in data work. While this is, in principle, distinct from bottom-up theory, the two usually work hand in hand, with some conceptual features being brought to data, and others being generated and modified through data work.

Variation theory – Tannen (2007) has used this term to describe 'a particular combination of theory and method employed in studying a particular kind of data' (2007: 5). So, any well-defined theory that is typically used in relation to a well-specified set of methodological procedures in order to produce a particular kind of data may count as an example of 'variation theory'. The discussion of critical discourse analysis that we provide in this chapter would be one such example.

Bottom-up theory is the creation of theory through the exploration of data. **Grounded theory** is the best known articulation of this view, but this is just one articulation of a general approach to conceptual and theoretical work through data.

There are other useful distinctions and descriptors that are important for reflecting on the various roles that theory can play in research. Grand theory and metatheory are both orientated towards examining and creating theory rather than being concerned with theory as a tool for doing empirical work. **Grand theory** refers to the process of theorizing, usually in overarching and very general ways (such as outlining a system of social organization) rather than in terms of a theory of a specific aspect of social life. C. Wright Mills (1959) famously warned against grand theory as a distraction from the real business of social science – namely, empirical investigation. As he put it: 'The basic cause of grand theory is the initial choice of a level of thinking so general that its practitioners cannot logically get down to observation … get down from the higher generalities to problems in their historical and structural contexts' (Mills, 1959: 23).

The term **metatheory** is used to describe the study of theory (Ritzer, 1990). Metatheory is typically directed towards improving our understanding of theory itself, to generating new theory, or to creating an overarching theoretical perspective. As George Ritzer makes clear, however, maintaining a hard distinction between grand theory and metatheory is not easy. In this text, we are not concerned with the development of theory in abstraction from data, but in the practical relation between theory and data.

It is common for researchers to situate their theoretical position within or in relation to specific **subject disciplines**. Researchers who identify themselves as cognitive psychologists, for example, identify with a defined area of interest that is likely to lead them to define their research questions (and, therefore, their research *answers*) in terms of, say, 'internal mental operations'. But while this may provide access to a range of concepts for making sense of the questions, and implies a particular level of explanation (in this instance, explanation at the level of the 'cognitive'), further conceptual specialization is required to be able to engage with the practical task of working with and analyzing data. A given discipline may delimit one's theoretical 'focal range', but it does not specify a particular focal point.

Of course, not all researchers are in the position of having such easily identifiable allegiances, and in such instances it can be difficult to find one's way through the very complex sets of strongly demarcated academic interests and concerns. It is important to emphasize that working with data is not contingent on being able to state a disciplinary orientation. Data analysis is undertaken through the use of very specific analytic tools, much more localized than general disciplines. A *discipline* only provides quite a general research orientation whereas *specific analytic tools* function as mechanisms for analysis. We will return to this point when we begin to look at particular examples of analysis.

Theoretical concepts

Specific theoretical concepts offer a much more focused route to conducting analysis. There is something of a definitional problem in describing what counts as a concept as the term simply refers to *a word or phrase that gives meaning to something*, and since all words give meaning it is not possible to separate out some words as constituting concepts and others that do not. Rather, in social research, a word becomes a concept when it is treated as such – i.e. when it is used to do some analytic work. The term 'concept' in the social sciences, then, means something like *a word or phrase that has been specially selected to make sense of a particular empirical area*. This is still not a particularly satisfactory definition, but hopefully things may become a little clearer as we move through this chapter.

By this definition, the use of concepts (or *words*) is not unique to the kinds of work that social researchers do, but is also a characteristic of normal everyday life. All language (be it the professionalized discourses of academia and research communities, or 'ordinary language' spoken in non-academic contexts) is made up of concepts/words that structure the ways that we make sense of the world: 'fast', 'policeman', 'pyjamas', 'brunch', 'mother', 'secondary school', 'newspaper', 'message', 'song', 'meeting', all serve as interpretive frames for labelling, categorizing, telling people about, analyzing and variously *giving meaning to* the world.

When social scientists speak of 'theorizing', they are talking about giving sense to a particular setting of investigation – and, ultimately, to their data – through some concept or set of concepts. While these concepts often look like the kinds of concept that ordinary people might use in their everyday language (think of concepts like 'reliable', 'identity', 'role', 'space', 'distribution' – all of which have some counterpart meanings in ordinary language and academia), their use in these professionalized discourses may or may not be similar to these everyday applications. Words provide us with ways of labelling and describing things, but they also *constitute* our world – as Ludwig Wittgenstein famously remarked, 'the limits of my language are the limits of my world'(Wittgenstein, 1961: 5.6). One way of characterizing what theoretical concepts do is *offering a way of providing a description of things, or an approach to constructing a language for giving new and different meaning of events or settings* (see Denzin, 1989, on this view). Box 2.2 provides a very brief example of the ways in which a conceptual language can help to re-present data and empirical settings in new ways for the purpose of analytical description. The point is much more general than the example of Erving Goffman that is provided here though, which relates to the ways in which researchers can use concepts to create different perspectives and views of the world.

Box 2.2   Conceptual language in Goffman's work

Goffman's (1959) work on the presentation of self has been particularly influential in qualitative social research, and provides a nice example of the ways that concepts can offer re-descriptions of the world. One of Goffman's interests was in the ways that people manage their social identity – the impression that they give of themselves to other people. A frequently used analytic trick for Goffman was to use metaphors to make comparisons between different social situations. One such metaphor is that of 'performance', and the ways in which a theatre stage is organized into a 'front stage' performance area and a 'back stage' area that is not visible to the theatre audience. Goffman used this to describe the ways that people organize their behaviour in other contexts, such as waiters in a restaurant. When they are working in front of customers (front stage), the waiters orientate to the production of a professional self, using particular kinds of language, forms of address, ways of walking, and so on. However, when the waiters are in other parts of the restaurant, such as the kitchen (or 'back stage'), they may well behave in very different ways in order to display other sorts of social status (e.g. as being 'a part of a working team' or 'good fun' or 'someone who takes their job seriously' or 'a boss' or 'a low status employee', and so on). Through analogies such as this, Goffman is able to give new ways of seeing particular forms of social life that, he suggests, may not have been evident otherwise.

Denzin's view of the role of theory is analogous to the role of some forms of psycho-analysis, where a patient's language is seen as constituting the 'problem' being dealt with, and the role of the analyst is to find a new language to use that alleviates the symptoms. As Brown et al. have put it, this form of analysis '… is achieved through the production of narrative in which the subject re-writes the story line of his or her life' (2004: 67). Here, the idea is that language can lead us to view ourselves in non-productive terms, and that by changing our language we may reach a more positive view of our lives. Heaton's (2000) comparison between Wittgenstein and Freud draws out nicely the ways in which these two very different approaches may be viewed as offering emancipation through their emphasis on language. Weiner (1995) has pointed out that this process of substituting an analytic language is also a good way of characterizing what social anthropologists do when they write ethnographies. Ethnographies are partial, culturally framed readings and renderings of views of the world (Clifford and Marcus, 1986). Ethnographic analysis involves providing substitute readings and 'tellings' that re-present the world in new ways.

Is one theory as good as another?

The description we provided in the previous paragraph quickly starts to sound very relativistic. Are we to say that 'one concept/theory is as good as another' or that 'theories merely offer different ways of looking at the same world'? Concepts in academia exist within particular paradigms or communities of understanding. Sets of theoretical practices converge around particular interpretations of concepts and preferences for ways of making sense of things. Answering the question 'Which theory is best?' inevitably involves invoking community-bound preferences of theoretical practice. While we certainly have our own preferences within these debates, this book is not an evangelizing endeavour (or at least not a disciplinary one); our aim here is to show how theory can be *put to work* or *built-up* in and through the processes of working with, and analyzing, data. We do not agree that all the analysis we present here is 'as good as each other' or even 'correct', but it would quickly become tire-some if we kept drawing attention to our own preferences. The reader is encouraged to make their own mind up about the persuasiveness and value of the various examples we include in this chapter, and indeed in the rest of the book.

Characterizations of the role of theory

There are a number of metaphors that try to outline the relationship between theory and data. Brown and Dowling (1998) refer to theoretical and empirical fields, and describe the process of research in terms of a dialogue between these fields: theoretical resources are specialized in defining a particular problem, and localization of the wider empirical field delineates the particular empirical setting in which the research is realized. Robert Alford (1998) refers to the movement between theory and data in terms of 'tracks of analysis', where researchers shuttle between theory and data in a mutually informative process. Howard Becker (1998) talks about a preference for thinking of theory as a trick (or set of tricks) for helping gain insights into the empirical world. For Becker, a 'trick' is 'a specific operation that shows a way around some common difficulty, suggests a procedure that solves relatively easily what would otherwise seem an intractable and persistent problem' (1998: 4). In this approach, theory is a practical activity and a way of thinking through problems or of looking at things in different ways. In all of these approaches, though, theory is a resource for doing things with data.

Box 2.3   Howard Becker's interactionist approach

Howard Becker is an extremely influential sociologist whose analytic concerns and approach are derived from the Chicago '**interactionist**' tradition of sociology. Becker's work exemplifies nicely the ways that particular academic concerns and disciplinary foci can be used in relation to different empirical domains. For example, one of the key concerns in this approach is with the analysis of work (see particularly E.C. Hughes, 1984). Becker can be seen to use this general topic of enquiry to examine areas such as drug taking (1953); musical performance (1974, 2000); and medical education (Becker et al., 1997). These various studies have much in common in terms of the application of a distinctively sociological perspective on the organization (and negotiation) of professionalized knowledge. Much of this work can be read as having a consistency in its commitment to the examination of 'conventions' of social practice.

To take an example, Becker's study of the 'career' of marijuana smokers was, in part, a reaction to psychologistic studies that characterized marijuana users as possessing distinctive psychological *traits*, which predispose them to such drug habits. In contrast to this view, Becker sought to show how the 'dispositions to engage in' (1953: 235) the use of marijuana are learnt through a process of socialisation, through which the user comes to view the taking of drugs as 'ordinary'. Becker employs a notion of 'career', as developed by Hughes (1984b) to characterize this process of learning to use and to account for differences in and changes in the perspectives and practices of drug users over time. Fundamental to the argument is that learning to become a drug user involves gaining knowledge about how to experience the drug's effects.

The intention of the preceding discussion has been to clarify some terms, and to describe the quite complex and diverse sets of theory-orientated practices in which social researchers engage. In what follows we offer some more focused reflection on these different conceptions of the relationship between theory and analysis. In the first section we describe some of the key issues involved in translating specific theoretical models into practical analytic strategies, and in the second we think about how to use data itself to generate theoretical ideas.

Top-down theory

To refer to 'top-down theory' is simply to describe any theory that has been formulated prior to empirical work, either by other theorists or by the researcher themselves. Theory in this sense may provide a way of posing empirical questions. For example, the famous social anthropologist Margaret Mead's (2001) interest in childhood among the Manus tribe of Papua New Guinea was framed by her reading of the psychologist Jean Piaget's writing on cognitive development. Piaget described the differences between the approaches to understanding the world of western children and adults, drawing attention to the ways in which children frequently invoke 'magical' causes as explanations (e.g. 'The water monster makes it rain', Mead, 2001: xvii), and 'animistic' explanations ('The clock ticks because it wants to', Mead, 2001: xvii).

Mead was interested in exploring how these ways of making sense of the world of western children may compare to the ways in which Manus children made sense of the world, and whether or not Piaget's ideas represented cross-cultural properties of childhood. For Mead, this theoretical interest presents a clear theoretical frame and an analytic focus for the examination of data. Animism, for example, was a clearly defined concept that could be explored in relation to specific sets of practices, and used as a way of categorizing certain features of observed behaviour for comparison with Piaget's observations. The pre-formulated theoretical frame, then, was a mechanism for categorizing, comparing and talking about the social world she was investigating.

Below we present an extended example of the use of theory in the development of analysis.

The example of critical discourse analysis

The following extended quote from Norman Fairclough (1995) provides a concise outline of his view of some of the key theoretical constituents of his interpretation of critical discourse analysis (CDA):

> I view social institutions as containing diverse 'ideological-discursive formations' (IDFs) associated with different groups within the institution. There is usually one IDF which is clearly dominant. Each IDF is a sort of 'speech community' with its own discourse norms but also, embedded within and symbolized by the latter, its own 'ideological norms'. Institutional subjects are constructed, in accordance with the norms of an IDF, in subject positions whose ideological underpinnings they may be unaware of. A characteristic of a dominant IDF is the capacity to 'naturalize' ideologies, i.e. to win acceptance for them as non-ideological 'common sense'. It is argued that the orderliness of interactions depends in part upon such naturalized ideologies. To 'denaturalize' them is the objective of a discourse analysis which adopts 'critical' goals. I suggest that denaturalization involves showing how social structures determine properties of discourse, and how discourse in turn determines social structures. (Fairclough, 1995: 27)

The principal analytic moves that we identify in this text are the following:

1 Ideology and language are intertwined.

2 Language may be used by people *uncritically*, without reflection on its ideological character.

3 Within a given institution there is usually one *dominant* ideology/language.

4 These ideologies often become 'the normal way of thinking' and are not usually regarded as ideological, but rather simply as 'the way things are'.

5   'Order' (which means here something like 'continuing as people expect things to continue') within an organization is a result of the dominance of a particular discourse.

6   CDA aims to show how this normalization of ideology and language occurs.

7   The explanation for this 'naturalization' uses a theory about the relationship between macro and micro social structures – the former relating to recognizable social institutions (such as 'schools' or 'the police force' or to 'systems of governance', etc.) and the latter to the ways in which people interact. In particular, the theory aims to show how language is conditioned by macro social structures and, at the same time, how language conditions those structures.

Fairclough approaches his analysis by examining transcribed sections of interactive talk and looking for the types of assumption and 'social bias' that can be seen within the exchanges. He does this by looking at the 'levels of naturalization' that can be found within the talk, i.e. the extent to which they may be unproblematically 'accepted' by members of a given community (which would count as 'high naturalization') or may, in contrast, be contested ('low naturalization').

Applying Fairclough's ideas to other empirical domains

In what follows we discuss the ways that a researcher may use Fairclough's ideas and approach as a means of investigating a particular empirical context.

The data extract below is taken from an ethnographic study of gender equality in the context of free primary education (FPE) in Lesotho in Southern Africa. This study is part of a postdoctoral research project conducted by Pholoho Morojele at the Institute of Education, University of London. The study aimed to examine ways of improving gender equality within FPE. Two important aspects to the context of this desire for improvement are the intersection of extremely patriarchal indigenous practices, which place tangible restrictions on the nature and level of women's participation within society, and the very high rates of HIV and AIDS infection within the region. The research aimed to empower women to be able to resist the forms of patriarchy that both limited their life chances and heightened their risks of HIV contagion.

The extract comes from a focus group that Morojele undertook with a group of girls in a co-educational primary school; the children are describing their participation in an after-school Christian group called 'Pledger's Group' that is organized by the school. The aim of the group was to provide moral education that could enable the girls to avoid the problems described above. The transcript is translated.

DATA EXTRACT 2.1

1	Int	What do you do during lunch time?
2	Girl 1	Me, every Friday after school there is an organization in the
3		school called *Maila-thoabalano* [Pledger's Group]. We have joined it
4		and our teacher Ms. Mary teaches why these people who fall in
5		love why they do so. And then we tell her.
6	Int	Okay she asks you why?

7	Girl 1	Yes, sometimes we do it in groups and tell her why when we
8		have sports trips girls like to walk with a boy.
9	Int	Okay when you have sports, boys like to go with* girls?
10	All	Yes sir
11	Int	And girls like to go with boys too?
12	All	Yes sir
13	Int	Why?
14	Girl 2	Its because they were being persuaded by love
15	Int	Okay, is that so?
16	All	Yes sir
17	Int	Who are being persuaded by love? Boys or girls?
18	All	Boys [Girls say in a chorus]
19	Girl 3	But no sir, girls also are persuaded by love [the girls laugh and
20		hide their faces]
21	Girl 1	Yeah even girls do
22	Int	Mamello, tell us how does this happen?
23	Girl 4	You see when one girl has a boyfriend and they go together
24		during sports and the friends of the girl also want to have a
25		boyfriend and so they don't come empty.
26	Int	Oh, girls are also like that?
27	All	Yes sir
28	Int	So when the teacher asked you [why people fall in love] what do
29		you tell her?
30	Girl 5	Me, I said its because these boys they only want to fall in love
31		with girls for a short while not for a long time.
32	Int	What about girls?

[Long silence]

33	Girl 4	No all of them they are the same
34	Girl 5	Yeah that is true (group laughter)
35	Int	Why do you think boys want to go out with girls for a short
36		while?
37	Girl 1	Its because they like girls
38	Girl 3	Yeah they [boys] won't go out with one girl
39	Girl 2	It's not like they [boys] love them [girls], they [boys] only lust
40		after them only. They want to misuse them so they become
41		miserable.
42	Int	Okay, what do girls think?
43	Girl 2	Girls think that boys really love them but its not like that
44	Girl 4	They deceive them
45	Int	Oh girls don't deceive boys?
46	Girl 1	Yeah
47	Girl 5	But there are others .....
48	Girl 3	There are those who deceive them (boys) and those who
49		don't.
50	Girl 1	Yeah, there are those who don't deceive them (boys)
51	Int	Those girls who deceive them why do they do so?
52	Girl 2	It's because they have seen that boys deceive them
53	Int	If boys don't deceive girls, girls also don't deceive them?
54	All	Yes sir [in chorus]

*'go with' here means not only 'be accompanied by' but has strong connotations of sexual intercourse.

If we were to apply the analytic framework used by Fairclough, we might reach the following analysis:

The formal institutional discourse of the Christian group (the dominant IDF) positions girls as abused and mistreated by boys (interjection 40 – 'they want to misuse them so they become miserable' and interjection 43 and 44 on boys' deception). However, the girls also display their own discursive frame, which positions themselves as operating with the same socially mediated desires as the boys for having a partner (interjection 24 – 'the friends of the girl also want to have a boyfriend').

Within the text there is a strong subtext, much more evident in the original language, that the discussion here is about sexual intercourse and not just 'being accompanied by boys'. Participating in the Pledger's Group involves learning, and becoming conversant with a discourse that positions boys as 'immoral' and 'deceptive', who are driven by this sexual desire. The aim of this discourse is to generate a change in the girls' sexual practices. While the girls show a conversance with this discourse, they also display an alternative ideology which positions themselves as operating with the same sexual desires as boys, as able to distinguish between deceptive boys and non-deceptive boys, and which comprises its own morality of retribution in which girls can be as deceptive as boys (interjections 46–54).

We may pose the following as questions for exploring other data within this study:

1   Is the Pledger's Group generally the subservient discourse, with the girls' own discourses operating as the dominant ones? How does context effect what is treated as 'dominant' or 'subservient' discourse?

2   Do the girls' discourses here display any similarity with wider discursive practices in other formal and informal settings?

3   Are there other instances of talk between girls within the school that also hint at the subservience of school discourse?

As with Mead's application of Piaget's theoretical orientation, the above example illustrates how the ideas presented in CDA offer a way of categorizing, describing and *talking about* data. CDA provides a conceptual framework for making sense of the data, and for working through it in a focused way. It provides particular concepts (e.g. 'ideology' or 'institutionalized discourse formation') and a particular set of aims (e.g. 'the ideological ideas implicit in language') that can be put to use to make distinctions, create categories, specify relations, make claims to the formations of tacit knowledge, or define sets of interest groups or typologies of interests.

In the analysis presented above, the concepts of ideology, dominance, ideological discourse formation, agency, and power serve as a ready-made system of concepts for exploring the research question. Language becomes the central focus for exploring the question of gender equality, and the analytic concern becomes understanding how that language, as crystallized in forms of discourse and particularly institutionalized discourse, serves to define the parameters of participation for women.

The relationship between forms of data and forms of theory

The analysis of extract 2.1 above is useful for highlighting that particular theoretical/ analytic frameworks imply preferences for certain sorts of data and certain forms of research design. The ideas that constitute the theoretical orientation of CDA cannot be pursued 'any old how', but require particular kinds of data – in the example above, questionnaires would not provide the level of detail needed to be able to answer questions about forms of discourse and specific discursive relations. This does not mean that only one kind of data can be valuable, as there are very often alternative data forms that one could use. However, the practicalities of research usually reduce these down to a small number of tangible alternatives. In the above example, then, the researcher might have asked the girls to record themselves talking about these issues, or he may have conducted interviews with individual girls instead of groups of girls. In each case, though, all kinds of ethical, methodological and practical issues would arise that would make such alternatives more or less doable or attractive. *Working with theoretical ideas, then, involves specifying a methodological framework in which such ideas may be taken forward.* We discuss this matter in more detail in Chapter 4.

The iterative nature of analysis and research practice

The analysis we provided of the data extract above shows also that, through analysis, researchers can specify new questions for further exploration. The analysis outlined implies that the institutional discourse of the Pledger's Group is competing with other forms of discourse that the girls use to make sense of and make decisions about sexual practices. Questions arise, therefore, about the origins and prevalence of these other discursive forms; these questions direct the researcher to investigate further forms of discourse through the collection of new data.

Analytic frameworks do not only provide possible concepts for shaping engagement with the data, but also offer mechanisms for designing, conducting and developing one's research. The analysis of data informed by a particular theory can impact on the whole research process and lead to new research questions and research designs. These points are explored in more detail in Chapter 4, when we turn attention to the role of research design in the specification of analysis.

It is very hard to talk in the abstract about the ways in which theory can be used in analysis, as theorization is always a contextual activity. The example of CDA provided above shows how that specific orientation might work in relation to a particular data set. Different data will offer alternative forms of application. Different theories will provide different conceptual specifications and analytic aims. The pre-specification of theory is not the only way in which theoretical frameworks may be used or developed. Just as theory is a resource for analyzing data, so data is a tool for the development and refinement of theory. In the next section we look at these issues in relation to grounded theory.

Bottom-up theory

Arguably one of the most influential discussions of theory in qualitative research came with the publication of Barney Glaser and Anselm Strauss's *The Discovery of Grounded Theory* (1999 [1967]), which proposed a move from what they saw as the 'testing' of theory in social research to the *creation* of theory. Indeed, grounded theory became so influential that it has almost become synonymous with theory-orientated work in qualitative research. The central thrust of the argument in *Discovery* was that theory that is developed in relation to a data set is more likely to do justice to that data than theoretical concepts that are imposed on data.

Box 2.4   Grounded theory

Grounded theory refers to the process of developing theory through analysis, rather than using analysis to test preformulated theories. Barney Glaser and Anselm Strauss' pioneered the approach in their early collaborative work, but the authors later parted company in quite dramatic fashion as their opinions and descriptions of grounded theory diverged. It is important to be aware, however, that the term 'grounded theory' is frequently used in a much looser sense to simply refer to the process of analyzing qualitative data. It is advisable, therefore, to reflect carefully on the particular claims that are being made in studies that describe themselves as using 'grounded theory'.

While the authors are clear that they intend their approach to be applicable to qualitative researchers in general, they do on occasion use the term 'sociology' instead of 'social research'. This is not surprising perhaps as the authors are both sociologists by training (although from very different stock). This slippage in terminology can be off-putting for those who would not regard themselves as sociologists.

As many authors have pointed out (e.g. Goulding, 2002; Charmaz, 2003; Grbich, 2006), grounded theory is not a unified approach to analysis as, after the publication of their extremely successful text, Glaser and Strauss developed distinctive approaches. The publication of Anselm Strauss and Juliet Corbin's *Basics of Qualitative Research* (1990) led Glaser (1992) to claim that the book represented a fundamental departure from the original grounded theory thesis. Glaser argued that Strauss and Corbin's text involved not the pursuit of a *grounded* analytic orientation through the careful development of concepts from data, but that it advocated the imposition of a priori analytic frames. Such was the intensity of Glaser's claim that he called for the withdrawal of the book and the wholesale reworking of the text. While there are indeed some clear differences in the author's later works, we are not particularly concerned here with outlining them in detail. Without wishing to deny the importance of their distinctive approaches, we want to suggest that there are also important similarities between the authors' various publications. Our discussion below deals primarily with what we see as the similarities within grounded theory.

A further area of debate within grounded theory has concerned the extent to which it can be seen to represent an interpretivist approach to research. Kathy Charmaz (2006) has argued that both Glaser and Strauss display positivistic tendencies within their work, evident in what she characterizes as a naïve epistemology in which the social world is regarded as being readily available for 'discovery' by researchers. Charmaz suggests that this position does not fit easily with interpretivist views of the constructed and contested nature of the social world. While we do not explore this issue in detail here, Charmaz's argument presents an important caveat for anyone working with grounded theory, as it highlights a tension between the frequently cited methodological underpinnings of qualitative research and the implicit aims of grounded theory.

Key features of grounded theory

Grounded theory is essentially an approach to creating theory from research and data analysis. Its basic principle is that all concepts and hypotheses, which are the key elements of theory within the approach (Glaser and Strauss, 1999 [1967]), should be generated from, rather than produced prior to, research – theory ought to result from an engagement in research, rather than being imposed on it. In their original text, Glaser and Strauss (1967) made heavy use of the distinction between theory **verification** – the approach normally taken in positivistic/hyperthetico-deductive paradigms – and theory **generation**. They suggested that, until their commentary on grounded theory, even within qualitative research the weight of emphasis had been on the former rather than the latter; on *testing* or at least examining/applying existing theories rather than on creating new ones. Strauss (1987: 12) later suggested that the emphasis on this distinction led some people to interpret grounded theory as involving disinterest in theory verification. This is a slight misreading of their argument, though, as the verification of any theory generated through research is a key aspect of grounded theory.

Box 2.5   Processes and concepts in grounded theory

Grounded theory can be characterized by the following processes:

- **Concepts** and **hypotheses** should be generated *through* the analysis of data.
- Theory development should involve the use of **coding, memo writing, theoretical sampling, triangulation** and the **constant comparative method**.
- These processes and procedures should be used to develop **categories, properties** and **theoretical relations**.
- **Hypotheses** should then be formed through both **theoretical induction** and **deduction**.
- Theory work should continue until **data saturation** has been achieved.

Strauss and Corbin's (1990) approach to grounded theory specified the following procedures for dealing with data: **coding** (the specification of categories within data); writing **memos** (keeping notes on what you are doing); **theoretical sampling** (choosing new sources of data or sites of data collection according to your theoretical interests); and **triangulating methods** (using different methods to investigate the same idea or concept from different viewpoints). All of these aspects are used within the **constant comparative method**, as outlined in *The Discovery of Grounded Theory*. The constant comparative method involves comparing findings or observation with other instances in which those findings might be applicable. Glaser and Strauss (1999 [1967]) characterize the constant comparative method in terms of four stages. We regard the first and second of these stages as overlapping, so we have condensed these 'stages' into three:

- Creating categories, properties and theoretical relations
- Solidifying the theory
- Writing.

Creating categories, properties and theoretical relations

This entails the generation of codes (or categories) that can be compared with other instances of their appearance. For example, Gibson's (2005) study of pharmacy practice entailed the creation of the category 'skills alienation' to describe the feeling of being overqualified for a particular task. When a particular section of data within an interview transcript suggested itself as an instance of this category, it was compared to other instances. This was not only to make sure that it was 'an instance of a similar type', but also to flesh out the **properties** of the category.

Strauss and Corbin (1990) define properties as the characteristics of a category. Properties can typically be described in terms of variations along a scale, i.e. in terms of the variation of particular dimensions, such as how long they take, how far away the deadlines typically are, or how difficult they are. For example, one of the aspects of pharmacists' work that was typically associated with 'skills alienation' was that of dispensing drugs. However, this work varied quite considerably depending on the setting in which the work was carried out. For those working in high street shops, there was little account taken of patient drug history within this process, and typically little interaction with other healthcare professionals. However, for those in hospitals, this could be a more involved role, in which the pharmacists may have been brought into contact with doctors or nurses within the hospital in order to build up quite detailed patient histories. These properties of the category of alienation ('interaction with professionals' and 'taking drug histories') became viewed as a sliding scale, at the most passive end of which professionals experienced alienation, while at the other professionals experienced fulfilment (see Figure 2.1).

The creation of **hypotheses** is also an important part of theory development and comprises the expression of relationships between categories and their properties. This is undertaken through the processes of **induction** and **deduction** – i.e. by pursuing intuitions about, say, the relationships between different categories (induction), and then formulating those intuitions in formal relational terms as hypotheses (deduction). Glaser and Strauss (1999 [1967]) emphasize that all of this 'theory work' ought to involve the use of memos – notes on how particular categories or properties relate, or explorations of a particular hypothesis or other theoretical specification.

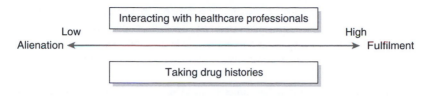

Figure 2.1 Theoretical relation between the properties and characteristics of pharmacists' work

Solidifying the theory

This entails the 'firming up' of a theory and its constitutive components (categories, properties and hypotheses). Here, the analyst begins to discard non-relevant properties and categories. A fundamental aspect of this later stage of theory development is that of **theory saturation**. A key concept in grounded theory, saturation refers to the point at which theoretical work (like applying a category) routinely involves seeing the same thing. Where an instance of a particular code comprises nothing new in the form of properties but simply reaffirms what is already known, then the data is seen as having reached saturation.

Writing

Glaser and Strauss propose that writing ought to be undertaken only once a theory has been fully developed. It comprises the collation of memos and data exemplars to *write up* a theory. In this model, then, writing very much involves the presentation of ideas rather than the exploration of them, which, the authors suggest, is much better accomplished through memos.

An important criticism of grounded theory

As we have seen, one of the key and defining features of grounded theory is the emphasis on generating theory through research rather than prior to research. One of the strongest examples of this view in Glaser and Strauss's work (both in their early work and in their subsequent divergent writings) is in terms of the uses of literature. For example, Strauss and Corbin make a distinction between technical literature and non-technical literature, the former referring to published academic work such as books and journal articles and the latter to diaries, documents, reports, etc. As with Glaser and Strauss (1999 [1967]) and Glaser (1978, 1992), Strauss and Corbin argue that for the purposes of grounded theory it is best to avoid using literature to generate theoretical or conceptual ideas for pursuit in relation to the research. In a particularly telling statement they argue that:

> ...if you begin with a list of already identified variables (categories), they may – and are indeed very likely to – get in the way of discovery. Also, in grounded

> theory studies, you want to explain phenomena in light of the theoretical framework that evolves during the research itself; thus, you do not want to be constrained by having to adhere to a previously developed theory that may or may not apply to the area under investigation. (Strauss and Corbin, 1990: 49)

An example of this view in practice comes from Weider's study of a drug addiction in a half-way house. Weider's aim was to understand why parolees who stayed in the house did not recover from their addictions. Weider notes that he had no knowledge of such environments when he began his study: 'I had read none of the literature in this area, and at that point decided … that it would be desirable, at least at first, for me to remain ignorant in that regard. We felt that my ignorance was desirable because, equipped with the literature, my observations might be pushed in the direction of the results of previous studies' (Weider, 1983: 79). Weider's study is a good example of why this approach can be useful, as his research resulted in a very nuanced understanding of the 'subculture' of the institution, and the maxims by which the residents orientated to their daily life.

Both Glaser and Strauss (1999 [1967]) and Strauss and Corbin (1990) also argue that it may be useful to use literature *subsequently* to compare the categories that the research has generated with other research in the field (see Goulding, 2002, on this point). In this respect, then, literature may be a good way of generating ideas in subsequent analytic 'phases', but not in the first instance.

A strong criticism that has been levelled at this version of grounded theory is that it represents something of a disingenuous view of how research typically proceeds. Goulding (2002), for example, argues that as experienced researchers, Glaser and Strauss's characterization of their research as closed off from other research belies the level of their research knowledge. Further, since the authors do not preclude the use of externally derived concepts at other stages of the research, their insistence on avoiding them at earlier stages can seem a little strange. It is particularly difficult to align this process with contemporary social research practices, where research is usually only permitted where researchers can show how their work fits within broader theoretical frameworks. Researchers are often required to explain in some detail the types of conceptual apparatus that they might use to analyze their data before funding, ethical approval or institutional agreement will be given for it.

This criticism aside, grounded theory approaches demonstrate clearly the ways in which theoretical orientations, such as concepts, hypotheses, relations and so on, can emerge or develop through research.

Generalized theory practices

On one level, grounded theory presents a strong alternative to 'top-down' theory orientations, where theory is used from the outset to inform or guide research design and organize data work. However, the commitment to using theoretical orientations to structure one's design and analysis, and the aim of developing analytic frameworks and theoretical conceptions through analysis – or, more nebulously, of using *data* to interrogate *theory* – need not represent competing commitments. Indeed, the idea that *theory can be both a resource for and a product of research* is a useful guiding principle when conceptualizing the relation between theory and data. These two conceptualizations of theory are intended as a resource for making sense of theory work. From these two positions we can generate the following list of practices which might be informed by theory:

- Formulating research questions
- Conceptualizing and critically engaging with relevant research literature
- Designing research
- Organizing data
- Analyzing data.

Formulating research questions – As we have seen with the examples of Mead's application of Piaget, and from our example of using critical discourse analysis in relation to a study of primary education in Lesotho, theory can inform the formulation of research questions. Through engagement with theory, researchers can create ways of asking questions by using the concepts and analytic focus specified by a given theoretical orientation. Where theory emerges through research – e.g. where concepts are created through the analysis of data – these theoretical orientations can be used to frame new research questions or to recontextualize existing ones.

Conceptualizing and critically engaging with relevant research literature – Because theory entails the specialization of interests, it can be used as a mechanism for defining what is to count as relevant research literature, and for developing a critical approach to managing that literature. Literature forms the context in which research is conducted, and so finding a way of sifting through and relating to this context is crucial. We will discuss this issue in more detail in Chapter 3.

Designing research – The specification of theoretical concerns is strongly implicated in the development of research designs. This 'working through of theory and design' may come at the beginning of the research process, by identifying the kinds of data that are required in order to address particular theoretical concerns, or it may come later on in the research when new interests and concerns are generated. In either case, theoretical concerns have implications for what kind of data is required and, consequently, for the types of method that are best used to generate data. We will discuss these issues in Chapter 4.

Organizing data – Theoretical concerns may present researchers with particular data categories and offer possibilities for labelling that data in ways that correspond to those theoretical interests. They may lead researchers to want to adopt particular methods of transcription, and to organize those transcripts in particular ways. In the critical discourse analysis example we discussed earlier, the theoretical interests are likely to lead researchers to use detailed forms of transcription, where some of the nuances of speech are captured. The organization of data through transcription is the topic of Chapter 7.

Analyzing data – Processes such as categorizing, describing, relating and interpreting data can all be undertaken through the orientation to theory. Theory may offer concepts for creating, labelling, subdividing and relating categories. Similarly, it may help researchers to describe particular features of the data they are dealing with, by providing a language for 'carving up' the data terrain. As we have seen, however, analysis is a two-way process, and just as theory is a resource for interrogating data, so data is a resource for interrogating theory. Whether those ideas are generated through the data or prior to it, data provide a way of working through theoretical ideas.

These processes represent some of the key ways that theory interfaces with the processes of working with and analyzing data. As we said at the beginning of this chapter, theory and analysis are contextually defined, so it is very difficult to create general statements of what these kinds of activities look like. In this chapter, we have presented two of the key ways in which theory is often thought of in research. The summary of practices presented above provides a way of moving beyond the confines of specific approaches, and to thinking about how to work through theory in particular contexts of operation. Where appropriate in this book, we will be giving examples of how theories may be worked out in relation to the contexts in which researchers work with data.

Concluding remarks

We began this chapter reflecting on the diverse ways in which the word 'theory' is used, and to the range of practices that can be characterized as 'theory work'. This diversity creates some ambiguity in decontextualized discussions about 'the uses of theory'. When formulating and conducting research projects, part of the work that researchers face involves working out what the theoretical orientation of the project is, and how that relates to the design of research and the management of data. The aim of this chapter has been to help researchers to do this work of 'contextualization' by providing them with examples of how theory and data relate to each other, and in so doing, helping them to work towards the establishment of coherence in their research. The examples in our discussions of 'top-down' and 'bottom-up' theory, and the summary of research practices in which analysis and theory interface, are intended as resources for these purposes. In the remainder of this book, we will be offering further discussion and examples of these particular ideas.

Recommended further reading

Charmaz, K. (2006) *Constructing Grounded Theory: A Practical Guide through Qualitative Analysis*. London: Sage. A theoretically nuanced and practical outline of the central issues in grounded theory.

Clifford, J. and Marcus, W. (1986) *Writing Culture: The Poetics and Politics of Ethnography*. Berkeley, CA: University of California Press. An influential reflection on the nature of ethnographic writing and analysis.

Fairclough, N. (1995) *Critical Discourse Analysis: The Critical Study of Language*. London: Longman. A detailed account of the practices and positions of critical discourse analysis.

Glaser, B. and Strauss, A. (1999 [1967]) *The Discovery of Grounded Theory: Strategies for Qualitative Research*. New York: Aldine de Gruyter. The original description of the rationale of the turn to grounded theory and its methodological procedures.

3 Engaging with literature

This chapter discusses the following issues:

- Exploratory literature reviews
- Focused literature reviews
- Conducting literature searches
- Bibliographic databases

Introduction

In this chapter we explore some of the ways in which researchers can productively engage with literature in their own field in order to develop their own analytic ideas and position their research in relation to other research and writing. By entering and interrogating the discursive spaces in which other researchers distribute and discuss their work, researchers can create opportunities for the conceptual and analytic development of their own research. We examine the process of undertaking literature reviews using both *exploratory* and *focused* review strategies, and explore some of the ways that researchers can use tools such as research indexes and bibliographic databases to aid this type of work.

One of the challenges that researchers often face when developing a research project is in working out what the distinctive features of their project are, in relation to other research and other writing in the field in which they are working. Social research is an ever-expanding enterprise, and the chances are that whatever the field, there will already be some considerable research available in that area. The sheer quantity of such published work, and the diversity of perspectives from which it is conducted, can make it difficult for researchers to work out how to situate their own work and to be sure that this work is going to make a distinctive contribution to knowledge in the field. Very often, this challenge is regarded in a rather negative way, and the difficulty of specifying the 'novelty' of a research project can be a very real cause for concern, particularly among doctoral researchers. In this chapter, however, we want to present this challenge in a very positive light, and to discuss the opportunities that engagement with published works provides. Rather than seeing the challenge as a matter of 'fitting one's research around existing studies', we want to describe the orientation to existing research as an opportunity to position one's work in a positive way and to develop one's analytic and conceptual schemas.

The uses of literature

Engagement with published research and other writing is clearly important in the early stages of any research project. Researchers coming to new projects will have, with varying degrees of certainty, clarity and detail, ideas about the substantive focus of the proposed research, the theoretical position that they might adopt, the analytic concepts that could be deployed, the possibilities for the design of the research, and the potential methods for collection of data. Identifying related research helps them to refine and extend their ideas and gives them a clearer sense of what has been achieved in the field in which they are proposing to work, and how it has been achieved. This engagement with literature, and the systematic recording of what has been read, where it was published and its relevance for the development of the researcher's own ideas, enables the researcher to become more confident that there is a space in the field for their research to contribute to knowledge. It also enables the researcher to demonstrate a good knowledge of relevant research and other work, which is an important part of being able to present work with authority and confidence and being able to participate productively in any research community.

Searching for and reading literature in the early stages of a project is likely to be exploratory. This initial exploration enables a map of the field of research to be built up and for the researcher's work to be positioned in relation to the work carried out by others. It also allows the development of a sense of the kinds of questions people are asking, why they think these are important questions, who the important researchers are in the field, the ways in which research is conducted, the kinds of concepts that people are using to understand the phenomena they are researching, and so on. In other words, it enables researchers to *position* their work.

We can illustrate this process by looking at one particular PhD study. Anna Cleaves (2003, 2005), while working as a secondary school science teacher, became concerned that a high proportion of school students who were very successful in school science at the age of 14, did not choose science when they selected their A level subjects at the age of 16. From this initial observation, she decided to conduct a study of the process of selection of A level subjects and the factors that influence students in making these choices. In an initial review of literature, it became evident that, while there had been a substantial amount of research on the choices that students make, existing research focused specifically on the accounts given by students at the point at which the choice is made; none of the research looked at the process leading up to the choice, or the stability or otherwise of students' intentions over a period of time. This initial engagement with literature, therefore, indicated that there was a space for a qualitative, longitudinal study of cohorts of students over the three years leading up to their choice of subject specialism at age 16. This created the opportunity to develop a more subtle understanding of how decisions are made and to explore with students the various influences that act to shape their aspirations and choices.

Engaging with these studies also gave a sense of the kinds of theoretical perspectives adopted in order to explore and understand the process of subject choice (which extends beyond a specific interest in science as a curriculum area). A number of studies, for instance, sought to understand the subject choices made by considering the images held by students of particular professions (such as scientists), and the extent to which the students were able to identify personally with these images. Addressing the strengths and limitations of existing studies began to open up both an empirical and theoretical space for the research. We can see, then, that this dialogue with other relevant research has a key part to play in these early stages, but it also continues as the study develops. As researchers work through their projects, they will continue to seek out and engage with literature and to build an increasingly rich picture of the context within which the research is carried out. Keeping abreast of research in the area is an important ongoing task that continually enriches the researcher's sense of their own work and its relation to other research.

Strauss and Corbin (1990) identify five potential uses of literature in research that extend across the life-course of the project:

1   To stimulate theoretical sensitivity (e.g. to generate concepts that can be brought to the empirical setting from the literature). We refer to this as a 'concept development' approach.

2   As secondary sources of data.

3   To compare alternative analysis.

4   To direct theoretical sampling.

5   To validate or compare theory or empirical claims in relation to what has already been said in the published literature.

Concept development

By 'concept development' we mean the process of developing mechanisms for describing or categorizing some aspect of the social world and, more specifically, of one's data. Published literature has an important role to play in the development of such mechanisms. Engagement with literature can either:

- suggest concepts for use in relation to one's data, or
- provide a resource for comparing one's own concepts with other people's formulations.

For example, researchers may use literature to:

- adopt the descriptive/analytic language and categories used by other researchers
- mark out their distinctive use of particular concepts in relation to what other people have said about those concepts/ideas
- formulate new concepts in relation to existing ones
- situate their work within an existing theoretical perspective or paradigm.

In all of these respects, the orientation to and engagement with the discursive space in which conceptual language is formulated and negotiated is a potentially rich activity. This is not to say that theory or conceptual development is *necessarily* developed in this relational way. It may be that one's central conceptual ideas are derived from the examination of data rather than through orientation to other people's work, but all of the above possible outcomes from engagement with literature are very good reasons for starting one's research with an examination of existing literature. These ideas are explored further in Box 3.1.

Box 3.1   Analytic outcomes of literature engagement

Adopting the descriptive language of other researchers – The application of an existing theory is a good example of this approach. The analysis of the extract provided in Chapter 2, where critical discourse analysis was used as a framework for analyzing an interview transcript, gives some illustration of how this process may work. In that example, some of the key concepts and analytic interests associated with CDA were used as a mechanism for focusing on, categorizing, prioritizing and describing particular aspects of the transcript. Where an existing analytic approach has been identified as potentially relevant, a part of the literature review process focuses on gaining a full understanding of the key concepts of that approach.

Marking out their distinctive use of particular concepts – As we noted in the previous chapter, adopting a descriptive language does not necessarily mean that that language is used uncritically, and one's analysis can be concerned with developing, amending or problematizing aspects of it. A literature review can be directed towards gaining a critical understanding by, for example, examining the ways in which different authors have applied or debated concepts, or thinking about how the particular empirical contexts of application may have impacted on the use or character of concepts.

Formulate new concepts in relation to existing ones – New concepts may be derived from either the analysis of data or through the interrogation of existing concepts. In either case, understanding the ways that existing concepts have been formulated can be critical to creating a clear picture of the distinctiveness of any conceptual innovations.

Situating work within an existing theoretical perspective – Researchers may not be specific in their orientation to existing ideas, and might simply adopt a general perspective rather than particular concepts (e.g. they might identify themselves as working within a psychoanalytic framework, but not, in the first instance at least, have strong ideas about which aspects of that approach they are particularly interested in). In such instances, a literature review may be directed towards discovering the work that has been undertaken in their empirical area and within that perspective as a means of developing more specific orientations.

Secondary sources of data

Published research can provide secondary sources of data for interrogation by a researcher. Not all published qualitative research serves as a good candidate for secondary analysis. To be able to reanalyze data, researchers need to have access not only to the analysis that was conducted, but also to the data. However, interview data, for example, is often presented in very brief form (usually as extracts) in qualitative research publications, so that the analytic work that went into the creation of its interpretation is not available for reinterrogation. In such instances, the analysis and the data are to some extent hidden from researchers, which makes secondary analysis difficult. The position is similar with observational data, where, typically, the description of the researcher's analysis is based around the presentation of a small selection of a large data set.

However, some forms of data and analysis are available for reinterpretation: in many forms of discourse analysis or semiotic analysis, for example, researchers often use quite small data sets that are included, sometimes in their entirety, within a publication, and which can be reinterpreted by others after publication. A researcher may attempt to find studies that are related to the empirical domain they are interested in, in order to uncover published data and analysis that they can reanalyze. For example, Walkerdine and Lucey's (1989) exploration of mother/daughter relations and learning was based on their analysis of conversations collected as part of an earlier study by Tizard and Hughes (1984), which was conducted drawing on a very different theoretical perspective and which reached very different conclusions. To be successful, these kinds of studies require more extensive access to data than that which is provided in published accounts of research. Facilities such as the Economic and Social Data Service (http://www.esds.ac.uk) increasingly provide access to qualitative as well as quantitative data sets, accessible online, for use (including secondary analysis) by researchers.

Alternative analyses

Published research in a very similar area to one's own research may provide different analysis of the same, or very similar, empirical phenomena. In Gibson's (2006) study of jazz improvisation, Ingrid Monson's (1996) work on improvisation in the jazz rhythm section and Paul Berliner's (1994) ethnographic work both provided data and analysis that interpreted some of the features under investigation in very interesting ways. In Berliner's case, the different location of the empirical investigation created an interesting comparison with Gibson's own work, while with Monson, the particular analytic interest (rhythm section improvisation) formed a useful counterpoint to Gibson's focus. In these sorts of ways, published work can provide researchers with material that can situate their own work comparatively.

Directing theoretical sampling

As we saw in the previous chapter, the term 'theoretical sampling' refers to the process of selecting participants in a study on the basis of their relevance for the research questions being posed. Published studies can provide information and analysis that helps the researcher to direct their attention to such potential relevancies. Berliner's (1994) ethnography provided key information for Gibson's study as it proved vital in helping to reveal key features of performance that could be taken forward as potentially relevant analytic issues. For example, Berliner showed how different performance venues sometimes encouraged particular types of performance (such as highly experimental improvisations or improvisations situated within a particular genre). This observation was used to try to examine the ways in which musicians organized their performances on the basis of the performance setting, and was developed through interviews with musicians who performed regularly at particular venues. In these sorts of ways, the empirical findings of existing research can be used as a springboard to develop one's own research design strategy.

Validating theory

Published literature can also be useful for helping researchers to validate their findings and theories. Published studies in similar empirical domains may offer support for particular findings that have emerged through a study. The validation often comes from research in empirical contexts that bear some similarity, but which differ in some distinct way or ways, and that enable the researcher to make comparisons between settings. Usually, however, researchers will go beyond simply conducting a study that merely seeks to replicate and validate an existing piece of research, and will try to advance that work in some way, for example, by developing new theoretical insights.

Literature searches

There is an important distinction to be made between 'exploratory' and 'focused' literary searches (see Box 3.2). Both approaches are potentially valuable to the research process, but they are conducted for different reasons and in different ways. We will discuss each in turn.

> **Box 3.2   Exploratory and focused literature searches**
>
> **Exploratory literature searches** are used to map out a general area of research whereas **focused literature searches** are directed towards answering particular questions in relation to published literature. A given research project may include conduct of both types of searches.

Exploratory and systematic literature searches

Literature searches are often conceptualized as a means of gathering together all of the published *studies* in a particular empirical area as a means of situating one's own research or of gaining a comparative understanding of the totality of *research knowledge* in a particular area. This view is particularly associated with approaches to **systematic reviews**, where researchers attempt to collate the findings of lots of research projects in order to generate summaries of specific empirical research areas. Implicit in this view is the idea that any study that is substantially different from one's own study (and forgetting for the moment that there is nothing particularly precise about the phrase 'substantially different'), or anything that is not a 'study' (again, a pretty vague term, unless some clear definition is provided) is somehow of less value to researchers. This view is partial as, while it is important to situate research within a broader field, there are, as we have seen, other functions that literature can have for research.

Box 3.3   Systematic reviews

Systematic reviews have been used to provide policy makers and professional practitioners with knowledge to help them to make sense of published research. They aim to summarize and evaluate published research and, where appropriate, to draw conclusions and suggestions for best practice. Systematic reviews commonly give priority to research that is conducted through a 'randomized control trial' model, and tend to treat experimental research conditions as the 'gold standard' for research.

However, systematic reviews have also been used in qualitative research, see for example Myfanwy Lloyd Jones (2004) and Mary Dixon-Woods et al. (2006). The process of using systematic reviews to synthesize qualitative research is extremely time consuming, due to the iterative nature of the review process, with review criteria emerging from the process. Organizations such as the Evidence for Policy and Practice Information and Coordinating Centre (EPPI-Centre) provide information and advice on research synthesis and the conduct of systematic reviews, and act as a means of dissemination of reviews (http://eppi.ioe.ac.uk).

Systematic reviews have been subject to strong criticism from those who see them as representing a limited conception of the role that research knowledge can play in social policy and professional practice. Martyn Hammersley (2001) has been particularly influential in this discussion, and has argued that social policy and professional practice cannot be proceduralized according to evidence of best practice, as such matters are reliant on experience and professionalized judgement, which are, Hammersley argues, *ad hoc* and circumstantially negotiated matters.

Exploratory literature searches can be carried out for a variety of reasons. For example, a literature search may help a researcher to:

- gain an understanding of a theoretical field
- help to understand an empirical field
- understand the ways in which an empirical field has been theorized

- explore the work of a particular author or set of authors
- develop a sense of the methodological debates in a particular area.

All of these functions can help researchers to work through their research plans and to place their research into a broader literary context.

The following provides an example of the role, practices and character of an exploratory literature review:

> In his study of jazz improvisation, Gibson spent considerable time researching in archives and libraries. This archival work was directed to understanding the field of 'jazz studies'. This process started prior to the research study itself, and continued throughout the research. The value of this part of the literature review was in helping to situate the study in a broader literary field. This archival work was not restricted to academic work, but also encompassed the exploration of media texts such as jazz magazines, CD liner notes, online jazz communities, biographies, collected letters and other historical documents. New articles and writers would suggest new areas of interest and new topical concerns that would lead the researcher to a different set of references and authors, and to new genres of writing. This exploratory review was not centrally related to the research focus: the central topic question being explored pertained to the social organization of improvised musical performance, but the exploratory literature review examined all kinds of topics, such as the biographies of particular prominent players; the description of music scenes; and the musicological analysis of tunes, sub-genres or playing styles. While there was no clear link between many of the literatures investigated in this review and the research question being investigated, the literature was nonetheless fundamental for helping to understand how the very narrow and focused issues being pursued in the research related to more general discursive terrains in the field.

Advantages and limitations in exploratory reviews

Exploratory reviews are very useful for helping to think around the contexts of a research topic and for reflecting on the relational nature of one's study. Their very 'undisciplined' nature can provide rich rewards in terms of generating inspiration for new ways of thinking about or analyzing problems. Indeed, apparently irrelevant literature can, on occasion, contain surprisingly germane discussions. In Gibson's unfocused review, numerous biographical sources and musicological discussions actually provided very relevant secondary data on the nature of improvisation in practice.

However, in most research projects, researchers do not have the luxury of conducting an exploratory review with the hope that focused research questions will arise from it. The simple but disciplining imperatives of time, money and institutional pressure usually restrict the amount of effort that researchers can spend undertaking such open reviews, and normally mean that a clear research focus is required 'sooner rather than later'. In the majority of cases, then, such open review processes will be accompanied by more focused literature reviews and are likely to be either short-lived or an extra-curricula activity.

The process of conducting unfocused reviews is difficult to outline in detail because it is, by definition, very much an *ad hoc* enterprise. However, the following resources may be useful sources for exploration:

- Biographies
- Novels
- Newspapers
- Specialist magazines
- Online communities and discussion spaces
- Specialist libraries and archives.

Focused literature searches

In focused literature searchers the aim is to find studies that are as closely related to a given set of interests as possible. 'Closely related' here, can mean that studies are similar in a number of focal areas:

- Asking the same kinds of questions
- Using the same kinds of research designs
- Using the same kinds of methods
- Using similar theoretical frames
- Operating in a similar empirical domain.

One way to think about the production of focused reviews is to look for research that fits as many of these areas as possible. Most commonly, researchers discover that there are a lot of studies that fit with one or other of these focal points, a small number that fit with three or four of them, but very few, if any, that completely match the list of dimensions of relevance.

The purposes of conducting focused reviews are:

- to work out the theoretical/methodological contributions that the proposed study makes to the field
- to work out what is already known about a given empirical area.

A useful way to conceptualize these aims is to assume that there is a study available that absolutely matches the various dimensions or areas of relevance of the research project, and that the aim of the review is to find that study. This is a *trick* that forces the researcher to concentrate very closely on the nature of their own research, and to compare this with the approaches/theories/empirical interests of the other types of research that are encountered. In all likelihood, this idealized and perfectly matching study will not be found, but the discipline of focusing attention on one's interests is very valuable.

Studies that closely match a researcher's interests

A study that closely meets the search criteria in a literature review is useful for helping to understand the nature of the contribution of one's research project and for thinking about how other people's work may inform one's own. The closer a study is to one's own interest, the more challenging it becomes to find the individual feature of one's research. Many postgraduate researchers have reported to us the experience of finding a study that 'has already done what I wanted to do'. However, while in the early stages of research in particular it can *appear* that one's interests have been entirely satisfied by an existing study, it is very rarely, if ever, the case that an empirical domain is entirely 'used up' by the presence of such work as, to put it simply, *there is always more to say*. The particular character of this 'more' comes from the distinctiveness of the empirical focus, the people being included in the research (the research sample), the types of data that are available and the specific theories or concepts that are to be used.

Returning to Gibson's study of jazz improvisation, Berliner's (1994) already published ethnography of jazz was both a help and a hindrance – this work comprised large numbers of interviews, participant observations and active participation in the jazz community over many years. The depth of the study very much felt like 'the final word' on the matter of improvisation in jazz. However, as Gibson's research developed and new foci emerged, it became clear that far from blocking the development of the research project, Berliner's study offered a rich resource for addressing the very specific and particular problems that the research ended up posing. The distinctiveness of Gibson's research was in the ways that particular theoretical orientations were brought to bear on the empirical subject.

Studies that do not closely match a researcher's interests

Studies that less closely meet a search criteria are not necessarily less relevant to a research project. A study from a different analytic perspective can be valuable precisely because it shows how other disciplines or researchers have addressed that issue. Similarly, the application of a similar analytic framework and research design in a closely related but different empirical setting may be useful for showing the value of the analytic approach being taken. Mapping out the literary terrain, then, involves working through the theoretical, methodological and empirical features of a project in relation to published studies, and this 'mapping' includes illustrating differences as well as similarities.

Clearly, the production of a list of focal relevancies requires researchers to have a very well developed sense of their research. As qualitative enquiry is so often methodologically, theoretically and analytically iterative, it can often be difficult to specify all of these areas in detail at the beginning of the research process. For this reason, focused reviews may need to be carried out several times during research, or at the very least need to be updated at several points.

Conducting literature searches

Literature searches should be conducted using a variety of tools and sources. Bibliographic indexes such as ISI Web of Science, ERIC, and Sociological Abstracts, are search tools that enable researchers to search multiple journals and databases at the same time. Different indexes search different journals and vary in their level of disciplinary specialization, so repeating the same search on more than one database will be likely to produce different findings. When deciding which databases to use, researchers need to explore the extent and nature of their coverage, and its 'fit' with their areas of interest.

When conducting a search, researchers need to begin by analyzing their research topic and to divide it into its component parts. This involves undertaking a concept analysis of the central aspects of the research. We discuss concept analysis in more detail in Chapter 4 in the context of formulating a research question. Here, we simply wish to discuss the ways in which concepts can be worked out and combined in the context of literature searches.

Combining concepts in literature searches

Say a researcher is interested in exploring the issue of computers in classrooms. The researcher may outline the key concepts under investigation as:

> Classrooms – Computers – Educational Tasks – Educational Aids – Success/Failure

Each one of these concepts becomes a central aspect of the search strategy for which the researcher needs to specify the synonyms and alternative phrases that might be used to describe them in published literature. For example, the term computer may be described as:

> Computer – OR – laptop – OR – PC – OR – information technology – OR – educational technology

The '*OR*' is a Boolean search function that will instruct the index to search for one or other of the alternate phrases that are specified. The researcher needs to think about all the ways in which a given term may be described. Some concepts are of course easier than others. The phrase 'educational tasks', for example, may be particularly difficult to specify because of the very wide range of things that may be classed as 'educational tasks'. For this reason, it can be more straightforward to concentrate one's search on very focused concepts rather than on abstract terms.

Truncation symbols can help to overcome the problem of words that have potentially different endings. For example, 'comput*' (with an asterisk in place of the final 'e') would pick up phrases such as comput*e*, comput*er*, comput*ing*, comput*ation*, computa-*tional*. The precise symbols that are used in databases for searching for multiple word truncations vary. Other useful parameters that can be specified within a search include:

- type of publication (journal article, conference, professional report)
- year/years of publication
- language of publication.

Further, researchers can define the part of the publication in which they wish to search for the phrases (e.g. in the title, the abstract, the keywords, the main text), and can delineate the proximity of the words to each other (e.g. within ten words, in the same paragraph, on the same page).

The delineation of the central search concepts may also include specifying the key theoretical or methodological features of the research. If a researcher is particularly interested in carrying out an Action Research project, for example, 'Action Research' may be a concept that is included in the literature search. Similarly, if a researcher has a clear theoretical concern, like exploring postcolonial discourse, then that too may form a central part of the search. However, very broad terms, such as 'psychology' or 'geography', would be far too general to be much use.

The main purpose of all of this is to be able to retrieve as many relevant research publications as possible. The more flexibility is put into the search, the more articles will be retrieved. Typically, the search results will take the form of information on the publication (such as author, date, title, publication type, place of publication) and an abstract. The first task is to search through this information and to assess how relevant the search results are. Often, researchers will realize at this stage that some phrase or other is 'skewing' the search by bringing in a lot of irrelevant literature. It can be useful to rethink one's research strategies if this happens in order to minimize the number of irrelevant hits. Researchers need to browse the results to determine which are to be regarded as relevant. In many cases this will be straightforward as the topic will clearly be irrelevant. Often, however, the challenge is in working out 'what is to count as relevant'. This is much easier in a very focused literature search where the aim is to find very similar studies, but in more exploratory searches there is often a temptation to read all of the potentially relevant studies. In such cases, it is frequently the time constraints of the project that delineates the decisions about what should and should not be read.

Conducting literature searchers involves, then, the detailed analysis and specification of one's own research interests. The very process of orientating to a community of other researchers, of trying to situate one's interests and concerns into a wider body of work, and of using published research as a source of analytic inspiration *necessitates* working out the central concepts being explored, the parameters of the empirical domain being orientated to and, to some extent, the theoretical resources to be employed. In these respects, literature searching is a fundamental aspect of the conceptual development of research, and of the initial specifications of some of the analytic interests and parameters of the research.

Bibliographic databases

Bibliographic databases are useful tools for storing the information that is found during literature searches. Such databases record the basic reference information as well as more detailed notes and review points. There are various commercial products that can be used for these purposes, such as Endnote and RefMan. These tools provide user-friendly interfaces for not only storing literature references, but also for searching library catalogues, for the automated download of references, for inserting references into written texts and for building bibliographies. However, researchers who are less interested in these more technical aspects can of course build their own databases using basic spreadsheet and database software.

Bibliographic databases constitute a personalized catalogue and review of all the literature that has been read on a given project. The database may include keywords for each source, information on the content of the literature, commentary on its relevance or use for the research, and reviews and descriptions of the theory/methodology used in the studies. The database is organized around the production of an analysis of the literature, and such analysis is always relational to the analytic aims and character of one's own research. It can be useful to organize such analysis around three basic sets of information:

- Methodology
- Empirical domain
- Theory/concepts.

The review should include both basic descriptions as well as a critical review of the character of the literature in these three respects. Commercial products often include a generic 'notes' field, where information like this can be stored, but they can also usually be customized so that researchers can create their own specialized notes fields.

Keywords are another standard field in databases, and act as a kind of metatag that makes it easier to find information on particular topics within the database. While there are likely to be a few obvious words that will be relevant to a study at the beginning of a review process, many keywords will emerge through the study. One of the difficulties of metatagging in this way is keeping track of the often quite large numbers of descriptors that are created. The more unwieldy one's collection of tags, the harder it is to use and apply them in consistent ways. While it can be tempting to spend a long time in organizing ones tags and in working through a database to use them systematically, it is something of a false economy to spend too much time on this. Because most databases include search tools that allow you to search all the text in a given database, the production of tightly applied metatags is arguably less necessary.

Literature reviews are an opportunity to work through one's own interests and concerns in relation to the work of other people in the field. The reviews are not just a matter of providing critique from an already formulated position, but are also ways of thinking through issues that may be undeveloped. This point relates centrally to the model of social research that we outlined in the introduction to this book, with each aspect of research (including design, data collection, analysis, writing, literature reviewing) informing each other. The review of literature and the close examination of how other researchers have tackled a problem or empirical domain, the types of methods that have been employed in a given area of study, the uses and value of different theoretical and conceptual schemas – all of these aspects are important material for thinking through one's own research. The word 'review' in the phrase 'literature review', then, does not necessarily refer to the production of critique from a preformulated position, but also describes the creation of ideas through the orientation to other work.

Concluding remarks

This chapter has aimed to show some of the key ways in which researchers can put existing literature to work in the course of developing their own research ideas. Literature is, we suggest, a potentially very rich resource that can help researchers not only to formulate their concerns but also to work out how to pursue them in their particular contexts of operation. Engagement with published work is a tool for and component of analysis not a competitor to it, and this productive and reflective engagement can help researchers to develop an array of nuanced analytic resources.

Recommended further reading

Hart, C. (1998) *Doing a Literature Review: Releasing the Social Science Research Imagination.* London: Sage. A detailed and practical discussion of the literature review process.
Rumsey, S. (2004) *How To Find Information: A Guide for Researchers.* Maidenhead: Open University Press. A user-friendly outline of how to find documentary information.

4 Research design

This chapter discusses the following issues:

- Formulating research questions
- Developing research plans
- Sampling
- Methodological debates
- Ethics

Introduction

Research design can be thought of as a matter of figuring out what kind of data is needed to answer a research question or set of questions, and specifying approaches for gathering or *generating* that data. In order to do this, researchers need to have a strong sense of their interests and analytic focus. Because there is always more than one way to produce data, designing research involves working through the various possible strategies that research might take, and creating a clear idea of how the research is to proceed and how the design relates to or impacts on the research interests. Like the development of an analytic focus, the specification of a research design is an iterative feature of research that develops through the research process rather then being entirely prespecified. This chapter aims to clarify some of the ways in which design and data are linked, and to help researchers to think about the relationship between their design and data work.

'Research designs' vs. the research design process

Before we begin this discussion in detail, it is important to make a distinction between *research designs* and *the process of design*. **Research designs** refer to particular approaches to research, such as experiments, case studies, ethnography, and action research. **The process of research design** refers to the practice of working through a given focus for research and the generation of a research plan and design for that topic. The design of research entails specifying analytic interests and working out what kind of data is required to explore those interests, and how it is to be generated.

Specific research designs can be thought of as rough templates that provide a broad structure for thinking about how to work through a research project. In each case, though, these 'approaches' contain many possible variations on how they can be taken forward. A case study design, for example, might involve a detailed exploration of a single case or of multiple cases; a 'case' might be a person, an institution, a profession, a role, or any other relevant comparative variable; the methods might involve interviews, questionnaires, focus groups, document analysis, or any other research method (see Robert Yin's (2003) influential text on case studies). These templates then specify only very loose research protocols. Table 4.1 gives a brief outline of some of the key characteristics for a number of design approaches. While some approaches do have particular research methods that are typically used when pursuing those designs, their design parameters are in general extremely open. Researchers undertaking an ethnography, for example, may well use interviews, document analysis and possibly even questionnaires to complement their observation work.

Precisely because they are so open, it is not always helpful to think about a given research project according to these templates. There is so much fluidity between different approaches that it can sometimes be difficult to decide which one a given research project best fits within. For example, action research may well take the form of an experiment and use broadly ethnographic methods to accomplish its aims. Sometimes, then, thinking in terms of these templates can be constraining rather than liberating. In this chapter we are not concerned particularly with thinking about research in terms of these specific designs, but rather with the process of working through research designs. However, we will refer, as appropriate, to these more general design templates.

Approaching the design of research

The idea that we aim to develop in this chapter is that research design can be usefully conceptualized as a matter of working out the relationship between data and research topics. Designing research involves the following:

- Specifying research topics and questions
- Choosing research sites and participants and thinking through how they are to be selected
- Thinking through the methods of data collection and working out how they are to be employed.

Like all aspects of research, design is not static or self-contained, and develops throughout the life of research. Research topics and questions are sometimes not finalized until the research is very advanced. The exact sites of research and the participants included within it are often not known in advance, and it is more common than not for a researcher's plans

Table 4.1 Key specifications of common research designs

Approaches	Defining characteristics
Ethnography	Involves a commitment to understanding from the insider's point of view.
	Traditionally (e.g. in anthropological research), ethnographies involve substantial time in the field (e.g. at least six months) and aim for full immersion in a fieldwork setting. It is increasingly common for research to be of an 'ethnographic style' and to be much shorter and less intensive.
	It usually involves observational work, but this is often supplemented with other methods, such as interviews and documentary analysis.
Case study	Involves an exploration of one or more cases or the comparison of two or more cases.
	Usually, the number of cases is not large as the aim is typically to examine each case in detail.
	It usually involves multiple forms of data and can include both qualitative and quantitative components.
Experiments	Involve examining the effects of some form of 'intervention'.
	Can occur in natural as well as contrived experimental settings, and can involve a wide range of methods of data collection, including interviews, questionnaires and observation.
	Qualitative experiments typically involve a small sample size.
Survey	Involves using questionnaires of some form, which may be self-administered or delivered by face-to-face interviews.
	Normally, questionnaires are administered to quite a large number of people as the aim is typically to gain an understanding of a cross-section of people.
Action research	Involves the informed formulation of some kind of action or intervention to address a particular problem or issue and examining the impact on participants.
	Conducting the research and analyzing the data occurs cyclically and recursively rather than linearly, with a continual dialogue between the statement of the problem, the formulation of action, data collection and analysis.
	Commonly involves practitioners and participants as researchers.

to change somewhat as the research unfolds. Similarly, it is common for the research focus and interests to change somewhat during research, and for new areas of concern to emerge, which may mean that changes to the original plans of participant inclusion need to be made. Further, the methods of data collection can frequently need some design tweaks as the research progresses. This may be because of a shift in interest, because of difficulties or challenges in recruiting the desired participants, or it may simply be that, for whatever reason, the methods didn't quite produce the data that they were supposed to.

Given all of this, it is perhaps best to think of design as a two-stage process. Researchers usually produce some kind of **preliminary design**, where the general topic, participants and methods are given some definition as a means of getting the project off the ground. These are the kinds of outlines that would be used for research proposals or bids for funding, and as working plans that provide clear strategies for moving forward. These preliminary designs usually need to be very well worked if they are to convince an institution/funding body/ethics committee to support, fund or approve the research, or if they are to be of value as a research blueprint. One of the key aspects of a convincing and useful proposal is that they are coherent – i.e. that the topics and/or questions outlined can be answered or dealt with through the specified methods and sample. This preliminary design is then used as a referent throughout the research, and is developed as a **working design** as the unfolding contingencies of the research bring new interests, foci and ways of working. This working design is, in essence, a matter of using a preliminary design to work through the alignment between research interests and data, the methods that will be used to produce data, and the people who will be involved in research.

Research topics, concepts and questions

Very often, researchers start their projects with a quite general topic of interest that, over time, gets turned into a much more focused research question or concern. Topics usually comprise some delineation of one or more of the following:

- The empirical domain to be researched
- The particular kinds of people that are of interest
- The types of practice associated with and enacted by these people.

In the first instance, these are likely to be quite loosely formulated. It is very common for researchers to be a little unclear at the start of their projects about what exactly they are interested in researching. It is important, though, to work through one's initial vague ideas at the very beginning of the research process in order to develop more clearly formulated research questions and interests.

From words to concepts

A useful activity that can help to move a general topic towards a focused area involves interrogating the constituent parts of the given area of interest. Let's say, for example, a researcher is interested in examining the role of computers in classrooms. It may be that a researcher has noticed that sometimes computers work really well as educational aids and that at other times they do not. The component parts of the topic might be formulated as:

Classrooms – Computers – Educational tasks – Educational aids – Success/failure

The key words of the topic are separated out as potentially distinct concepts. The next step is to interrogate each one and to reach some further specification of what the particular interest is. For example, what does 'classrooms' mean in this context? Does it refer to a particular age of learner (such as those between six and seven years old), phase of education (such as primary or elementary education) or attainment level (such as low-achieving students)? Is the interest in comparing different ages/phases/levels or with examining just one particular age/phase/level? Is the interest in mixed attainment or differentiated classrooms, with learners of particular socio/cultural/economic characteristics, or with male and female students? Asking these questions shows that one of the constitutive features of 'classroom' is of course 'learner', and that defining the former involves defining the latter. Interrogating a concept, then, may well reveal that it points to, or is constituted by, other concepts that themselves need to be worked through.

The next concept outlined above is 'Computers'. Is the research interest in the computer itself as a physical object (e.g. its spatial impact on the learning environment) or is the interest in software? If the latter, is the concern with particular software, with a comparison of software types, or with software *in general*? If the interest is in software in general, how is this 'in general' going to be taken forward? As it is not possible to investigate all software, some decisions need to be made about what sorts of software are of interest (e.g. subject specific educational software, computer games, word-processing tools).

The general aim in this process of examining concepts is that each of the words within a given topic area are subject to the same sort of interrogation. In this way, researchers create a conceptual focus for their research – they narrow down their area of interest from something quite vague to something much more specific.

It might be that some of the words/concepts are either not relevant or are implied by one or more of the other concepts being used. In the above example, the concept of 'educational aid' might actually be covered by the words 'computers' and 'educational task' (e.g. it might be that 'educational aid' actually means 'computer software' in this context). The point of writing out the words like this is to be able to find a way to work out one's research interests in more detail. The idea is not to tie yourself to your concepts, but to work out which of them are significant, and what potential research issues they lead to or imply.

From concepts to questions

By interrogating concepts in this way, researchers can move from general topics of interest to much closer specifications of their research concerns. The next step is to try to move further on by articulating these concepts in the form of questions. Not all qualitative research necessarily involves formulating research questions in a very formal way, and can be more concerned with a general issue, conceptual problem, area of interests, and so on. Further, neither is it the case that the research process is best thought of as involving and being guided by a prespecified research question. Sometimes research is more iterative than that, and takes an exploratory path rather than one driven by specific questions. In their influential discussion of ethnography, Hammersley and Atkinson comment that 'Much of the effort that goes into data analysis is concerned with formulating and reformulating the research problem in ways that make it more amenable to investigation' (1994: 31). In this view, the analysis of data is directed towards working through a problem and research question as much as it is to answering that question. We wish to suggest, however, that precisely because analysis is not bounded and is an ongoing feature of research work, it can be very useful to think about research concepts in terms of questions as means of specifying and thinking through the research focus. These questions may well change and develop, and need not be treated as immutable, but the presence of some focused interest in the form of a question is very useful for working through a research design.

The form that a question takes will delimit the research interests in very clear ways. Any set of concepts can be formulated in a number of question forms. For example, Figure 4.1 shows four questions that could be developed from a set of specific concepts related to the above general research area. All of these questions pertain to the issue of 'gender', as specified under the 'classroom' concept. In the first question, gender is treated as something that might impact on the successful completion of a task, but no articulation is given of how that might be measured or examined. 'Impact on' is an extremely vague phrase and there is no indication in the question of what 'impact on' might look like. This does not mean that question 1 is bad; it simply implies that further specification may be required in order for it to be taken forward in a research design.

The second question is a lot more clearly articulated. The question sets up two groups of interest – single gender groups and mixed gender groups – and asks about their comparative abilities within interactive computer-based maths tasks. The clarity comes from the fact that we know that the interest is in a comparison of groups along their gender formation. The third and fourth questions turn gender into something that the students (question 3) and teacher (question 4) might be concerned with. Here, the concept becomes something that the research participants *do* rather than being something that *makes* them do something (i.e. be successful at the task). In comparison to the first question, the last three questions all treat the examination of the concept of gender as part of the research interest rather than merely as something that causes something else.

In all of these questions 'gender' seems to be *the* key or at least *one of* the key concepts. The maths–computer–success/failure issues could be thought of as the *context* in which this central issue is being explored. Of course, this need not be the case as any one of these concepts or issues could be treated as the central concern.

The point of developing research questions is that they facilitate the creation of a research plan. It is very difficult to design research if it is not clear what one is looking for so plans, even if they are partial and subject to change, are very important.

While there is a functional value in being able to create a question in the first instance and in having that question to orientate to throughout research, the fact that questions may well change should be expected and even embraced. Research is about discovery, experimentation and exploration. As researchers approach research settings wanting to find things out, it should not be surprising if one of the things they find is that there are more interesting things afoot than they first thought, or that some of their initial assumptions were incorrect.

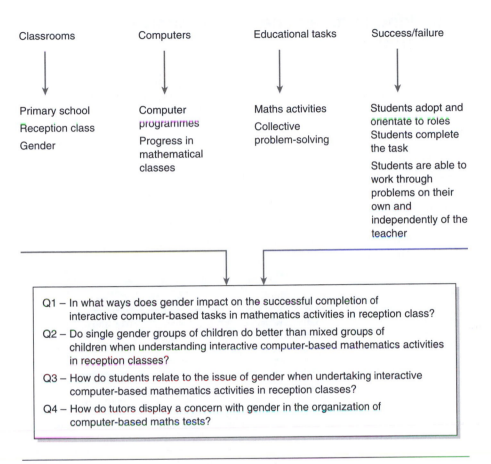

Figure 4.1 Research questions from research concepts

From research questions to research plans

Research questions provide a focus for the development of research *plans*. Ultimately, a research plan is a strategy for gathering data to help address a particular research issue. It is only when one knows what kind of data is required that it is possible to develop a strategy for gathering it. 'Knowing what you are looking for' does not imply that you know which direction your research will necessarily take, but simply that you have a directed interest and a preliminary sense of how you might begin to explore it. Research plans comprise two key things:

- A sense of what kind of data is required to answer a question
- A plan for gathering that data.

What kind of data is needed to answer a question?

Data is relevant if it enables the researcher to answer the question(s)/address the issues that they have posed. Making sure that relevant data is gathered involves aligning one's data and research questions/issues. A useful heuristic for creating such alignment is to make the assumption that any method could be used to deal with a given research problem, and then to work out which method is the *most* appropriate, practical and feasible.

Table 4.2 outlines a way of thinking about research methods that involves creating three categories of methods: observing people; asking people questions; and reading. This characterization has some similarity with the way that other researchers have described methods (e.g. Wollcott's (1994) 'experiencing, enquiring, examining' idea, where 'experiencing' refers to observation, 'enquiring' to asking questions, and 'examining' to textual research).

Table 4.2   Categorizing research methods

Category	Characteristics	Methods
Observing People	Watching what people do	Observational research
Asking People Questions	Asking questions about orientations, practices, experiences, etc.	Interviews Focus groups Questionnaires
Reading	Reading or examining documents and other textual resources	Documentary research

Let's take a practical research example in order to think through the differences in data forms within this three-way distinction. Say a hospital is concerned with examining the ways in which a new computerized information system may impact on the work of its various personnel. Question-asking methods (i.e. questionnaires, interviews, focus groups) can give information on the ways in which these various personnel may experience this new technology, and provide insight into how they may be affected by such implementations. Observations of work practice may also enable researchers to examine the impact of a given technology. It may be possible, for example, to look at the particular tasks that different personnel undertake and how they collaborate with each other, and to analyze the changes that a given technology might have on those practices. Similarly, by looking at documents such as time sheets, work logs, work protocols, or minutes from meetings, a researcher can also gain quite a good understanding of the potential impact of the computer system. Each of these general categories of method may well result in appropriate data for answering the research question.

Thinking through the ways in which these different methods can be put to use in a given setting is very useful for creating a preliminary map of the research setting, and for generating initial ideas for how that might be explored. This map helps the researcher to delimit their interests, and to focus on the types of area with which they are most concerned. Importantly, by producing this type of methods map, researchers nearly always generate a lot of questions, usually related to gaps in their knowledge. To continue with our example, the researcher in our hospital would have to gain a good knowledge of the types of document that are used in the settings they are interested in so that they could make informed decisions about which documents they wanted to use, which ones they would be likely to get access to, and how they might go about getting that access. In some instances it may be possible to conduct a **pilot study** as a means of answering these types of question. Our researcher may be able to conduct some preliminary interviews in order to get a better sense of the setting, so that they can design a study that is based on some knowledge rather than on guesswork. Alternatively, the researcher may need to build such preliminary 'fact finding' into their research. When writing formal research bids, it can be very useful to have completed any relevant pilot work as it is often more persuasive for funding bodies to receive bids that show some knowledge of the setting being explored.

A plan for gathering data

A plan for data gathering (or generating) will usually involve some detailed specification of:

- the methods to be used and the ways in which they are to be employed
- the people to be involved in the study (i.e. the sample)
- the timescale and costs of the project.

Using methods

The three-way methods categorization that we provided above is useful for thinking through ideas, but a research plan needs to be much more detailed than that. If conducting question-asking research, the researcher needs to think in detail about what is to be asked, why, and how those questions relate to the data. In observational research, the researcher should think through the particular features that are to be observed, why, and how they relate to the research interests. These issues are dealt with in detail in Chapter 6. In documentary forms of research, researchers need to think about what can be learnt from documents, the types of knowledge that is needed to understand them, the sorts of document that are available. All of these issues are discussed in detail in Chapter 5.

Advantages and disadvantages of particular research methods

Because decisions about research methods are always contextual, there is, in some senses, little point in thinking about research methods in terms of inherent advantages and limitations; the advantages and disadvantages are derived from the *particular* context in which they are being used. For example, in some instances it may be a disadvantage that questionnaires do not enable interviewees to probe the data, while in others the possibility of research participants writing freely without a researcher's interference may be perceived as an advantage. The alignment of research interests entails working out what are to count as advantages and disadvantages in particular contexts. We discuss this issue in more detail in Chapter 6.

Free choice and 'motivated' choice in methods selection

It is naïve to think that researchers always have a 'free choice' regarding the methods that they employ as it is quite unusual for researchers not to have some kind of research specialization and commitments that lead them to one choice rather than another. Indeed, many ethical guidelines promote professional standards by suggesting that researchers should only participate in research within their areas of expertise (i.e. to refuse work that they are not qualified to do). Further, researchers tend to develop preferences for particular modes of investigation – preferences that are often tied to epistemological conceptions of the nature of knowledge or particular orientations to methodological debates. Also, and as we saw in Chapter 2, the uses of particular theoretical ideas and positions may be more compatible with some forms of data than others.

Designing research, then, very often does not involve an open selection between possible methods, but is rather a matter of working out how a particular researcher or research team's skills, preferences, theoretical concerns, and practical interests may be used to answer a given question. However, even where such preferences are present, there is value in thinking through research strategies in these kinds of pluralistic ways, as researchers can generate a deeper understanding of how their own preferences and skills may relate to broader modes of enquiry. This is a very important feature of one's analytic focus as analysis is defined as much by research *limitations* as it is by research interests.

Selecting participants – sampling

Sampling refers, in broad terms, to the points of data collection or *cases* to be included within a research project. These points of data collection may be a person, a document, an institution, a setting, or any instance of information or data gathering. Samples are formulated in relation to the interests and concerns of the researcher and the logic of the research design adopted. The terms **theoretical sampling** and **purposive sampling** both describe the process of selecting research participants on the basis of their relevance to the research. The aim is to select possible research participants because they possess characteristics, roles, opinions, knowledge, ideas or experiences (or whatever else) that may be particularly relevant to the research. The **sampling frame** is the range of cases from whom the participant cases can be selected.

In some instances there may be formal documentation that could help to identify the cases of inclusion. In the hospital example discussed earlier, there may be a register of employees from which the researcher can draw a specific sample of relevant people. The researcher may be interested in the experiences of nurses of a particular specialization, and can use this list to select this sample. In other instances, the broader population might be quite opaque and hard to formulate. In his study of poolroom hustlers, Ned Polsky noted the difficulty of discussing the relationship between the sample he drew and the broader population of pool hustlers in the

USA. 'It is not possible to demonstrate the representativeness of [the] sample because the universe (all US pool and billiard hustlers) is not known exactly. But the hustlers I asked [...] generally agreed that today the number is quite small' (Polsky, 1971: 47). It is interesting that Polsky discusses the issue of his sample in relation to the matter of **representativity**. This refers to the link between a researcher's sample and the broader population to which it refers, with the idea that the sample 'represents' the wider population from which it is drawn. Where the *generalization* of research findings is a key concern, then the issue of 'representativity' can become important as the sample 'stands for' and is being used to *speak about* a broader population. However, it is not always the case that qualitative researchers are interested in speaking generally, or at least not in statistical terms. The aim of producing 'thick description', and nuanced understandings of social practices and situations that capture the details of those contexts often take priority over an attempt to strongly relate those findings to broader contexts. In Polsky's case, his use of this language of generalization perhaps reflects the time in which he was writing, when researchers using qualitative methodologies were still in many ways rather defensive and deferential to those using more quantitative approaches. In contemporary qualitative research, it is common to speak of generalization through theory (see Flick, 2004), where the conceptual apparatus of a project is used to infer relations between particular settings. The term 'qualitative inference' is occasionally used to discuss this notion of conceptually moving or 'inferring' between distinct cases or settings (see Reichertz, 2004).

In the beginning of research, when formulating a research plan, the research concepts and question(s) will form the central referent for constructing the categories of participant or 'case' relevance. In Gibson's (2006) study of jazz musicians, the initial sampling frame for interviews was very loose, as the interest was simply in understanding the performance perspectives of different musicians. The aim was to be able to interview people who played a range of musical instruments. As the study developed, though, other issues became relevant, such as whom those musicians had played with, their level of experience, their background in formal musical education, and their role as educators. Because analytic concerns are iterative, so too are sampling procedures. It is very commonly, or even *usually*, the case that as data is gathered and examined, so new ideas and interests for people to include in the study develop.

The nature of the population being studied has implications for the design of the research. Where the population of interest is large, and the range of variables of interest are quite broad, then the number of cases that need to be dealt with in the research increases. So, if the concern in our hypothetical example was with all personnel types within the hospital and not just doctors and nurses, and with all departments and sections within a hospital, the number of cases that need to be accessed is much higher. This, of course, has practical implications. If interviews are used, the time needed to interview potentially large numbers of people will increase dramatically. The more complicated the population of interest is, the harder it will be to develop a manageable sample. One common pitfall in constructing samples is to assume that all social variables must be considered all of the time. So, researchers frequently think that variables such as gender, social class, age, and other central demographic descriptors are necessarily important in social research. When operating with this assumption, it is easy for a sample to rapidly increase, as more and more cases are required in order to examine those variables. However, as Flick has put it:

> ...it is important to check critically the extent to which the classic demographic dimensions need to be considered in every study: do phenomena being studied and the research question really require a comparison according to gender, age, town or country, East or West, and so on? (Flick, 2004: 150)

Variables should only be included as features of sample selection if they are of clear analytic interest to the project.

Timescales and costs

Time and money are two of the most delimiting aspects of research. It is very easy to come up with elaborate plans and creative uses of methods, but these must be situated in the constraints of the project. While they can often be experienced as *constraints*, time and money are actually extremely useful considerations that can help to make selections about what to concentrate on and how to undertake a possible research project. A project that needs to be completed in three months will of course need to take a very different design from one that is to last three years. In our hospital example, a three-month project that managed a review of the literature and conducted some preliminary interviews with a very small number of key personnel would be doing extremely well. Over three years, this same project could conduct quite a large number of interviews, undertake some observations of practice, and conduct a much more thorough analysis of its data.

Similarly, thinking through the financial resources available enables researchers to know what is and is not possible and to design their study accordingly. If you have the money to pay for another researcher, then suddenly the person hours available to conduct research increases and the possibilities of what can be accomplished in the time grow. Likewise, if you have the money for extensive travel, for buying expensive technologies and software, for travelling to conferences to present and discuss the work, to put on international symposia with high-profile invited guests, then the possible research designs and research products are very open. In most cases, though, budgets are quite restricted, and these limitations mean that decisions have to be made about where efforts are to be concentrated.

Triangulation

The exploration of potential data characteristics can also be used to reflect on how different methods may be combined to create different types of data. This type of **triangulation** of methods is a common practice in qualitative research. By gathering data through different methods, researchers can compare different forms of data against each other. Focus groups may be a useful way of gaining an overview of ideas in the first instance, which can be subsequently followed up with focused individual interviews. In this way, collective discourse can be compared with individual opinion and experience. This may be very enlightening for examining how particular sets of personnel are represented within institutional discourse. Similarly, one may examine the relationship between how people *document* their practices in particular forms of work logs with how they *perform* them. This may help to show the strengths and limitations of systems of documentation, and the restrictions that they place on work practice. Triangulation can be useful for checking the **trustworthiness** of different sources of data (e.g. how accurate a data source is) or for examining the same phenomenon from different points of view.

Box 4.1   Trustworthiness

The notion of **trustworthiness** is used by Egon Guba and Yvonna Lincoln (1982) and is useful as a means of side-stepping the thorny issue of 'validity' in qualitative research and the connotations of 'truth' that come with it. Validity refers to the aim of 'measuring what you claim to be measuring'. This analytic aim can fit uneasily with the idea of the constructed nature of accounts to which much qualitative research is committed. Since meaning is constructed and open to a multiplicity of interpretation, the notion of 'truth' becomes something of a difficult concept to pin down. In contrast to validity, trustworthiness focuses on the context of data collection and the methods of the generation of data rather than on its inherent 'truthfulness'. This helps researchers to reflect in detail on how data is generated and on the relevance of that for the character of the data. To take a short example, say a researcher is interested in the impact of a new regime of airport security checks-in on passengers and decides to interview 30 people who have gone through those checks. The trustworthiness of the data may be compromised if the interviews are carried out a long time after the checks (i.e. so that it is hard to remember exactly what happened); while passengers are in a rush for a flight (so that they don't have time to reflect properly on the questions); if the interviewees are not told about the context of the research – i.e. who it is for and why it is being conducted (so that they don't know how to pitch their answers, e.g. as a customer satisfaction survey, as a review of security effectiveness, as a test of the people carrying out the security checks, etc.).

Other ways in which the notion of validity has been approached in qualitative research is by checking the relation between researchers' accounts and the common-sense knowledge of the members of the communities being researched, (see, for example, Frake, 1964). In such approaches, research participants or community members must be able to recognize the accounts being produced for the research findings or claims to be regarded as valid. Michael Bloor (1983) provides a very interesting critique of this approach, and points to the differences in the purposes of social research description and 'lay' description, and the problems of treating the latter as 'tests' of the former.

Returning to our hospital example, a researcher may choose both to observe practitioners working with computers and to interview them about their work. In such a technical domain, where the researcher is unlikely to have the expert knowledge necessary to understand the practices of the personnel, this approach can be very valuable for helping the researcher to understand in better detail the things they have observed, and for looking at the things that interviewees talked about in practice.

It is important to emphasize that this approach to triangulation involves an attempt to gain detailed understandings of research settings, practices or participants, and not an interest in trying to *verify* the findings of one method with another. As Flick (2004) has pointed out, the term 'triangulation' has been used in many different ways in social research, and often as an orientation to verification and validation. This is not the way we are using the term, and is not the usual way in which it is discussed in qualitative approaches. See Flick (2004: 178–9) for a more detailed discussion of these debates.

Ethics and research design

In making decisions about the design of a piece of research, it is vital to consider the ethical dimensions of the approach to be taken and the specific ethical issues that might be raised in working through a project. The general issues that need to be thought through are:

- informed consent
- confidentiality
- avoiding harm
- integrity and professionalism.

Various professional bodies provide ethical guidelines for researchers to follow in the design and conduct of their research. Awareness of and affiliation to such guidelines has become standard practice, and the completion of a formal ethical review through the host research institution (i.e. the institution to which the researcher is affiliated or where they are to carry out their work) is now normally a condition of applying for funding to conduct research. Such guidelines have the general aim of protecting the research participants and other interested parties to the research, including the researcher, as well as helping to maintain professional research standards, promote public confidence in research, and minimize legal risk. Ethical guidelines comprise statements of intent and appropriate practice that can be used to help researchers to work through the ethical dimensions of their research.

Whether funded or not, research nearly always needs to pass through an ethics committee before it can go ahead. It is very common for social researchers to experience these committees as a hurdle that needs to be cleared, rather than as an opportunity to reflect on their research and to engage in genuine debate about ethical practice in social research. In their very influential text, Israel and Hay (2006) promote an orientation to research ethics as an integrated aspect of research practice; as something that concerns every feature of research, and as an ongoing concern that does not end once a research council or ethics committee has given permission. They illustrate that it is very common for research to diverge from the practices that were agreed by funders or other bodies, and for new and unanticipated dilemmas and concerns to emerge as research progresses. They also emphasize that in contemporary social research, which is, in some cases, still dominated by models of research ethics developed in biomedical sciences, it is important to continue to have nuanced debates about ethics.

Ethics is a very broad area of research concern, and one that space restricts us from considering in detail. We would like to confine our discussion of this issue to data work. While it may seem strange to discuss this in a chapter about research design, researchers do need to give consideration to these matters while thinking about design not only because research ethics boards expect them to, but because doing so helps them to anticipate and minimize possible problems later on.

Ethical considerations in research design and data work

Anonymity of participants

It is very often the case that researchers want to hide the identity of their research participants. Importantly, though, it should not be assumed that anonymity is essential in ethical research, as there are certainly instances in which visibility may be entirely appropriate (see Israel and Hay, 2006). Where anonymity is preferred, researchers often choose to use pseudonyms to mask particular biographical features or other obvious identifiers. While in principle this can work, there are frequently occasions where such details are fundamental aspects of the data, where it matters who is saying what. For example, in our hospital example, a senior consultant in a particular area of specialization may make comments about the benefits of a new computer system that strongly reflect his institutional position. Analytically, it may be important to reveal the institutional role of the person as it shows something about how that group of people regard the organization of hospital work, but making this public may make the person identifiable. Similarly, the ways that people speak, the topics that they discuss, the sorts of stories that they tell – all of these things can make the participants identifiable by other people (particularly in small samples or in tightly-knit communities). Further, it can be difficult for researchers to know which features of the data would be recognizable by others. It may be that one of the anecdotes told in an interview is widely associated with a given person (who has told it on other occasions to other people) and by using and citing it as data, the researcher inadvertently reveals the identity of the person who provided it. In short, it is easy to promise anonymity, but in practice it can be much harder to safeguard.

Data manipulation

The use of pseudonyms and the hiding of other biographical features are, in essence, a matter of manipulating data. But there are lots of other ways in which data might be manipulated. A researcher might deliberately not select sections of data that obviously reveal an identity, that deal with a sensitive issue, or which contradict an emerging argument, for example. Researchers might be tempted to provide small manipulations of talk or observations so that they fit more closely with their emerging ideas, or so that they support an emerging case. Perhaps an interviewee has said something in a slightly unclear way that can be remedied by changing the words in order to preserve and clarify the intended meaning. While some of these practices are easily seen as unethical (it is hard to imagine what context could possibly justify making up or changing data to support an argument), others are a little less easily classified as 'definitely' or 'definitely not' appropriate.

Data storage and management

The protection of data is a key issue in social research. The nature of research work, and the fact that it involves lots of travel, working in more than one place, and often requires researchers to share their data (in part or in the whole) with other people (e.g. by presenting at conferences or colloquia, discussing with colleagues or supervisors, or working in research teams), all mean that the location of data can be hard to specify and contain. It can easily end up on various internal hard drives, external disks, as email attachments, in printed form as a handout or a working paper. Very careful thought needs to be given to how data is stored and distributed, and the mechanisms that are used to contain it within the bounds of the researcher's control.

The life of data

It is also very important to think about what happens to data after a project has finished. A common approach is to assume that the best policy is to simply destroy data once the research is complete. The wide dispersal of data that we discussed in the previous paragraph can make it difficult to be entirely sure that all records have been destroyed. Further, it is not always obvious that the 'destruction' of data is necessarily the best option. A researcher may have an interest in preserving data so that they can show how they reached their conclusions, or in order to revisit their analysis later in order to clarify or develop it. Even research participants may have an interest in having access to such analysis so that they can trace their presence within an analysis. Research funding councils can occasionally make requests for research data to be stored in 'data repositories' so that other researchers can use them. There are also instances where researchers may be asked to share their data with the police and other formal institutions. Van Maanen's (1983) ethnographic work as a police cadet provides a famous example. Some years after completing his work, Van Maanen received a subpoena to present his data to a court as it had a bearing on an important legal case.

These examples illustrate the complexity of issues that researchers face when reflecting on the ethical dimensions of their work. The four general concerns of informed consent, confidentiality, avoiding harm, and integrity/professionalism are not in any sense straightforward ideological aims, but extremely complicated and contested issues that are read differently by different people, and which take different shape in different contexts. In some cases, the general moral codes may operate in contradiction of each other. Returning to Van Maanen's (1983) study, the subpoena for data was made in order to investigate some of the claims made by a newspaper reporter who drew on his informal conversations with Van Maanen to produce accounts of police brutality and corruption. Van Maanen's data did contain detailed accounts that corroborated these accusations, but revealing them would breach the trust of the research participants, who had accepted him as one of the police community. Van Maanen did not submit his materials. This example shows the importance of Israel and Hay's argument that ethics is far from a static or 'solvable' feature of research, but is, like analysis, iterative, circular and multifaceted (Israel and Hay, 2006).

Research design and the analysis of data

The process of designing research is intimately tied to analysis as, in the end, design is about formulating a strategy for collecting data in order to explore a set of analytic concerns. A research design can be thought of as the crystallization of abstract interests and questions into tangible approaches for generating data. The process of working out these abstract interests into practical plans and strategies will result in quite detailed research specifications. These specifications will include the following:

- A well formulated set of research concepts
- A research question or set of research questions
- A detailed sense of who might be included in the study and how their selection relates to the research questions and concepts
- A knowledge of the type of data to be generated through the research
- A knowledge of the methods that are to be used to gather that data
- A rationale for why the chosen data gathering methods are being employed rather than others
- An awareness of the limitations that these methods will place on the research and how this focuses the analytic concerns of the project
- A sense of the methodological issues implicated in the research methods and an outline of possible strategies for responding to them
- An understanding of the ethical implications of all aspects of the research, of how they may be managed, and the implications of these responses for the research process and the data gathered.

As we have said, the preliminary design plans that are developed through these specifications are iterative, and are modified and reworked as the research progresses.

We noted in Chapter 1 that one of our key aims is to encourage an approach to data work that is about conceptual problems and not exclusively about techniques. The description of research design that we have provided in this chapter shows the ways that conceptual problems are used to fashion data; to sketch out the basic character of the required data and its relationship to a research problem. When working with data, then, researchers do so with these specified interests, questions and concerns in mind, trying to answer the questions and deal with the problems that they will have posed while designing and collecting that data. Researchers who get to the stage of having some data and then think 'what now?', can very usefully begin by recalling the very many decisions and delineations they made in the process of getting that data.

Concluding remarks

We have spoken in this chapter about the ways in which researchers 'design' the basic character of their data so that it can be used to address a particular problem. The processes of specifying a research question, of selecting the methods to be used in research and, where relevant, their relation to each other, of thinking through the sampling strategy for research, of working out the budgetary and temporal limitations of the research, of carefully considering the ethical dilemmas raised by all of the above – all of these are undertaken *iteratively* through a process of trial and error, and with careful thought about how each one impacts on the others. All of these aspects relate to data, and to its use in answering a question or dealing with a problem, issue or area of interest. In the next two chapters we look more closely at the process of actually collecting data in relation to documentary research (Chapter 5), asking questions and observational research (Chapter 6), and explore the ways that the actual experience of research can also be conceived as a matter of generating data to deal with a specific research problem.

Recommended further reading

Alford, R.A. (1998) *The Craft of Inquiry: Theories, Methods, Evidence*. Oxford: Oxford University Press. A widely cited text with some interesting reflections on the intersection of theory and method.

Cresswell, J. (2007) *Qualitative Inquiry and Research Design: Choosing among Five Approaches*. London: Sage. This text provides an accessible overview of a number of approaches to qualitative research, including ethnography, case studies, phenomenology, and narrative/ biographical research.

Flick, U., von Kardorff, E. and Steinke, I. (eds) (2004) *A Companion to Qualitative Research*. London: Sage. A wide-ranging discussion of issues related to design and data work in qualitative research.

Israel, M. and Hay, I. (2006) *Research Ethics for Social Scientists*. London: Sage. This book provides a guide to thinking through ethical issues in relation to research practice in productive and thoughtful ways.

Marshall, C. and Rossman, G.B. (2006) *Designing Qualitative Research*. London: Sage. An elegant and expansive discussion of issues in research design and practice.

Silverman, D. (2005) *Doing Qualitative Research: A Practical Handbook*. (2nd edn). London: Sage. A thoughtful and accessible introduction to some of the key issues faced in designing research in qualitative approaches.

5 Using documents in research

This chapter discusses the following issues:

- Analytically filtered and analytically focused data
- Documents as primary data and secondary data
- Analyzing and categorizing documents
- Types of document

Introduction

A central aim in this chapter is to demonstrate the analytic value of documentary sources of data. The general point that we emphasize is that documents can offer distinctive analytic possibilities, particularly when combined with other data generation methods.

Documentary research refers to the process of using documents as a means of social investigation and involves exploring the records that individuals and organizations produce. Documents are, as Gary McCulloch (2004) makes clear, a ubiquitous feature of social life that can be used by social researchers as an important empirical resource for their enquiries. Such documents might include letters, diaries, maps, minutes from meetings, social registers, governmental reports, emails, websites, posters, wikis, blogs, and any other record of social practice. Through documents, researchers can gain detailed insights into people's lives, and to the workings of organizations. One of the distinguishing features of documentary methods is that they can be *either* **analytically focused** *or* **analytically filtered**. Analytically focused methods involve creating strategies for generating data that is relevant to the research question(s) being asked. The interview method is an analytically focused method because it entails the creation of a discourse that is designed, through the engagement of both parties with the specific questions being asked and the responses given, to answer the research question. The data that results from an interview – namely, the *talk* – is structured either tacitly or explicitly in relation to the research question. Similarly, observations involve researchers selectively generating recordings of data, usually in the form of fieldnotes that can be subsequently interrogated. Documentary research can also have this character. To take an example, researchers might invite their participants to keep diaries of a particular feature of their life, or to take photographs of their work practices. In these ways, the data from the method is generated to answer particular questions or address a particular problem.

Box 5.1   Analytically focused and analytically filtered methods

Analytically focused methods are those that generate data in a way that is focused on the research problem at hand. Crucially, data is a *product* of the implementation of the method. **Analytically filtered** methods do not generate data, but select or *filter* data according to their relevance to the research problem.

However, much documentary research – and probably the majority of work that researchers do with documents – is not analytically focused but analytically *filtered*. Many of the documents that researchers use as sources of information pre-exist the researcher, and are remnants or features of the social worlds/lives/practices being explored. In other words, the documents as *data* are produced through the practices being researched, rather than in order to answer a research question. In this form of documentary research, creating analytically focused data is essentially a matter of *choosing*, rather than *generating*, the right data. To put the matter like this makes data 'selection' sound like a very passive process. In reality, of course, achieving an 'appropriate selection' involves a significant amount of analytic skill and focus. In documentary research, as with any other method, analysis is a lived part of the working through of the method, and *not just* a tool that is used to make sense of the data once it is created. Relevant data is an emergent property of this 'lived analysis'. A key part of the aim of this chapter is to reflect on the process of data selection in documentary methods.

Primary and secondary data

Another distinction that is relevant for thinking about the nature of analysis in documentary research is that of primary, as against secondary, data.

The term **primary data** is typically used to refer to data that is generated either by the researcher, a research participant or by someone relevant to the research question (such as a historical figure). Primary data is *first hand* in that it is a product of a researcher's or a research participant's practices or reflection. **Secondary data** usually refers to commentaries or claims made on other data by other researchers, reporters or commentators. In documentary research, it is common to distinguish **primary**

documents, which have the character of primary data, from **secondary documents**, which typically take the form of newspaper articles, academic work and other forms of commentary or reportage that are secondary with respect to the events and accounts with which they engage and on which they report.

While this is a common distinction to make, one of the problems with it is that it can lead researchers to think in a rather polarized way about their own research projects by potentially ignoring sources of information that may be absolutely central to their research. Secondary data, such as newspaper reports, are, of course, not produced to answer the questions that a piece of research is asking, but they can nonetheless be fundamental for informing researchers of particular events, or for leading researchers to think about issues in new ways.

Further, secondary data can, on occasion, *become* primary data. Say a researcher is investigating the impact of the introduction of parking restrictions in a particular residential area. A project may start out by using interviews as a means of data generation. The researcher may subsequently discover the importance of news coverage in local and international papers as a means of understanding the impact of the parking restrictions. That data could be regarded as 'secondary', as it simply contextualizes or 'frames' the research. On the other hand, those newspaper articles could be treated as data in their own right: as a form of politicized discourse that is a *resource* used by the interviewees in their discourse in the interviews. The newspaper reports could even be presented to interviewees as a means of generating discussion on the topic, perhaps in the context of focus groups. In these sorts of ways, the newspaper reports move from being a contextual object to a data-generating resource in their own right.

In addition, researchers may choose to subject the newspaper reports to analysis through some form of discourse analysis, like critical discourse analysis, as a means of understanding how the reports construct and use particular versions of 'reality'. They may then decide to analyze, for instance, transcripts of council meetings, where particular policies were formulated and implemented as a means of understanding how the new procedures came about. As this example shows, there is a difficulty in conceptualizing and discussing the matter of secondary data use, as the things that count as either 'primary' or 'secondary' are dependent on the way a given research question is framed. What is secondary data to one project may be primary data to another.

In this chapter we are not particularly concerned with the primary/secondary distinction, but we will inevitably refer to it at various points. Our aim is to show the ways in which various documentary sources (some forms of which are often thought of as 'secondary sources') may be used to work through and develop one's research, and to explain how they can be put to analytic use.

Choosing and working with documentary sources

The sources of information that are included in a research project very much depends on the questions being asked. Just as one selects interviewees on the basis of their relevance to a given project, so researchers choose their sources of documentary evidence according to how well they relate to the central research questions. However, with documentary research, it is not always easy to tell whether or not a given document will be relevant. A researcher may discover a diary in an archive kept by someone centrally related to their topic, but which contains little information relevant to their question. It can take a significant amount of work to find appropriate materials for one's research.

There are two possible complementary strategies available to researchers in trying to map the terrain of documentary sources available to them: **brainstorming** and **exploring**.

Brainstorming documentary sources – The first is to think about what kinds of documents might be useful to help them answer their preliminary research questions. Say, for example, a researcher is interested in exploring the quality of life in a care home for the elderly. They may begin by assuming that diaries of both the people who live in the home and the staff would be a very useful resource. They may also want to look at the operational policies of the home, and the ways in which the home is organized by examining the work schedules or the reports made by staff on the residents. They may also look at any letters that residents have written to their families or friends, or at the diaries of relatives who regularly visit the home. Constructing such a list can help to creatively focus one's thoughts on the types of evidence that may inform one's research.

However, such a list is, in many respects, a work of fiction (or, more accurately, of *fantasy*) – it is a *wish list*, not a list of known existing sources, and its generation merely a precursor to more active research. It is very difficult for researchers to diplomatically enquire into the existence of diaries or personal letters, let alone gain permission to actually look at them. The value of this kind of brainstorming, however, is in thinking about how particular institutional/individual practices, attitudes, experiences (or whatever) may be manifest in documentary form, and the ways in which such documents might relate to their research questions. The list itself is not what is of interest; it is the detailed reflection on the ways that documents may relate to research questions that is of importance.

Exploring documentary sources – A second and complementary strategy is to try to identify the kinds of documents that are actually available. Again, this is by no means easy as, in most settings, there is no list that sets out the range of documentary sources that might be accessible. Researchers can usefully start with some of the more obvious forms of documentation. In our example of an elderly care home, a researcher might begin by looking at minutes of staff meetings that have been held, or by looking at reports made by the staff on particular residents. It may be that by reading the minutes of meetings, researchers discover that there are particular policy documents outlining the mission statement of the home or health and safety procedures or principles of professional practice.

Brown (1999), in a study of social class and parental participation in schooling, focused on a particular project that was set up to help primary school teachers involve parents in the mathematical learning of their children. This included mathematics activities for parents and children to do together, which could be added to teachers' schemes of work. In order to understand how the project worked and to get a feel for possible sources of data, Brown spent a period of time with the project directors and others involved in the project and attended meetings for teachers and parents. Documents relating to the project were collected, including published and less formally produced and distributed material, which helped Brown to gain an understanding of the origins and ethos of the project and how it operated in practice. In addition to this contextual material, other sources of data, relating more closely to the central focus of the research, came to light. For instance, many of the schools taking part in the project produced booklets for parents which were designed to explain what parents were expected to do, how this would benefit their children, and so on. These booklets gave insight into the manner in which teachers conceived the relationship between school and home and the ways in which parents could legitimately participate in supporting the progress of their children at school. A more systematically collected sample of these booklets had the potential to contribute more than contextual background to the study. Closer analysis of the booklets could show how teachers construct domestic practice and the activities of parents in relation to schooling. They could also show how this varied from school to school and the extent to which any variation might be related to the social characteristics of the community served by the school.

Other documents available within the project held even greater potential for exploration of key research questions. Parents and children were, for instance, asked to complete simple diaries relating to the mathematics activities that they carried out together, and the project directors had collected sets of these for the purposes of evaluation and research. Analyzing the content of these diaries in relation to the intake characteristics of the schools constituted a substantial component of Brown's subsequent research project.

A key issue in gaining access to documentary sources (which includes the more preliminary issue of simply finding out about their existence) is the matter of **building trust**. The overall aim of gaining trust is to assure one's participants that the research is ethically sound and that any documentary sources will be used with sensitivity in respect of the ways that they may affect the community or individuals being researched. All research should attend to ethical codes as guides to and checks on the conduct of the researcher in achieving those aims. However, the *practices* to which such aims and ethical standards pertain are somewhat slippery. It can be very difficult to describe general approaches to building trust that will work in *all* instances. Working out how to develop trust is a contextual matter, and the role of ethical codes and guidelines is principally as a *guide*, not a rulebook. Research will commonly give rise in practice to ethical questions and dilemmas that do not have off-the-peg or easily codified solutions, and which require creative thought and engagement on the part of the researcher.

Combining documentary and other empirical sources

The interrogation of documents may well occur in conjunction with other forms of data collection, including interviews and observational work. Documents can be used to compare, for example, how some people explain an issue and how they document it. This may be used to 'cross validate' or *triangulate* one's data, but it may also simply be a means of exploring the ways in which different contingencies or contexts place different requirements on how particular issues are to be recorded, represented or talked about. In other words, that a document does not match another form of evidence may not necessarily *invalidate* another data source. To return to our example of research in an elderly care home, a researcher may find that an official report on an elderly patient's health conflicts with how that patient has described those problems to a researcher in an interview (e.g. in a more simplified form, or with some details being omitted). Thinking about this as a matter of 'validation' may take one's focus away from interesting reasons for such differences. By combining documents with other data sources, researchers can explore their research setting in a comparative way, and help them to look at their setting from more than one perspective.

In Brown's (1999) research on parental participation in schooling, banks of mathematics activities, notes from meetings, booklets for parents and diaries completed by parents and children were combined with interviews with parents and teachers. The interview material enabled Brown to move beyond the representation of the activities relating to parental participation in these various forms, and to examine the expectations of teachers and how they interpreted what parents produced with their children and the comments made in the diaries. It also enabled him to explore with parents what they did with the activities sent home with the children and how they thought the activities would help their children at school. It was possible to explore with parents how they made decisions both about doing the activities and what they would write in the diaries. Interviews facilitated the collection of information about their occupational and educational background and other biographical data that could contribute to a more nuanced understanding of the complex relationship between social class and schooling than would be possible from documentary sources alone. Analysis of the differences in the perspectives of parents and teachers, and differences within these groups, enables the researcher to explore and explain how a particular set of practices can generate distinct patterns of social differentiation and stratification.

Some documents may actually require the insights of insiders in the community to help make sense of them. In Gibson's (2006) study of jazz improvisations, Gibson used interviews to discuss recordings of particular performances, and to analyze music scores. In this way, the insider knowledge of research participants was used as a resource to interrogate the documents that were being analyzed. Similarly, Brown (1999) presented examples of activity sheets sent home to parents to explore how they interpreted these sheets and to gather accounts of how they went about doing the activities with their children.

Analyzing documents

Sometimes researchers choose to use documents as a primary form of evidence because of the difficulties of using other methods. Historical researchers, for example, very often have very little option but to use documents and artifacts as their primary form of data. Similarly, where researchers are exploring contemporary practices, the difficulties of gaining access to some areas of social life may mean that documents are the only source available for interrogation. In such instances, documents must be considered on their own, using whatever analytic resources may be at hand to make sense of them. While the analysis that researchers undertake in relation to documents is of course contextually specific, there are a number of general features to which researchers can usefully pay attention. Table 5.1 provides some examples of the types of question that a researcher might ask when examining a document for the first time.

Table 5.1 General questions that are useful for examining documents

Time	When was the document produced?
	How long did the document take to be produced? How does that timing relate to other key events?
Author	Is there a single author or multiple authors? Is the author operating independently or as a member of an institution or organization? Is the document produced through sponsorship or funding from other bodies, or in association with other bodies? Has the author produced other documents that are of relevance, and how does this document compare/relate to them? Does the author have some public notoriety/institutional role/relation to other people that may be relevant?
Purpose	What is the document for? Why is it structured in the way that it is? Why was it produced when it was? Does/did the document achieve its aims?
Audience	Who is the document for? Is the audience diverse or homogeneous? Did the document reach its audience? How did the audience respond to it?
Relation to other documents	Is the document part of a collection of documents? Does the document develop something that was started previously or is it a new document? If the document is a stand-alone object, why is that the case?
Ownership	Who owns the document? Has the ownership changed, and if so, who owned it previously and why did it change? Are the owners the same people as the producers or the audience?
Alteration	Has the document been changed at any point? If so, who changed it, how and why? Does that alteration reflect some change in function/role/status?

To take an example, establishing the *author* of the document is very important for working out the way it is to be read, e.g. as voicing the opinions of an individual or as outlining an institutional perspective; as part of an institution's work; as a document for public consumption or as a record for the individual. Not all of these questions will necessarily be relevant to all researchers, and there may well be other questions that are not included in this list that are of central importance.

When preparing to work with documents, researchers may usefully try to construct a list of their own questions, which they can take to their analysis. In the early stages of research this may be quite difficult, but as research progresses, researchers are likely to become more focused in their investigations and have very specific reasons for wanting to look at documents. It is also likely that different documents will be relevant for different reasons, so that it is difficult to treat all questions as relevant to every document.

It is important to make individual **record sheets** for all documents. A useful way to organize such sheets is to use three separate sections, with the first containing the general questions to be asked of all documents and the answers to those questions; the second containing the specific questions being asked of *that* document and the answers to those questions; and the third containing all the action points or new questions that emerge through the analysis. This format makes it easy to see the similarities and differences between the analyses conducted of different documents, and to keep track of how the analysis develops in terms of specifications of new research questions and foci.

Categorizing documents

In addition to asking questions of documents, researchers can often find it useful to make analytic distinctions between the types of document that they are looking at. The document types that we discuss below (such as diaries, letters, newspapers, etc.) comprise one kind of distinction, but there may be other distinctions that can help the researcher to make sense of their data. To repeat, all analysis is contextual and so the particular ways in which such distinctions are made will always be worked out in the context of a particular project. As a means of illustration we provide two examples of some distinctions that have been used in documentary research.

Two examples of document categorizations

Hakim (1983) distinguishes 'routine', 'regular' and 'special' documents. **Routine documents** are those that are produced in the normal functioning of a given institution. So, in the context of a shop, the various inventories of goods received and sold would be routine documents within the institution. Routine documents are useful for examining the functioning of an organization and its general procedures of operation, the ways that it manages its business, and its level of stability over time. Precisely because they are routinely produced, such documents are often reasonably complete and reliable, as they are often produced according to strict procedures.

Regular documents are those that are created through an institution's response to external factors. Such documents are not fundamental to the ongoing business of the particular institution, but are a by-product of their relations with others. These may be forms of record-keeping that are imposed by others (such as when regulatory bodies insist on certain bureaucratic procedures being undertaken). Clearly, there is a rather opaque relationship between regular and routine documents, as the former can quickly become institutionalized and be produced as a matter of course, therefore becoming *routine* documents. The distinction is perhaps not best approached as a hard-and-fast one, but merely as a tool for thinking about the relationship between different organizations.

Finally, unusual or unique circumstances, such as changes in organizational structure, procedure or responses to emergencies or unusual situations, result in **special documents**. Special documents are a record of how an organization responded to or coped with a particular change. This form of distinction may be quite useful when a researcher is interested in the documentary sources in an institution, and in trying to make sense of the various roles that the documents play and how they came about.

Another approach to categorizing documents comes from John Scott (1990), who uses three document categories that are cross-referenced with particular levels of access to those documents, from entirely closed access to published public resources (see Table 5.2). This categorization makes an initial distinction between personal, individually owned and produced documents on the one hand and official/institutional documents on the other. Official documents are then subdivided into **private** or **state** authored documents. Table 5.2 represents a coding scheme for categorizing documents according to how they fit within this descriptive scheme. In Scott's approach, an archived personal letter would be coded as '3', while an official document, produced by, for example, a member of government and held in a private collection, would be coded as '5'.

Table 5.2 Scott's document classification schema

Access	Authorship		
	Personal	Official	
		Private	State
Closed	1	5	9
Restricted	2	6	10
Open – archival	3	7	11
Open – published	4	8	12

The classification of documents in these kinds of ways gives researchers a conceptual schema for making sense of the terrain of the documentary resources available to them. Very often, a researcher's own analysis may involve working out how they can categorize their documentary sources. Of course, categorization is a means to an end: namely, being able to put the documents to work in saying something distinctive about a given empirical setting.

Forms of documentary data

Digital, electronic and online

The internet provides an extremely rich resource for researchers as it offers easy access to commentary, public debate, published and unpublished reports, to libraries and archives, and very many other document sources. Through the web, researchers can gain information and resources that, as recently as five years ago, would have been much more difficult to access.

The websites of all kinds of organizations offer links to a large variety of documents. To take an example, most university websites will include links to mission statements, guidelines of ethical practice, conditions of employment, the organizational structure, the history of the institution, the courses and modules offered, complaints procedures, application forms, maps, guides, staff curriculum vitae, research papers, and much more. A quick visit to a website might produce immense amounts of documentary material for researchers, much of which may be only peripheral to the central interests of a research project.

But the web is more than simply a portal to documentary sources; it is a documentary source in its own right. Web pages constitute perhaps the most ubiquitous form of documentary evidence in contemporary society, and many organizations and social groups are entirely constituted by web pages and online activity. Further, it is not only documents to which the web provides access, but also computer-mediated discourse through discussion boards or real-time text chat. This has rather clouded the concept of 'documentary research' as these documentary sources actually *constitute* the discursive practices of many forms of social activity and, as a result, have changed the landscape of documentary research quite dramatically. Much of what we say below about different forms of documentary data is relevant to associated online or other digital resources.

Newspapers

Our comments in this section are primarily directed towards newspapers, but they may be relevant to other forms of textual print media, such as magazines. They are also relevant to the digital counterparts of and adjuncts to these media, such as websites associated with newspapers and magazines, and other means of online news reporting. The value of newspapers for researchers is often overlooked as the concern with creating a research design for collecting primary data and with engagement with published academic work often takes precedence. This set of priorities may be appropriate in most cases, of course, but newspapers are nonetheless potentially very valuable resources for researchers. While there are distinct conventions for the production of news reporting, and while these conventions often do not involve the same concerns with methodological rigour found in academic work, newspapers offer diverse forms of discourse on a wide range of issues.

The value of newspapers

Newspapers can be valuable to researchers in a number of ways. First, reporters will very often have access to parts of society that academic or commercial researchers do not have. Newspapers may publish interviews with political leaders, heads of industry or other high-profile people who may be unreachable to researchers. Secondly, popular media is a much more rapid form of production and distribution of information, knowledge and opinion. Academic publishing, which is a key forum for social research distribution, is very slow – it can take as long as two years from the submission of an article to a journal and its actual publication, and books often have a similar production time. Newspapers, on the other hand, can produce pieces in a matter of days (sometimes hours), and are therefore much more up to date. As a device for finding out about contemporary events, newspapers are extremely valuable.

Newspapers provide researchers with material for thinking about research problems from different perspectives. News reports are typically politically charged, and presented in a distinctively journalistic manner. Reports on domestic politics, for example, are very often imbued with implicit, and sometimes explicit, support for particular types of position (which frequently manifest in support for particular political parties or candidates). This form of rhetorical positioning can help to reveal some of the ways in which, for instance, morality is normalized into dimensions of 'ordinary and taken for granted positions'. Social researchers frame their research within this field, sometimes even allying themselves with one or other of these existing positions. To take an example, two contrasting moral positions in immigration are that, on the one hand, immigrants are essential for the health of the economy of 'first world' countries, and, on the other, that they are a potential stress on the economic resources of the country. Researchers who are involved in investigating this area inevitably come into contact with these distinctive positions. This does not mean that they need to take one or other of these stances, but simply that these popular opinions are likely to shape the empirical domain in which the researchers operate. An engagement with the media discourse in this area, then, sensitizes the researcher to these positions, and gives an awareness of the popular discourse which will constitute one of the resources on which their research participants draw to make sense of that and related issues.

The limitations of newspapers

Quite clearly, the information included within newspapers must be treated with extreme caution and will typically not form the central data source for researchers. Newspapers are politicized and often sensationalized forms of discourse that do not present a balanced view but offer particular perspectives on the events being reported. Newspapers do not provide information on how their data was gathered, or even on what constitutes data in their accounts. They are, by definition, produced with the aim of selling newspapers, and therefore are always subject to the suspicion that a story may have been manipulated, or even manufactured, in order to make it interesting. Newspapers are far from being unproblematic resources. The suggestion, then, is not that newspapers form a primary means of data, or even that they form a primary resource for reflecting on a given issue, but simply that the pervasiveness of newspapers as a context for public debate and the dissemination of common knowledge makes them very important for researchers trying to understand those phenomena.

While they may not usually be the main form of primary data, the use of newspapers can be improved by systematizing the way in which one searches them, and by carefully selecting the newspapers that are used to inform one's research. Many newspapers now have online search tools that can be used to look at back issues, and good libraries will carry microfiche and digitized catalogues that can be explored and, in the case of digital information, searched, for relevant information.

In sum, the role that newspapers can usefully play for researchers is as a means of contextualizing one's primary data gathering, by framing the understanding of an issue, and its manifestation in distinct questions and research strategies, within an awareness of a public discourse of that general area.

Diaries

Diaries can potentially offer rich insights into the lives of their authors. Where they are not produced specifically as part of a given research project, their content is not likely to address directly the researcher's interests (or at least, they are not likely to *consistently* do so). In such instances, the content of diaries will probably be only partially relevant to a research project.

Clearly, and as we discussed briefly earlier in this chapter, there are important ethical issues in using diaries that are produced for purposes other than the research. Diaries are, by definition, usually private documents whose function is to record private thoughts and interpretations; their use as data for producing publicly available research findings is therefore problematic, as such use may be contrary to the author's intention. Where diaries have been donated to an archive or other public information source, researchers are of course free to use them in accordance with the specifications of use outlined in the archive (see Lynn Bloom's (1996) discussion of the public and private status of diaries). However, where they remain the property of individuals, researchers need to be much more careful and their use must be agreed with their owners/producers. In addition to ethical use, researchers face the difficulty of gaining access to such sources and, even more problematic sometimes, of becoming aware of their existence. Precisely because they are private, it is often the case that researchers do not know that such documents exist.

Because of these difficulties, the decision of whether or not to use diaries as data is contingent on circumstances: where they become available, and where clear and agreed terms of use can be established, diaries can provide useful devices for framing and developing one's ideas. This is, as we discuss below, particularly the case in historical forms of documentary research.

Diaries as analytically focused documents

Diaries are frequently used as a means of *generating* data, rather than as gathering existing accounts, i.e. as *analytically focused* forms or, as Heather Elliot (1997) has called them, research-*driven* documents. One of the most common approaches to diary research is to invite participants to keep diaries that record particular events or that capture the author's feelings at particular points in time or in relation to specific interventions.

Diary research can, like all forms of primary data collection, be either prestructured or open. In its prestructured form, diary research involves specifying the types of data that are relevant. For example, researchers exploring the ways that family and friendship groups are used as resources for coping with terminal illness may ask patients undergoing treatment to keep diaries that record their daily lives and the practical and emotional role that the family plays in their treatment. The researcher may pre-specify particular aspects and contextual information that they wish the respondents to record, like the date and time of the entry, or the people who were involved in the event being reported.

The analytic focus that is provided is, of course, related to the research interests being explored. In the above example, the 'specification' of interest is still quite loosely formulated, but researchers could go further and provide more structured formats for the diary's production. The diary may contain particular sections for each entry that need to be completed. In this way, researchers can create a very neat and systematic set of data, with each data instance (i.e. each diary entry) covering the same topical issues. Such specifications aid the subsequent comparison and help to ensure consistency in the data. The diaries analyzed by Brown (1999), for instance, were designed specifically to provide feedback on mathematics activities carried out by parents and children. They contained both specific structured items on, for example, the level of perceived difficulty of the tasks and the opportunity to make open-ended statements about whatever aspects of the process participants wished to comment on or describe.

Box 5.2   Structured and unstructured diaries

Structured diaries provide an analytically focused data-gathering instrument that enables the researcher to collect data on very specific features. **Unstructured diaries** enable researchers to discover things of interest about the life of a person or group of people. Designing diary research involves thinking through the relation between these two forms of data for the particular research project. It is important to remember, though, that these are not necessarily mutually exclusive forms as:

- unstructured forms can lead on to using structured forms
- structured forms can include unstructured sections.

With unstructured diaries, the aim is usually to iteratively develop the themes of analysis from the data, rather than pre-specifying them. In this approach, research participants are given much more freedom to decide what they want to record in the diaries. With unstructured diaries, the flexibility of the format means that researchers may discover thematic relevancies that could have been overlooked with the use of predefined structures. Unstructured approaches are often used as preliminary forms of data gathering, and as a precursor to the creation of more structured interventions and forms of data collection. In diary research, then, researchers may use an analysis of unstructured content to create a more focused data-generation method or strategy.

The dilemma in deciding on the level of structure in diary research is the same as that faced with any primary data collection method (such as observations, interviews or focus groups): too much structure may limit the iterative development of ideas, but too little may hinder the comparability or *coherence* of the data. The puzzle of how to relate to the level of predefined structuring is a matter of working through the research interests and the particular focus of the project being undertaken. The *design* and *application* of diary research is most successful where it is directed by a conception of the nature of the data required and its relation to the questions being asked. We discuss this issue in more detail in Chapter 6.

Advantages and limitations of diary research

At their best, diaries can be a fantastic way of generating detailed data at regular intervals. Unlike interviews, which usually occur only once or on a small number of occasions, diary data can be gathered over a much longer timeframe. Entries can also be made in close proximity to the occurrence of the events that they describe or address. Diaries can also be quite empowering methods for research participants, who are able to use and develop their own voice more easily than they can in interview settings. However, the success of the method very much relies on the comfort that the participants have with the written form. Researchers who suspect that written diaries may be problematic for their purposes may wish to use devices such as audio/video recorders as a means of capturing the data. Indeed, such forms can be richer than the written diary as tone of voice and facial expressions can be useful for gaining more of a sense of the person and their feelings at given points in the research.

Another form of diary research involves inviting participants to create photo diaries, by regularly collecting data on a video or still camera. Still cameras in particular have become prominent data collection modes in visual research, where the collection of images in people's lives has been an important means of documenting and analyzing the material culture of different social worlds. Nässla and Car (2003), for example, used photo diaries of the ways in which families used a bulletin board in order to help the researchers to reflect on the design of an electronic version of the bulletin board. Such forms provide media-rich insights into social practices that may be missed by written diaries. By combining a variety of forms, researchers can create analytically insightful data that allows them to explore the relationship between the different representational modes. They may, for example, ask participants to take photographs and to write commentaries on the pictures that they take. As with other diary forms, though, researchers need to think carefully about the nature of the instructions that they provide to research participants so that the data that is produced is analytically appropriate to the research aims.

Letters and other forms of communication

In the pre-digital communication age, paper-based letters were the primary means of written communication between people. Historians have long relied on records of this form of communication to find out about the lives of the people who wrote them, and the nature of the social contexts in which they lived. McCulloch (2007), in his study of the prominent English educator Sir Cyril Norwood, draws on a range of public and private documents, including letters made available to him by Norwood's family. These letters include correspondence between Norwood and teachers at the school where he was headteacher (Harrow School) and other colleagues, letters to a solicitor and memoranda to the school's Board of Governors. In attempting to build as rich a picture as possible of Norwood's controversial time as headteacher of Harrow, McCulloch engaged in written correspondence with some surviving pupils from Norwood's time at the school. To comply with current legislation on the use of data, before he was able to write to these former pupils, the school had to ascertain that they were agreeable to being contacted by McCulloch for research purposes.

With the remarkable rise of the internet as a medium of communication, new forms of knowledge exchange are now dramatically expanding the range of resources that researchers have for investigating social practice. Email is one of the dominant forms of written communication in the twenty-first century and, as a result, is a fantastically rich source of information for social researchers.

Other forms of communication include chat-room discussions (either written or audio-video based), blogs and wikis. Blogs are single-authored webpages that are frequently used as a form of online diary. Often, blogs include comments facilities where other people can comment on the blog's content. Discussion boards are another common form of online communication. Many web forums include discussion boards as a means of asynchronous communication between the site members. Wikis are multi-authored webpages that constitute a record of a group of individuals' work, and can be analyzed to explore the ways in which particular ideas have evolved and been constructed among the group, as well as simply for the nature of their content as a collaborative production.

Natasha Whiteman (2007) analyzes this kind of data in her comparative study of two internet fan communities. Her data comprises the postings made to discussion groups on two internet sites, one concerned with a television series (*Angel*) and the other with a video game (*Silent Hill*). Whiteman's study alerts us to a number of distinct issues that have to be addressed by researchers analyzing this kind of data. One is the instability of the documents. During her study, one of the sites was attacked by hackers and taken offline, requiring Whiteman to work from an archived copy she had made of the site. Her data had thus changed from being publicly available to being a private archive. Another issue relates to the authorship of the postings. No association can reliably be made between a given username (under which the postings are made) and a unique, known individual. The researcher can clearly not make claims to know anything certain about personal characteristics associated with any given username. Furthermore, postings made under the same username do not mean that they are made by the same person. Whiteman thus had to consider the discussions that take place on the sites as interactions between 'avatars', i.e., between usernames, not people. These decisions, which relate to the units of analysis of the study, are clearly analytic in nature, and display further the ways that engagement with research resources and the working through of research leads one's analysis and focus to develop.

Practical and ethical issues in analyzing electronic forms of communication

There are, of course, a number of other difficulties associated with such research. First, researchers commonly have to cope with a massive amount of very dispersed information. For example, the sheer quantity of emails that can build up on an individual's email account, and the often haphazard approach to organizing and archiving these, makes it very difficult for researchers to know where to start with such information. Secondly, there is the ever-present difficulty of gaining access to such information. The ubiquitous nature of email communication means that it is used as a form of exchange within and across institutions and within friendship and family networks. Thus, gaining access to an email account may mean gaining access to very many aspects of an individual's life, and not just the particular aspect that a researcher may be interested in. Unless the particular user has been very systematic about their storage of their email, it is often very difficult for a researcher (or a research participant) to filter this information.

The ethical implications of this are immense. Even if an individual agrees to participate in a given research project, the various institutions or other individuals with whom they communicate may not, and as email frequently involves records of their conversations too, it can be difficult for researchers to exclude them from their investigation. Very similar issues apply to other forms of electronic discourse. Sixsmith and Murray (2001) show that the dynamic nature of many online communities makes it very difficult to gather consent from all community members within a given discussion group.

While there are ethical and practical problems associated with the examination of all of these communicative and collaborative modes, there are also distinctive opportunities. Some forms of collaboration, such as blogs and wikis, are usually public environments so, practically speaking, researchers can very easily access the data that they require. The data is also often the entirety of the social world being investigated. In other methods of investigation, such as interviews for example, the data is a guide to things that happen in other, inaccessible social worlds and practices. In some forms of online documentary research, the entire social world is visible to the researcher. Even in the most successful of ethnographic forms of investigation, researchers frequently only have access to certain parts of the social setting.

Photographs and other images

Images, in the form of photographs, maps and drawings, are an extremely useful documentary resource for social researchers. Images can be used both as data and in presenting the outcomes of research. As data, images can provide a means of moving beyond written descriptions and provide a richer access to the people, places and practices being studied. By presenting their data in visual form, researchers can also provide their readers with a depth and nuance of insight that is hard to achieve with text alone. Description is, of course, an analytic endeavour as it involves providing guided insights and characterizations. The use of photographs as an aid to description is a means of analytically drawing attention to particular aspects rather than others.

Where they are treated as a form of 'evidence' about the social world, photographs must be dealt with carefully. The myth of the truthful image – as in 'the camera never lies' – is nicely illustrated by Howard Becker's (2002) reflections on the impact of a piece of photojournalism that *mischaracterized* the town that constituted its subject matter as 'deserted' and 'run-down'. The photographs created a narrative that completely misrepresented the social and economic realities of life in that small town. Becker uses this observation to illustrate that, as with all forms of evidence, it is important to be sure that photographs are representative of whatever it is they are supposed to depict. This basic point is useful for drawing attention to the fact that, when using photographs, the same principles of research design and data collection that we have discussed in this and the previous chapter are applicable. When using photographs researchers need to:

Be clear that the photographs have a role to play in the analysis – Ethnographic work can particularly benefit from the use of photographs as the aim is often to explain and depict forms of life, and the inclusion of photographs aids the creation of a 'thick description' (see Sarah Pink's (2001) discussion of visual ethnography). The value of photographs is not restricted to ethnography, however. Any form of research where the description and analysis of events and practices will be enhanced by images may benefit from including this form of data. For many approaches to research, photographs may not provide much additional information to other data sources. Photographs are only relevant where they aid the production of a detailed description or play some analytic role that cannot be achieved by other forms of data. In some instances, of course, photographs might constitute the principal form of data in a study. Burke and Ribeiro de Castro (2007), for instance, analyze books of school photographs as a way of exploring the relationship between the school and the community.

Be sure to map the relationship between photographs and other data sources, and be clear about the distinctive functional role that the photographs play in the analysis. Where photographs are being used in conjunction with other data (such as interviews or observation schedules), it is important to be clear how these data forms relate to one another. Two particularly important questions to consider in this respect are:

- What do photographs provide that the other data do not?
- Can one type of data inform the understanding of the other?

Reflect on the structure of the photograph and its implicit meanings – Photographs are partial, focally restricted, two-dimensional representations that show the world from a particular angle and visual perspective. The implicit meanings within a photograph are a result of this combination of factors, and researchers need to be careful that the pictures that they take or use do not *misrepresent*.

Select the photographs that are included in the study according to a clearly articulated sampling rationale – Photographs are typically used to tell a story about the social world that is being investigated. Where this is the case, the images must be selected to tell that story in a representative way. Just as individual photographs can mislead, so the cumulative effect of photographs can create false impressions, as in Becker's (2002) reported example.

Design the study so that the analysis of the photographic material can inform the design of the research – The iterative nature of social research means that analysis often leads to new interests and foci. When using photographs, it is important to integrate the close examination of photographs with the process of their collection. This quite simply involves starting the analysis of images as soon as they have been collected.

Photographs and images can be used to provoke and sustain discussion with research participants and as a resource for sparking ideas, comparing perspectives and generating alternative analyses. Andrew Pollard (1996), for instance, used photographs of classrooms and school activities to initiate a discussion with young children about their perceptions of schooling. This kind of approach might be extended to look at how people make sense of images created by other people. Photographs might also be solicited from research participants rather than being produced or provided by the researcher, creating a context for a discussion that gives the researcher insight into the lives of these people and their practices. A very interesting example of such collaboration comes from Caroline Wang and Mary Ann Burris's 'Photovoice' projects (e.g. Wang and Burris, 1994, 1997; Wang et al., 1996). Wang and Burris gave cameras to disenfranchised communities and invited them to collect visual images of their everyday lives. These images were used as resources for discussion with the researchers and helped to create detailed and contextualized explorations of some of the issues involved in the research participants' everyday lives. A similar approach was adopted by Diane Mavers and colleagues (Mavers et al., 2002), who invited school children to produce concept maps that pictorially represented their experiences of using computers and then undertook interviews with the children to explore further the rationales behind the images they produced. In these sorts of ways, texts can be used to collect further data, rather than being simply treated as 'meaning-ed objects' that need to be interpreted by the researcher.

The practice of integrating images into the research process in these sorts of ways fits well with interpretivist views of the world, which regard the 'myth' of the researcher as an unbiased observer looking in on research sites and *gathering* data to aid their analysis as, at best, disingenuous. The notion of a researcher's privileged position is firmly deconstructed in these approaches, as research knowledge comes to be seen as a negotiated creation rather than a researcher's discovery. Researcher and participants work out *in situ* the relevance and meaning of data, and discursively think through the implications and relevancies of particular forms of analysis. This epistemological position should not, however, compromise the researcher's integrity in the gathering and use of data. As we have seen, photographs can be used *mis*representatively, and it is the job of the researcher to use their reflexivity and developing knowledge and awareness of the issues being researched to select the images that are to count as data appropriately.

Concluding remarks

In this chapter we have sought to outline some of the ways that documentary sources can be put to work in social research. One of the purposes of the discussion has been to show that even where they are not doing 'documentary research' as such, the examination of documents can be a very useful way for researchers to explore or develop their ideas. Newspapers, for example, can be used to help researchers reflect on how their research topic relates to wider societal discourse. As we discussed in relation to photographs, documents can also be valuable resources for generating discussion with one's research participants and as a stimulus to further discourse. As a result of the developments in the World Wide Web, documentary research is now a very different proposition both in terms of practical organization and the breadth of materials that are available. In the next chapter we move from this very focused discussion of documentary sources to reflect on the relationship between analysis and data gathering more broadly.

Recommended further reading

McCulloch, G. (2004) *Documentary Research in Education, History and the Social Sciences.* London: Routledge Falmer. A thoughtful and nuanced account of documentary research.

Pink, S. (2001) *Doing Visual Ethnography: Images, Media and Representations in Research.* London: Sage. A detailed and insightful investigation of the use of images in ethnographic research that has relevance not just to 'ethnographers' but to social researchers in general.

Scott, J. (1990) *A Matter of Record: Documentary Sources in Social Research.* Cambridge: Polity Press. An analytically rich account of the uses and possibilities of documentary sources.

6 Generating data through questions and observations

This chapter discusses the following issues:

- The generation of interview data
- Structured, semi-structured and unstructured approaches to interviewing
- Interview modes
- Structured and unstructured observations
- Participant and non-participant observation
- Covert and overt observation

Introduction

Some approaches to research design have taken forward the view that the processes of data collection and data analysis can be mutually informative. Action research, for example, with its cyclical approach to data gathering and analysis, and grounded theory's iterative drive to the construction of theory both involve working through the relationship between analysis and data collection in non-linear ways. In both approaches, the logic of data collection is shown to be closely tied to the analytic concerns of a given research project. Both approaches show that the demarcation of a clear dividing line between 'getting data' and 'analyzing data' can be unhelpful as it involves treating analysis as an afterthought, rather than as an integral aspect of how to think about the question 'What counts as relevant data?' and how to manage the data-gathering process.

One of the criticisms that has been made of both grounded theory and action research is that they often formulate their methodological approaches in rather impractical ways. Some of the more extreme versions of grounded theory have been criticized for implying that the process of developing research *plans* may run contrary to the development of theory, as any plan would involve the specification of theoretical interests rather than allowing those interests to iteratively develop through research (Goulding, 2002). On a purely practical level, undertaking research without a clear methodological outline of the process is simply not an option for probably the majority of researchers, as institutions very rarely support research unless such plans have been specified and approved. Action research similarly relies on an approach to research that requires continual movement between data analysis and data collection, which can be impractical for some research projects as this significantly increases the duration of the project (see Box 6.1).

Box 6.1   Action Research

Originally formulated as an offshoot of 'positivistic' experimental research, **action research** has become a very influential approach to research design that can involve a number of key features:

- A cyclical approach to research design, with data analysis informing data gathering, research design and research aims
- The aim of producing a change in some aspect of the research setting
- The aim of enhancing some aspect of professional practice.

Action research has been particularly influential in the healthcare (e.g. Hart, 1995) and education (e.g. Elliott, 1991; Tomal, 1993) fields, but the range of disciplines in which it is applied continues to grow (see, for example, Berg and Eikeland's (2008) discussion of action research in organization research).

While still associated with constructivist notions of culturally situated meaning and value judgements, action research is frequently directed towards the improvement of professional practice and social action.

Such impracticalities aside, grounded theory and action research are valuable for drawing attention to the iterative nature of analysis and its relationship with data collection. Very often, a researcher's conception of their research focus changes or shifts emphasis during the research process, and one of the common points of such shifts is during the collection of data. As we outlined in Chapter 4, there is an important difference between a preliminary research design and the working out of that design in practice.

Social research is ultimately a matter of discovery, and it is to be expected, therefore, that the process of conducting research sometimes leads to a change in research plans. One may discover that the initial research interests were poorly framed (e.g. that they were not specified precisely enough or involved assumptions that have proved to be problematic) or that there are other issues emerging through the research that were not initially conceptualized and that are more interesting or relevant than the initial focus. It may be that the research strategy itself becomes problematic or unworkable for some reason (e.g. through a lack of access or poor levels of participation). In all these ways, the practice of doing research may lead researchers to reframe their interests and their plans for exploring them.

Critically, and as we also outlined in Chapter 4, a researcher's empirical interests and their formulation as an *analytic concern* help them to conceptualize what is to count as data and analysis. The analytic concerns specify the focus of a given project and, through the lenses of theory and method, crystallize in very specific empirical focal points. In this chapter we focus on the relationship between analysis and data collection, and on the ways that generating data relate to the specification and working through of analytic concerns. The discussion that follows is divided into two main sections. The first discusses methods of data collection that are based around asking research participants to provide answers to questions (e.g. interviews, focus groups and questionnaires). The second section looks at data collection through observation.

Asking questions

The aim of methods that involve asking direct questions to research participants (such as interviews, questionnaires or focus groups) is to create analytically focused discourse that provides insights into specified research questions. It is important that researchers are reflexive about the nature of the data collection process in order that they can be sure that the data they produce through such methods is relevant to them. In this section we will look at a variety of methods of asking questions and explore the intersection of analysis and data collection within them. To do so, we make use of Nigel Fielding's (2003) distinction between **modes** of interviewing and **types** of interview. An interview *mode* is the format in which it is conducted (e.g. face to face, telephone, online chat-room, email, etc.) and the *type* is the form of organization (e.g. structured, semi-structured, unstructured).

'Idealized' interview types

When research texts make reference to interviews, they very frequently do so in terms of structure, with some approaches being pre-defined, rigidly structured and tightly followed, and others being only very loosely specified and essentially *improvised* in the interview setting. Box 6.2 outlines some of the main distinctions that are commonly made. In this section, we provide a brief discussion of each of these, and then look at how these different structures may work in practice.

Box 6.2   Types of interview structure

Structured interviews – The wording of questions and the order in which questions are asked is predefined and non-variable. All participants are asked the questions with exactly the same wording and in the same sequence.

Semi-structured interviews – Interviewers prepare a list of questions, but these can be asked in a flexible order and with a wording that is contextually appropriate. The aim is to ask all the questions on the list with sensitivity to the developing conversational structure, but not necessarily in any particular order.

Unstructured interviews – No pre-defined questions are created and the interview is treated as an occasion to have a conversation about a particular topic or set of topics. Participants are given the conversational space to address the issues that they see as relevant to those topics in the manner that they desire.

Structured interviews

Structured interviews involve formulating, prior to the interviews, the precise questions to be asked, the order in which they are asked, and potentially even the wording of the questions. Researchers use their research interests and knowledge of the topic to decide the exact areas into which they are going to enquire. All subsequent analysis is dependent upon, and therefore built around, the analytic concerns represented in the interview structure. In this respect, analysis is pre-defined and constrained through the topical issues that have been developed as questions. These questions/topics will be carried through as concerns to be worked out in the examination of the data that is created.

It is useful to bear in mind the following questions when designing structured interviews:

- Are all of the questions clear and unambiguous? It can be particularly useful to pilot the interviews, or at the very least ask colleagues to read through them before undertaking the research, so that clarity can be maximized.
- Are all of the relevant analytic matters included in the interview schedule? This is an obvious point, of course, but it is also surprising how often researchers make a mistake in this respect and fail to include questions about key issues in their research.
- Are only those matters that are of interest part of the enquiry? It is important not to waste time in interviews, so while there can be some value in having questions that are directed to building rapport, or to 'easing into' the central concerns, it is important to think carefully about which ones are really necessary.
- Is the order of the questions appropriate? There may be some matters that are more logically discussed before others. Maybe some topics are a good opening to the interview and others good 'closers'. Again, piloting can be very useful to make sure that one gets this right.

Once the interviews have been conducted, analysis will be undertaken around the themes represented in the question topics. Very often, this will involve some form of thematized analysis of each individual question by comparing the ways in which respondents have answered the questions and using either preformulated or emergent codes to categorize that data. The rigidity of the question-asking structure helps to ensure that the data gathered is topically consistent, and makes the application of such codes for comparative analysis more straightforward than in less structured approaches.

There are significant issues involved in using a highly structured approach. First, by prespecifying one's interests, researchers minimize the extent to which research findings can be iteratively developed. While discoveries can be made in the confines of the questions being asked, the closed structure does not allow new issues to evolve very easily. Researchers can minimize this by including some open questions in the interview schedule that ask quite explicitly about matters that may not have been covered in the interview. Secondly, however, highly structured interviews disrupt the natural flow of conversation so that topics can only be discussed at the point at which the interview schedule specifies, rather than when the interviewee may be thinking about them. The potential result of this is that participants may forget or ignore things that could have been relevant to the interview.

Semi-structured interviews

Like structured approaches, semi-structured interviews involve specifying the key themes of the interview that are, in turn, formulated as key questions. Unlike structured approaches, however, researchers are usually more flexible in the way the interview schedule is used. For example, researchers can vary the order of the questions according to the 'natural flow' of conversation. Researchers try to fit their pre-defined interests into the unfolding topics being discussed, rather than forcing the interviewees to fit their ideas into the interviewer's pre-defined question order. Interviewers are also free to probe the research participants for more information on particular points, to explore the topics more discursively than in structured approaches, and even to explore topics that may emerge that were not included in the interview schedule.

This form of interview requires distinctive skills on the part of the researcher, who needs to be able to:

- remember the questions they need to ask
- ask questions at appropriate times
- bring the conversation around to their own topics of interest without disrupting the natural flow of conversation
- sense when a topic of enquiry has been exhausted
- help the participants to make links between the topics being discussed
- manage the duration of the interview
- evaluate the analytic relevance of the information as it is being produced.

The last item in the above list is key from the point of view of analysis. Like all interview forms, semi-structured interviews are conducted with the researcher's interests in mind. The whole interview process is managed and negotiated in relation to the concerns of the project and therefore requires the researcher to make judgements 'in the heat of the moment' about 'what counts as relevant'. This is no small matter as it involves the researcher thinking beyond the unfolding structure of the conversation being held and reflecting on the overall aims of the research. Clearly, the question topics provide some guide, but as part of the aim of the process is the iterative development of ideas, this structure is only a loose guide. In semi-structured interviews, analysis can be a *lived* aspect of the data 'gathering' process, and not just a preformulated strategy. Researchers *perform* their analysis during their interviews, working through ideas with their research participants, improvising their data as an analytically mediated outcome. This approach to interviewing is much more common in qualitative research than the more rigidly structured forms precisely because the iterative nature of the data generation and analysis fits well with the overall aims of qualitative enquiry.

Semi-structured forms of interview organization often involve a less formal distinction between interviewee and interviewer. James Holstein and Jaber Gubrium describe what they call the 'creative interview', which entails the production of 'a climate of mutual disclosure between interviewee and interviewer by allowing the latter to have a deep involvement in the conversational development' (Holstein and Gubrium, 1995: 119). Interviewers may offer their own experiences of whatever it is that is being discussed, or provide evaluations of a particular issue. In these ways, the interviewer both removes the interactional barriers of the attitude of 'interviewer as an objective outsider' and creates discursive resources for the other participants to use in the course of their own formulations.

As analysis can be a lived feature of semi-structured interviews, it can be extremely useful to examine interviews immediately after they have been conducted. This can help to establish whether there are other topical issues that have emerged that might be worth exploring in other interviews, and ensures that analysis informs the data-gathering process. Table 6.1 outlines some questions that can be used to help focus one's exploration of interview data. The analysis can be used to evaluate:

- the relevance of the sample being used and to develop new approaches to sampling
- the value of the interview mode being used (see our discussion of these matters later in this chapter)
- the appropriateness of the questions being asked and whether there are new issues to be dealt with
- the approach to interviewing being used, and whether the interviewer's mode of engagement is facilitating the development of relevant topical talk.

Unstructured interviews

Unstructured interviews involve asking questions without any or with very little pre-definition of the topical concerns of the interview. This approach may be used in long term ethnographic research, where a researcher's need to familiarize themselves with a given research setting may mean that they simply need to 'figure out how things work'. Unstructured interviews may also be used as a form of pilot (or perhaps more accurately, as a 'pre-pilot') to try to find out what might be of interest in a given setting. In their study of the culture of training in medical schools, Howard Becker et al. (1977: 18) describe the value of unstructured methods as helping them to uncover data that would enable them to work out what types of question they should be asking in their research.

However, the term 'unstructured' is a little misleading as it implies that researchers have no particular interest in a given research setting. As Brown and

Dowling (1998: 72–3) suggest, interviewers always have some motivated interest, even if it is simply to 'figure out how things work' or to 'think about why a given setting might be interesting'. This is an important point: the idea that an interview might have 'no structure' is something of a misnomer, for there would be little point in conducting an interview if the researcher had no particular interest that they wished to pursue within it. That said, it is perhaps appropriate to conceptualize interviews as having a sliding scale of rigidity in the ways in which they are organized. Decisions about the level of prestructuring to be adopted need to be made in relation to the distinctive research interests being examined. An 'unstructured' approach is appropriate and more common where the analytic concern is in the process of being formulated or involves quite an 'open' question along the lines of 'how does such and such work?', or the exploration of the personal experience or biography of an interviewee where the interviewer can have little or no prior sense of what are key events for them.

Where the aim of an unstructured interview is to find out how something or some setting works, or to explore possible lines of interest, the interview commonly resembles an 'ordinary' conversation in the sense that the interviewer is not directing the conversation by their questions, but is simply trying to engage the respondents in discussion about their practices or activities. As with semi-structured interviews, the interview is managed according to the interviewer's sense of 'what might be relevant or interesting'. The interviewer will probe areas that they regard as being of particular analytic merit, and may well try to sideline issues that they regard as less relevant. The interactional encounter of unstructured interviews is therefore structured by the unfolding sense of analytic relevance, as conceptualized by the interviewer.

As unstructured interviews are typically undertaken as a means of working out what might be interesting, researchers analyze an interview directly after conducting it. The precise nature of such reflection will of course be contextual, and it is therefore somewhat artificial to specify areas that researchers should concentrate on in such analysis. Table 6.1 is intended as an heuristic to help reflect on some of the aspects that may be relevant. These questions can also be valuable for exploring semi-structured interviews.

Interview structures in practice

These distinctions between structured, semi-structured and unstructured interviews are very rough characterizations. It is quite conceivable, and indeed quite *usual*, that a given research project has aspects of all three 'approaches': some well worked out, pre-defined questions, some loose topical interests that have been dealt with in no particular order, and some discursive spaces that are rather 'circuitous' in character. It may be that a researcher begins their research in a broadly unstructured way, and moves to an approach that resembles a structured approach. We suggest that instead of thinking of these characterizations as representing formalized research methods that implicate particular and defined research strategies, it may be more productive to reflect in detail on the ways in which the relationship between data and research topic may implicate a more or less structured orientation. Let's look at an example.

Table 6.1 Reflexive questions for undertaking unstructured interviews

Action	Questions
Produce a list of the topics covered in the interview	Were there issues that were raised by the interviewee that were not explored in detail in the conversation? Was there anything that was particularly strongly emphasized within the interview (e.g. topics that were particularly prominent)? Is there anything particularly unexpected or surprising about what the interviewee said?
Compare the interview content with other interviews that may have been conducted	Are there obvious overlaps in the things that different interviewees have said? Can you think of an explanation for such overlap? Are there any differences in the content of the interviews? Can you think of a reason why there may have been differences in content? For example, where interviewees raised different issues, try to reflect on whether there is an explanation for those differences (e.g. that they occupy different institutional positions, perspectives or have distinctive biographical differences).
Think about the way in which you as an interviewer played a role in the development of the conversation	Did you show more enthusiasm for some topics rather than others? Why, and was that appropriate? Was there anything about the context of the interview (e.g. time constraints or the way the interview was introduced) that may have led the interviewer to respond in particular ways? Were there points raised that you did not pick up on sufficiently?
Reflect on how your answers to any of the above questions may be used to take your research forward	Are there obvious themes that you could take forward through particular questions? Are there issues that are clearly not relevant that you would like to avoid discussing? Are there particular people that may be interesting to talk to? If so, why are they interesting and what would you like to know from/about them?

Interviews in practice – an example

Imagine a researcher is looking at the problems of implementing fire safety legislation in private companies. The researcher may rather arbitrarily identify a small
number of companies (perhaps on the basis of the places they have access to,
rather than anything more technical or theoretical), and begin by talking to the
health and safety officers and managers in those organizations, trying to understand quite broadly the procedures that these companies have in place, the kinds

of training regimes they implement, their safety review procedures, and so on. These might resemble very loose semi-structured interviews, with discussions with key personnel being organized into particular topical areas, but with no firm or formalized structure. As more and more data is collected in the different companies, a more or less formalized interview schedule is developed. The schedule ends up being implemented in fairly regular ways, taking pretty much the same order, and even with the questions being phrased in similar ways. Perhaps it turns out, however, that one of the organizations has actually had the experience of dealing with a fire, and one of the interviewees suggests talking to some of the people that were involved in it (the fire officers on duty, the security staff, some of the people who were evacuated from the building). These discussions might begin in quite open terms, with the very general aim of finding out what happened, and what the people's experiences were. These may be very loose conversations because of the distinctive perspectives of the people and the need to simply understand their point of view. Through these interviews, the researcher may build something like a 'case study' of a fire event. They may then carry on with their initial mapping of procedures, but with a slightly more nuanced understanding of the problems that can emerge in real fire situations.

The example shows that as understanding of and familiarity with the settings grows, and as new issues and questions arise, so the researcher's need to use more or less structured questions changes. Where the researcher has a good idea of what they want to find out, and clear categories and questions to ask, then the interview is likely to become more structured; where the questions are of a more open type, so the interviews become more open. Some of the key questions that are likely to drive this analytic reflection are:

- What is the problem here?
- What data am I getting?
- How does that data relate to the other data?
- What other questions or issues come to mind as I generate or think about that data?
- What do I need to do to address those questions or issues?

The diverse character of data

In our example, the interviewer would end up with quite a diverse data set, with direct answers to direct questions, and discursive, meandering 'informal' talk. They would have transcripts that looked very structured and formal, and transcripts of a more 'narrative' nature, with long passages of talk and interactive dialogue between the interviewer and the interviewee. We have found that this kind of situation, which is entirely normal, is often quite concerning for new researchers who tend to wonder how to deal with this very varied material. One very important point to emphasize is this: *the data is varied because it has been produced in different ways and for different reasons. The question of 'how do you deal with it?' is in many ways the wrong question. A better question is 'why is it varied?', and the answer will nearly always be because of the particular setting and issue being dealt with within it.* How you decide what to do with it depends very much on the questions you are left with once you have the data. In other words, a useful question to ask at that point is: 'Now that you have generated some data you know more things than when you did when you started. What other things do you want to know or find out about that the data might be able to help you with?'

But this might still be a little vague. Let's return to our example.

Interviews in practice – an example continued

The researcher ends up with 34 interview transcripts, of varying sorts, from three different organizations. Having conducted these interviews, the researcher knows a lot more about the different practices in the organizations; about rationalizations for 'why things happen as they do'; about the different contingencies faced by different personnel; varying attitudes to the procedures by these different personnel. Some of these aspects they really understand quite well and could almost write up immediately (although to do so would involve pulling the data together, and organizing it into different parts). But others require some more work. Perhaps they have a suspicion that there are some key differences between the ways that fire officers in one organization and fire officers in another have spoken about the role, but they are not quite sure what that difference is yet. They noticed that some of the terminology was different and that the attitudes seemed to vary, but this is all a little unclear still. Some more comparative work will be required before it can be characterized properly.

This example shows the problems of treating analysis as a distinct stage of research. Clearly, the working through of the research design, and the iterative production of data, has involved a good deal of analysis. Some clear understandings have emerged that need to be pulled together by using the data to tell the stories of how various things work or what people think and why. This 'pulling together of data' might proceed by using codes to categorize the interview transcripts, and comparing the content of those codes in order to produce a coherent narrative. But there are also some questions that remain not only unanswered, but also quite underdeveloped. To recall Hammersley and Atkinson's (1994) quotation, the 'analysis of data' is very much directed to figuring out what these questions might be, whether or not there is value in pursuing them, and how that might be undertaken. It is easy to imagine that in doing so, the researcher may realize that they need some more data or data of a different kind so that they can properly deal with these newly emerging issues.

Modes of interview

New communicative modes, such as forms of web-based communication, have dramatically enhanced the range of media through which interviews can be conducted. Some of the key modes are shown in Table 6.2. All of these modes have their own advantages and disadvantages, the relevance of which for a given research project are very much dependent on the empirical context being investigated and on the nature of the research interest in that setting.

Table 6.2 Characteristics of interview modes

Mode	Pros	Cons
Face to face	A communicatively rich mode of exchange in which the gestural aspects of the discourse are visible to the participants Data can be recorded with video or audio devices Other materials, such as documents or photographs, can be easily used in the interview as a resource to aid discussion	May require either the interviewee or interviewer to travel and can therefore be expensive and time-consuming Require interviewees to come up with answers 'on the spur of the moment' and do not enable interviewees to reflect for long on their answers
Synchronous online chat	Researchers have a choice in the modes of communication they can implement as the discourse can be audio, audio-visual or text-based Some software saves the chat history for subsequent analysis The mode facilitates communication across large distances	Real time, very often has a slight delay in the relay of information which can result in interactional difficulties Does not give participants time to reflect on their answers Even in the most 'data rich' of environments (i.e. video chat), the verbal cues are limited to the angle provided by the camera. In non-video modes, the communication is not contextualized by other communicative modes
Email and other asynchronous modes such as discussion boards	Gives participants the time to reflect on their answers May be more convenient for interviewees because of the flexibility of the time of participation Interviewers have the opportunity to reflect on answers and to develop questions to probe on the basis of such reflection	A much slower form of discourse than co-presence or telephone interviews The 'flow' of conversation is very disjointed and it may therefore be difficult to create coherent discussion
Telephone	May be more convenient for interviewees than face-to-face discourse Can be quicker and easier to conduct a series of interviews than through face-to-face methods Data can be recorded with an audio recording device (with interviewees permission)	There are no non-verbal cues to contextualize the talk There is little opportunity for the interviewees to reflect on their answers

The advantages and disadvantages of different modes of interviewing can be thought of in terms of the following kinds of issues:

- Convenience for the interviewer
- Convenience for the interviewee
- The presence or absence of verbal cues
- The amount of time that participants have to formulate their answers
- The amount of time the interviewer has to reflect on the answers
- The speed of the communication.

It is increasingly common for researchers to use more than one discussion mode for their interviews. For example, a researcher may conduct their interviews face to face, and then have follow-up email conversation to explore some ideas. Alternatively, a researcher may begin by posing some questions and having some preliminary discussion through email, and then following up through face-to-face discussion. In these sorts of ways it is possible to maximize the benefits of different modes of discourse.

Interviews in practice – an example continued

Our researcher has conducted some interviews with very busy managers via email. Some managers have written quite long emails about general topics. Others have written much shorter exchanges, like text messages, with quite direct answers to questions. On a few occasions the researcher managed to speak to these managers on the phone after the email conversations. Most of the other people were interviewed in person in various settings (offices, work cafeterias, restaurants). Not all of the people agreed to the conversations being recorded, and some did not want to be mentioned by name (although most did not mind).

Again, it is very common indeed for researchers to have data recorded in various ways, with different levels of detail, and with respondents giving different permissions of use. Where no recording device is used, a researcher may have to rely on a general sense of the ideas discussed. This will mean that no quotations can be used in the writing-up, of course, which may limit the ways researchers can use those accounts but does not necessarily mean that they can't use them at all. In other words, if the interviews were not recorded, then they cannot be subjected to scrutiny for their structural elements, for example, but they can still be used as illustrations of particular attitudes or opinions, providing the interviewer is confident that they have remembered them in sufficient detail for them to count as such.

Interview analysis sheets

It is a useful discipline to create a set of analytic notes to accompany each interview. These notes may include an outline of the following:

- Any problems faced in the interview (e.g. the intelligibility of particular questions, the length of the interview, the focus of the discussion, keeping the discussion on track, etc.)

- Any particularly useful aspects of the interview (questions that worked well, or answers that were especially valuable)
- Any points that were similar to points made in other interviews that have been conducted
- Any points that were different from points made in other interviews that have been conducted
- How the interview process may be developed on the basis of the experience of conducting that interview.

Interview analysis sheets help researchers to adapt the research process as the analysis is conducted. It is useful to have some standard form to the sheets so that they can be compared; this is best achieved by making the sheets as simple as possible. Box 6.3 gives an example of an interview sheet used as part of a project examining pharmacy work practice. As they are typically orientated to producing an analysis of interviews in comparison to other interviews, analysis sheets are likely to become more detailed as research progresses. It is worthwhile completing such forms directly after the interview and comparing them with the other sheets that have been produced straight away, while the interview experience is fresh. Using such tools helps to make the research process centred on the analysis of data, and comparative in its orientation to the data it produces.

Box 6.3   Exemplar interview analysis sheet

Participant: xxxx
Date: 04 November 2000
Location: xxxx Hospital
Interviewer: xxxx

Similarities
Questions that seemed to produce similar answers to other interviewees were:
   Collaboration with other professionals – emphasized the problems of working with doctors.
   Wide range of roles and responsibilities – again relating to the relevance of university training.
   Detailed induction process at the hospital – see interviews xxxx and xxxx.

Differences
xxxx emphasized their lack of ward-round experience. It seems that the structure of training here may be different from other hospitals. What is the rationale for that? What impact might it have on the process of acquiring expertise?

Problems
Question 4 produces very monosyllabic answers – consider revising.

Implications
The notion that hospital-based practice may be more involved and varied than other forms of pharmacy work.
   That hospital work may vary considerably between hospital institutions and is contingencies on managerial support.

The organization of the interview setting

Most of the decisions about where to conduct an interview are likely to be practical rather than analytic. Considerations may include convenience for the interviewee or interviewer, the appropriateness of the environment for recording the talk and, the level of privacy that the particular setting affords. However, research interests may also play a part in selecting the setting of an interview. In Gibson et al.'s (2001) pharmacy study, for example, interviews were generally carried out in the pharmacists' place of work. The rationale for this was not only that these settings were practical for interviewees (although this was certainly the case), but because these settings helped to give an understanding of the working environment. As the analysis was concerned with 'what postgraduate pharmacists did in their training environments', gaining a sense of the physical space, the local area in which the pharmacy was situated, and the colleagues that the pharmacist worked with helped to generate a broader understanding of the work contexts. This information helped to make sense of the dialogue produced in the interview, to understand the people being discussed and the way the work was organized.

Contextualizing research

A widely discussed issue within question-asking research is how best to contextualize the research issues for participants. Like so many research issues, there is no general 'correct' answer to such issues. In some approaches to interviews, researchers aim at something like 'neutrality', and attempt to avoid the imposition of ideas. In other instances, researchers are much less cautious and provide quite detailed outlines of their interests and aims. For example, in his study of craftwork, Mishler notes that he was very explicit about his theoretical concerns, and introduced the participants to some of his theoretical ideas and how they would be used to make sense of the interview narratives (Mishler, 1999: 5).

One way to characterize the dilemma about contextualizing research is as follows. Interviewees need to know what the research is about so that they can direct their responses according to the research interests. As studies of the organization of conversation have shown, people *design* their talk on the basis of what they know the other person needs/wants to know (Sacks, 1995). So, the researcher needs to give the interviewee information so that they can design their conversations accordingly. However, precisely because they are directing their answers to the interests of the researcher, interviewees may leave out other important information that they may regard as 'irrelevant' or 'not on topic' etc. To put it another way, if you ask interviewees specifically about 'x', they will tell you about 'x', but it may be that neither of you knew that 'y' and 'z' were also relevant to the problem. The researcher's aim, then, is to be able to frame the research questions or interests so that the interviewees can orientate their answers towards those concerns but without excluding other areas of discourse.

When reflecting on this issue, it can be helpful to keep in mind the following questions:

- What do the research participants require in order to appropriately direct their questions to you?
- Are the questions being asked likely to be issues that the research participants have reflected on previously? Do they require prior notice of the questions in

order to give them time to reflect on their answers before the actual interview? (This is only appropriate in some interview modes, such as face-to-face interviews.)

- How experienced are the research participants at participating in research? Do they require any kinds of instructions on how to answer the questions and on the type of data you are interested in gathering, on the organization of the research process in general?
- Would it be helpful for the research participants to know about the context of your work and the background to how you developed it as a topic? Why?

Narrative analysis

A term that is often strongly associated with the conduct and analysis of 'question-asking' methods, such as interviews and focus groups, is 'narrative analysis'. Like so many terms in qualitative research (think of 'grounded theory', 'triangulation', 'interpretive', 'discourse analysis'), narrative analysis is a very broad term that can, depending on how it is being used, both delineate something quite specific or describe a very vague interest.

In general terms, the phrase usually refers to the idea that narrative is an important component of how people make sense of themselves and their lives. Narrative analysis is an interest in the ways in which people build and use accounts and narratives. Much like discourse analysis, there are a wide range of approaches to the examination of narrative, which represent very many disciplinary perspectives and which involve taking forward more or less defined concepts and areas of interest. In a classic, early discussion of this diffuse area, Riessman notes that many approaches to narrative analysis are critical of the ways in which other approaches to qualitative analysis 'eliminate the sequential and structural features that characterize narrative accounts' (1993: 3). In other words, the ways in which they fail to pay attention to the structures used by participants in the construction of their discourse. Narrative analysis is typically more concerned with accounting practices than with the events to which those accounts may relate.

Examples of narrative analysis

Emerson and Frosh (2004) describe one approach to narrative analysis that they call **critical narrative analysis**. They provide an example of this approach that involves using interviews to investigate the ways in which teenage boys involved in sexually abusing other boys built accounts of their sexually abusive behaviour and made sense of their own behaviour. Critical narrative analysis looks in detail at how people produce accounts of their lives and experiences, usually concentrating on quite a small number of research participants, so that their narratives can be examined in detail – this is quite a common feature of narrative analysis more generally conceived. As Emerson and Frosh put it, narrative analysis 'asks specific questions about particular lives: how does this person, in this context, get to give the account she or he does? How is it constituted, what does it do, what psychological processes can be seen at work in it?' (Emerson and Frosh, 2004: 11). We can see immediately that the nature of the theoretical interest (narrative and discourse) is used to frame the research topic – 'the production of narrative accounts in sexually abusive boys'. The research question *comes from* or is *structured through* the lens of the conceptual schema brought to it. A part of that conceptual schema is the interest in 'psychological processes'. This refers to the processes by which the boys make sense of themselves, their behaviour and life contexts, and to the relations between those and the wider 'social discourses, beliefs and assumptions that may be organizing and sustaining these accounts' (Emerson and Frosh, 2004: 11).

Elliot Mishler's study of craftworkers is another interesting example of narrative analysis, in this case driven by an interest in identity, craftwork and forms of social organization. It is insightful to quote at length from Mishler here, as his description of his early formation of his research interests shows some of the ways that the quite loose idea of 'narrative' is given a more specific focus:

> [My interest] began with a quotation from William Morris, the godfather of the late-nineteenth-century Arts and Crafts Movement, that valorized 'handicrafts' in the context of a critique of the dehumanizing impact of industrialization and mass production (Morris, 1966/1883). I made the bridge to the Marxist concept of alienation via C. Wright Mills's analysis of the loss of craftsmanship in modern bureaucratic society (Mills, 1953). The aim of the proposed study, reflected in its title, 'Work and identity: The lives of craftspersons', was to contribute to research and theory on the crafts as a form of creative work and to reflect on the general problem of relations between work and personal identity. (Mishler, 1999: xiv)

Mishler creates a theorized reading of craftwork as a 'critique' of industrialized work practices and used this focus to speak more generally about identity and work in society. Mishler defines identity as 'a collective term referring to the dynamic organization of sub-identities that might conflict with or align with each other' (Mishler, 1999: 9). In this view, the identity of an individual is pluralistic, and characterized by numerous overlapping, mutually informing, conflicting and changing conceptions of self. Mishler outlines three themes that emerged from his work: 'the similarities and differences between individuals' identity formation'; 'the continuity and discontinuity of work identity over time'; and 'identity as a relation between people through discourse'. Consistent with Riessman's critique of 'thematized analysis', however, working through these themes does not involve sidelining the structures of the narratives being investigated. Mishler's theoretical ideas are used to structure his work, and to provide a thematized discussion of the narrative interviews that formed the primary data of his study. While Mishler does not try to create an enshrined and bounded approach to analysis (as Emerson and Frosh do with their 'critical narrative analysis'), he does create a theoretically specialized approach through the use of particular commitments and interests.

Methodology and analysis in narrative approaches

In terms of methods, the interest in the structures and uses of narratives and accounts means that prestructured forms of interview are inappropriate, as this would not enable the researcher to look at how research participants use and build their own accounts. Some researchers have used visual as well as verbal narratives as a component of their data and analysis (see Newbold, 1996), which draws the method closer to some of the documentary approaches we discussed in Chapter 5.

Analysis begins with the production of transcripts. The level of detail required within the transcripts depends very much on the type of narrative approach being used and the nature of the empirical questions being asked. Using transcripts, researchers then work through their data, attempting to identify and delineate the structural features of the narrative, 'the boundaries of narrative segments' (Riessman, 1993: 58). These segments are then subjected to further analysis or 'rediscription', by, for example, specifying the functional elements of that redescription.

Observation

Observational research can be conducted for many reasons, but it is very often a part of a general interest in understanding, for one reason or another, what people do and why. Frequently, this is expressed as being part of a broader concern with gaining insight on the insider's point of view (Emerson, 1983), or understanding the meanings that those activities have for the participants who enact them (Blumer, 1969). While it is common, this focus is not the only reason why researchers undertake observations, which might simply be directed at 'seeing how things happen', without any particular concern with the meanings attributed to them, or the understandings that people have of those things. In this section we will explore some of the key features of the ways that social researchers have talked about observations, and reflect on the ways that researchers might orientate to these areas of debate and practice in their work. A central area of our interest here is to show the ways in which data analysis is worked through during observational research.

Levels of structure in observational research

In **structured observations** researchers prespecify features of the behaviours or practices being observed that are of interest to them. This typically involves constructing an **observation schedule** that is used to direct attention to particular forms of information. Observation schedules are analytically focused resources that help researchers to pay attention to particular aspects of the practices being observed. They are designed to pick up the key features of a given setting as they relate to a researcher's analytic concerns.

As with structured interviews, then, structured observation schedules typically need to be piloted in order to:

- check that they are sensitive enough to pick up the required forms of data
- check that there are no issues that may be relevant that are not included in the observation schedule
- make sure that they can be easily followed and filled out by the researcher(s).

Structured observations are carried out once a given set of analytic interests has been developed and confirmed, which often involves the use of less structured modes of data collection as a starting point.

Again, as with structured forms of interview, the analytic structure specified in an observation schedule forms the basis for all subsequent analysis. The observational focal points are created because they are relevant to the research topic and these relevancies are then taken forward in subsequent data work. Researchers need to have a very good understanding of why they are interested in the particular features defined in their observation schedule. Where researchers are unsure about what these interests might be, they may find it much more productive to start with unstructured observations and, if it becomes appropriate, move to using structured forms later on. Structured observations are appropriate where researchers have a very clear idea of what they want to look at and have a well-formulated rationale for why it is relevant to them.

In **unstructured** forms of observation, researchers do not follow a tightly defined schedule of observation, but work in a more iterative fashion to find out about a particular setting or set of practices. The aim is very often to gain an 'emic' or insider understanding of how the setting works. This does not mean that unstructured forms necessarily involve using less strongly developed analytic concerns. As we saw in Chapter 2, Margaret Mead's observational work in Papua New Guinea was very clearly theoretically defined, but still used a more flexible approach to observational work. Like unstructured interviews, the structure of data 'collection' is not absent, but is simply worked through in practice. As the data is produced, the researcher is thinking through the relevance of that data by, for example:

- trying to understand why things happen as they do
- thinking about which aspects are particularly interesting to their research
- comparing the unfolding data with other data they may have generated
- reflecting on the relationship between what they observe and their research questions and interests (as far as they have defined them).

Table 6.3 provides an outline of some of the ways in which researchers might take forward these concerns as critical questions.

As with interviews, the titles 'structured' and 'unstructured' observations are slightly misleading as all observations are directed to some interest or other. In what we have described as 'structured' approaches, that interest is prespecified and built into the design of the research (or into *that part* of the research); in 'unstructured' approaches, the interest is worked through in context. Also like interviews, these different terms should not be seen as delineating formalized and distinct sets of methods, but as approaches to gathering data that researchers can move between and that can become more or less relevant, depending on the context.

As more observations are undertaken, a researcher will normally create more focused ideas about what is of interest, and their observations may well begin to resemble structured approaches. They will probably enter observation settings wanting to know more about one thing than another, with the aim of generating data on a particular aspect of behaviour. They will, in other words, generate analytic focus that will translate into observational focus. But by carrying out these observations, new interests may emerge that direct the researcher to some more open questions which imply a less structured approach. The 'structured/unstructured' distinction is one that is worked through by the researcher as the research progresses.

We would like to emphasize at this point that this description of observation and the notion of 'structure' as an unfolding concern shows clearly that data analysis is an integrated feature of observational work – the data is analytically 'dealt with' as it is produced because *producing data* necessarily involves detailed reflection on its character, its relevance for the project, and its relationship to other data.

Table 6.3   Questions for interrogating unstructured observations

Central question	Sub-question
What features of the observed actions were interesting?	What things in particular did you notice?
	Why were they interesting/relevant?
	How do those things relate to other things that you have observed in other instances?
Was there anything that you didn't understand?	Would understanding those things help you to formulate your research interests?
	Is there someone who can explain them to you?
If you have a recording of the observation, what happens when you show insiders the things you observed?	Do they see things you didn't see?
	Do you see things that they don't see?
	Do they agree with your observations? If not, why not?
How do the different observations you have conducted compare with each other?	Are the data similar or different?
	Do they support the same suppositions/ideas/rationales?

Participant and non-participant observation

It is common to make a distinction between forms of observation in which a researcher is a passive and known observer looking in at the setting and one in which they attempt to be an active participant within it. In participatory research, the researcher aims to be a part of the practices being observed as much as possible in order to gain an understanding of the insider's perspective. Being a part of the activities enables the researcher to see what it feels like to do such and such, to understand the experiences of the participants, and to get close to understanding the meanings that participants give to their activities. Very often, such research is a long-term project that can last for many months, as the requirement of 'seeing what the participants see' demands significant socialization into new areas of social life.

As we have already commented, while these types of approach to observation are common, 'gaining an insider's perspective' is not necessarily the objective in all observation research. Merrett and Wheldall (1986) conducted a study that involved an observation of teachers' approval and disapproval of children's work. They were not concerned with understanding the participants' views on the activities being observed, but simply with categorizing them in a way that facilitated cross-case comparison between different classrooms and institutions. Now, one might question how 'qualitative' this study is if it did not involve much of an interest in the character of the activities, but it does reveal that, in the abstract, researchers might orientate towards very different research aims when undertaking observations.

The detailed ethnographic studies characteristic of social anthropology are often conducted with the aim of deep socialization into a community. This does not typically involve 'becoming a member of a community' or 'doing exactly what the research participants do', but simply getting as close to those practices as possible and being accepted as 'someone who is around'. Kelly's (2005) ethnographic work on an urban brothel in Mexico is an example from social anthropology where the researcher became a part of her community under study but with no attempt to engage in the key business of its population. Similarly, in his highly influential study of criminality in an urban Italian community in Chicago, William Foote Whyte (1955) was able to 'hang out with' the members of the group without actually engaging in criminal acts. The participation in the acts would not only have raised serious ethical issues, but would probably not have aided his analytic concern all that much. Whyte was interested in understanding the motives for the actions and their relationship to the structures of social organization in the community. Because of the types of relationship he had been able to build with the research participants in the setting, Whyte was able to carry out his research and address its central concerns without 'membership', which would entail actually engaging in the acts under study.

A widely discussed problem in participant observational research relates to the relationship between a researcher's motivated concerns and the perspectives of the participants in the setting. In many forms of qualitative work, observations are employed in order to 'see as the research participants do', and to understand the meanings that those settings/practices/behaviours have for the people who are part of them or who produce them. The issue of 'going native' (see, for example, Adler and Adler, 1987) refers to the idea that the researcher actually *becomes* an insider and loses the original perspective that drove their enquiry.

The dramatic cases of researchers entirely losing their original perspective is illustrative of a more common problem – that of maintaining or working out a focus in the context of a distinctive empirical environment. A frequently discussed issue in observational fieldwork is the discontinuity between the methodological and theoretical concerns of academia and social research, and the practical issues of research sites (e.g. see Kurotani's (2005) description of the difficulties of explaining the purpose and role of 'fieldwork' to Japanese housewives in the USA). The duality (or multiplicity) of perspectives that the researcher tries to inhabit can create real problems for forging and holding on to clear analytic concerns. We have spoken at length in this book about the way in which research problems and issues are key resources for analysis, but it is by no means the case that these concerns are always *clear*. However, it is precisely because this is so often the case, and because data work and research practice are about 'finding a focus' and 'working it through' that it really makes no sense to think about data analysis as something distinct from other aspects of research work. Data work is very much a matter of perspective development. In observational research, this data work is an absolutely integrated feature of data generation.

Covert observation

Covert observation refers to the process of conducting observational research without the knowledge of the participants. Most commonly, this involves participating as a member of a group without letting the group know that the participation is part of a research project. A much less common form of covert observation might involve observing some practice or other through hidden cameras or inconspicuous vantage points.

The most significant sets of issues in this mode of research are of course ethical in nature. As we have already commented in this book (see Chapter 4), some ethical guidelines explicitly prohibit conducting any research without consent from participants. The underlying issue here stems from the notion that all research participants have the right to know that they are taking part in research. Other approaches are more lenient, however, and propose that the relevance of a given ethical issue (e.g. consent) must be worked out in relation to a particular project goal. In this view, the relevance of a covert form of research comes from a consideration of the benefits that such an approach may have for the research findings and their potential wider social interest.

Laud Humphreys' (1970) highly contentious study of homosexual activity in public spaces in the late 1960s involved him participating as a 'watch queen', and observing the sexual practices of men in public toilets. Humphreys suggests that he had no choice but to hide his identity as a researcher, as revealing it would have immediately deprived him of access to key research data. For Humphreys, the driving force behind his decision was that he needed data of a particular type that could only be gained through covert means.

In terms of analysis, covert participation usually involves participating in a setting in one particular role, and the nature of this participation will frame a researcher's findings and analysis. In Humphreys' study, for example, he describes the limitations he faced that arose in understanding the activities in their entirety because of the particular observational perspective and role that he adopted. Precisely because the researcher needs to protect not only their interests as a researcher but also their very *identity*, it can be difficult to gain insights from others on their activities without raising suspicions about the reasons for that interest. Indeed, Humphreys ended up revealing his identity to some of his participants in order to try to gain data other than his rather one-sided observation perspective. Ethics aside, then, there are important implications for the adoption of covert forms of observation that can offer real restrictions to the types of understanding a researcher can gain from a given setting.

Recording observational data

Fieldnotes are records of observational work. They can take a variety of forms: highly structured records of the event, loose analytic notes, or a combination of the two. Fieldnotes may be produced during an observation or afterwards, depending on the pragmatics of the setting and on whether or not other forms of data collection are being used, such as audio or video recorders.

One of the dilemmas that researchers face when producing fieldnotes is how to represent the difference between **description** as an account of what happens and the **analysis** of that account. Of course, to put the matter like this immediately creates problems as it suggests that there is a clear distinction between these two things – i.e. that description can be unmotivated and can stand apart from a researcher's interpretation of it. Interpretivist critiques of what are regarded as 'naïve' realist positions about the status of 'knowledge out there' that is separable from the individual and community perspectives that produce it are key components of methodological discourse in qualitative approaches. This is not the place to be sidetracked by these undoubtedly important areas of discussion (although readers might be interested in the following references: Bittner, 1973, 1983; Cruickshank, 2003). Regardless of the way these issues are played out in epistemological debates, researchers often need to make a practical distinction between what happened and what they think about what happened.

Where they are being used alongside other modes of data collection, fieldnotes might be employed as a kind of 'analysis *in vivo*' and not as a record of events (see Sanjek's (1990) insightful volume of collected writings on this point). The researcher might use the notes to remind themselves of particularly interesting features of the setting that they should check on the recording, or of ideas that occur to them while in the setting that they might take forward later on when they work through the data. Even here, though, researchers might also want to record observations of happenings in a more descriptive way in order to complement the other data. For example, when using video recordings, the partiality of a camera angle may not reveal other aspects of the observation setting that are useful, and the researcher may use fieldnotes to record these events.

If the fieldnotes are the only data record, then the researcher may well want to focus particularly on noting what happened rather than on producing an analysis of it. Becker et al. (1977) describe the value of writing fieldnotes as close to the events to which they pertain as possible in order that they can be as accurate and complete as possible. This recording will be *motivated* and directed to particular features that are of interest rather than on trying to record *everything*. Indeed, fieldnotes can only ever be a very partial and analytically directed recording of a given observation setting.

Given the importance of the difference between description and analysis, researchers often separate their fieldnotes into different sections or areas so that these components do not get mixed up. Quite how they are organized is very much a matter of preference – the important thing is that the researcher finds a way of working that helps them to manage these different components.

Researchers often find it useful to make a distinction between contextual/background information (e.g. the time, date, venue, purpose or participants in a given activity) and the details of one's notes on those things. The detailed notes may include, for example, the key structural features of the event, problems that may arise, things that are not intelligible to researchers, or unexpected aspects of behaviour. However, the research interests of a given project will help them to decide more firmly about the features of behaviour they are interested in recording.

To give an example, Gibson's (2006) study of jazz improvisation involved making fieldnotes after performances in which he was participating as a member of a band. The study lasted for more than three years and involved many observations of participation in performance settings. In the early part of the study, the fieldnotes were very unfocused, and simply acted as a kind of 'diary of events', with reflections on factors such as the repertoire of tunes played, the nature of the setting, and the researcher's feelings on how well the performance went (see the extract below for an example of these fieldnotes). However, later on in the study, the fieldnotes had gained greater focus and tended to be concerned with particular issues. One key concern, for example, was the analysis of how particular musical problems were resolved during the performance. The notes typically took the form of a 'stream of consciousness' record of a given event. An extract from one of these later fieldnote entries is also provided.

Example of topically unfocused fieldnotes from Gibson's study of jazz improvisation

06.07.01 – Playing at xxx Hotel in Manchester. (NAMES OF PARTICIPANTS OMITED). Two-hour lunchtime gig in the restaurant. Room about half full of diners (businessmen and tourists?). Played normal range of standard tunes. Had a request for Girl from Ipanema (which none of us were happy about apart from THE DRUMMER who likes playing Latin Rhythms). As there was no piano today it was easier to accompany (as a guitar player), and nice to have the space to develop harmonies without worrying about clashes with piano chords. xxx said he liked playing against the guitar chords too. Nobody played particularly well, and there was nothing very exciting about the gig. I didn't feel like I got to grips with much in terms of my solos and felt like I overplayed most of the time. I was trying to use some of the ideas I was working on with xxx last week in some tunes, but I haven't really got those sounds under my fingers yet.

Example of topically focused fieldnotes from Gibson's study of Jazz improvisation

05/03/02 – Missing out choruses on 'Yardbird Suite': I forgot to count the number of A sections during Bill's [saxophone] solo. I was listening to the others for a cue as to whether we were going to go to the B section or repeat the A section. Bill played something that sounded like the B section but the bass repeated the A section. I followed Bill and Bob subsequently heard the change and altered his bass line accordingly. Bob and I exchanged looks at that point, and we were all careful to look again at each other at the end of the chorus. … During my [guitar] solo I got lost and had to listen out to the others again to determine the section change. This created some inconsistency in the solo as the pause didn't really fit the line I had been developing.

The structure of fieldnotes, then, is itself an iterative feature of research. One way to conceptualize fieldnotes is that they involve a working out of the analytic focus of a study. Fieldnotes provide a way for researchers to think through their setting and their analysis of it on paper – to discursively explore the things they are observing and their connection to the researcher's interests.

Analyzing observational data

The previous discussion showed the artificiality of a distinction between data collection and data analysis in the context of observational work. Apart from instances in which the researcher is not present in the setting, and is relying solely on video data, all observational work involves the working out of analysis in the research setting. It is very unhelpful to create a dividing line that separates data collection from analytic work, as doing so leads to exactly the type of confusion over the processes of data analysis that we described in the introduction to this book. Observational work *is* data analysis – it involves thinking through what is being observed, why it is interesting, how it is to be categorized, what its relevance is to the problems at hand, how it might be thought through in relation to other data, which aspects of it are unintelligible or confusing; how it contrasts with or supports existing ideas/propositions/data/assumptions, and so on.

The varied character of observational work, with some observations being quite formally structured and others more open, means that researchers very often end up with a range of data. Upon reviewing their materials, a researcher may discover that they have some structured observation schedules, some fairly messy observation notes, a couple of video recordings of a particular setting, and maybe one or two audio recordings where video was not permitted but audio recording was. (However, to reiterate the point we made earlier, the *revision of* such data should be an integrated part to data collection, and not an afterthought.) This is probably quite an extreme example, as normally a researcher would expect a little more standardization than this, but it is certainly not uncommon.

The purpose of research is not to end up with a body of unified data materials, but to understand an empirical domain for some motivated reason or other. The variation in one's data materials should not therefore be a cause of concern, but they might be a source of enquiry. A researcher might start by thinking about the reasons why their materials are varied:

- What is it about the particular settings/people/practices that were observed and the specific contexts of that research work that led the data to take the form that they did?
- Were there any defined questions or issues that were being explored when the researcher started the observations, and does the data help the researcher to deal with those questions/issues?
- Is there anything that the data shows that was not part of the formalized research interest prior to the observation but which is nonetheless interesting and relevant?
- What are the strengths and limitations of the data gathered and what other forms of data might complement them?

These types of question can be usefully recorded on some kind of **observation analysis sheet,** like those used in interviews. An observation analysis sheet is different from a fieldnote as it concerns observations that are recorded about the data (about the fieldnotes) in a separate document.

Concluding remarks

This chapter has been concerned with exploring the role of data analysis in and through methods of data collection. The discussion focused on interviews and observations and showed how conducting research using these methods involves researchers engaging with analytic issues and problems and working actively with the data as an integrated feature of using those methods. The general point being made here is that 'collecting' or, as we prefer, *generating* data through any method of engagement with the social world is an analytic activity: researchers do not passively 'gather up' information from the social world, but are active participants in the construction of the discourse and observations that constitute the 'data' for analysis. 'Analysis' is not separate from this activity, but is rather a basic feature of it.

The limitations of space have meant that we have had to be very cursory indeed in our treatment of these issues. The methodological debates and procedures of research methods are complicated and expansive, and we could not possibly offer an overview of all of the issues here. The intention has been to exemplify the relationship between data work and research methods in order to demystify the practices of data analysis. Hopefully, our discussion has achieved that and readers will be able to take forward this general view into their own exploration in other contexts.

Recommended further reading

DeWalt, K.M. and DeWalt, B.R. (2001) *Participant Observation: A Guide for Fieldworkers*. Palo Alto, CA: AltaMira Press. A thorough reflection in the issues and practices of participant observation.

Gubrium, J. and Holstein, J. (2001) *Handbook of Interview Research: Context and Method*. London: Sage. A rich collection of essays covering every aspect of interview research methodology.

Holstein, J. and Gubrium, J. (1995) *The Creative Interview*. London: Sage. A concise and engaging description of the issues involved in interpretive interview practice.

Humphreys, L. (1970) *Tearoom Trade: A Study of Homosexual Encounters in Public Places*. Chicago: Aldine de Gruyter. A classic and highly controversial piece of observational social research.

Mishler, E. (1991) *Research Interviewing: Context and Narrative*. Cambridge. MA: Harvard University Press. Mishler offers a productive account of the interview as a 'discourse event', and some intricate discussions of methodological issues in interview research.

Riessman, C.K. (1993) *Narrative Analysis*. London: Sage. A short but nuanced introduction to narrative analysis.

Robben, A.C.G.M. and Sluka, J.A. (2007) *Ethnographic Fieldwork: An Anthropological Reader*. Oxford: Blackwell. The inclusion of 'anthropology' in the title here should not put off readers who do not associate themselves with the discipline. The collection of texts included in this edited reader covers a very broad scope of issues from some important authors.

7 Transcribing and representing data

This chapter discusses the following issues:

- Forms of transcription
- Technology and transcription
- Transcription and epistemology

Introduction

> Transcription is translation, and all translations are partial; the partiality in the case of research derives from the theoretical perspective of the research. Transcriptions are never value free; they are theory laden. (Kress et al., 2005: 10)

Transcription is a form of *representation* and must be considered as such. The process of transcribing is not best conceptualized as a matter of simply 'writing down what someone or some people said or did'; it involves making analytic judgements about what to represent and how to represent it, and choosing to display or focus on certain features of a piece of talk, action or interaction rather than others. When researchers speak of a **transcript**, they are referring to a mode of representing a piece of data that has been gathered. **Data** refers to material that has been collected (or *generated*) in the course of research, while **transcription** is the process of rendering that data into a new representational form. Through transcription, researchers *represent* or better still *re-present* the data that they have gathered.

Box 7.1   Re-presentation

The notion of **re-presentation** draws attention to the fact that transcripts are not 'neutral' but are an analytically guided *version* or *rendering of* data. Transcripts are data presented in a new, analytically focused way.

The comparison with the process of translation is particularly useful here for drawing attention to the interpretative process involved in producing transcripts: translations involve the intersection of culturally distinct knowledge, practices and modes of expression. The production of a translation can be seen as an attempt to re-present a particular way of life within the parameters of another (see Venuti's (2000) collection of work in translation studies). Good translation has sensitivity towards the cultural fields within which it is being operated.

Similarly, transcription in social research should be conducted with a reflexive eye on the role of culture (both that of the researcher and of the research participants) in the creation of meaning in the transcript and in the discourse and actions to which it pertains. This should not be taken to imply that researchers can either 'step out of' their own culture any more than they can unproblematically 'step into' another, but the epistemological conundrums that these limitations imply should not prevent a reflexive awareness of the operations of culture as features of meaning-making.

Through transcription, researchers specify particular aspects of data as relevant to their analytic purposes. The process of doing transcription involves deciding on 'what is to count as relevant' for the purposes of the project being conducted, and filtering out and emphasizing particular features of the data rather than others. Transcribing, then, involves two separate aims:

- Deciding which features of the data are relevant
- Finding an effective way to represent those features.

Both of these processes require a high level of *reflexivity* if they are to be effectively accomplished. This chapter is concerned with examining these processes in relation to a number of approaches to transcription.

Analysis in transcription

There are two interrelated aims involved in the production of transcriptions:

- To provide a guide to a given set of data
- To produce an analytic focus on a given data set.

We will discuss each of these in turn.

Transcription as a guide to data

An important role for transcripts is as a resource to help researchers to find their way around their data. The transcription acts as a kind of shorthand version of the data that is more practical to work with than the data itself. As guides to data, transcripts can of course save researchers a lot of time as re-playing recordings of interviews or videos of observation can be a lengthy process; reading is often faster than listening or watching.

However, when using transcriptions in this way, researchers do need to take care that they do not become too reliant on the transcriptions themselves. It can be tempting, particularly when using a lot of data, to simply use transcripts without returning to the data, but this can lead to problems. Precisely because transcriptions are *re-presentations*, they do not carry the detail of information represented in the data. Below we outline three different general approaches to transcription that vary in the level of detail represented in the transcripts. Even in the most detailed transcription, however, any given transcript will not include all of the nuances of speech, and yet those nuances are important signifiers of meaning. By regularly revisiting their data, researchers can check the accuracy and appropriateness of their transcriptions; it is surprising how many mistakes can be made when producing transcriptions, and it is very common to be correcting mistakes in transcripts some time after they have been produced.

Transcription as analysis

Transcription is not just undertaken in order to serve as a guide to data; it is also a way of analytically working through some problem or other in relation to data. As Riessman has noted, 'Analysis cannot be easily distinguished from transcription. … Close and repeated listenings, coupled with methodic transcribing, often leads to insights that in turn shape how we choose to represent an interview narrative in our text' (1993: 60). Transcription enables researchers to focus on data, and to draw out particularly relevant features of it. Transcription is perhaps best thought of as an approach to generating analytic focus, of pointing to particular features of data and of filtering out less important ones. All transcripts produce analytically focused renderings of data, and they do so by imposing modes of representation and/or categorization that display and draw attention to some features of the data rather than others. Even a 'simple' transcription of talk between two people makes numerous analytic distinctions: the representation of conversational turns in a linear manner; the naming of participants in a particular way; the use of punctuation to generate meaning; the sidelining of visual forms of communication. All of these produce selective ways of reading and seeing which both focus attention on some things rather than others and specify, either explicitly or implicitly, ways of interpreting those things.

In this chapter we discuss these aspects of transcription in some detail in relation to three distinct approaches. Before we do so, however, we will discuss the relevance of transcription to different forms of data.

Transcription and forms of data

The analytic focusing that transcriptions provide is relevant to a wide range of social research data. Photographs, videos or documents can all be analyzed through the production of transcriptions that both form guides to that data and analytic renderings. In this brief section we give an example of this in relation to a photograph, but it should be emphasized that this same form of representation applies to many data types.

Figure 7.1 is a photograph taken as part of an analysis of how flows of 'people traffic' are organized at public events. The problematic behind this research concerns the ways that people can try to negotiate the boundaries of specified queuing spaces.

Figure 7.1   Photograph of queuing behaviour

The photo itself is the raw data that is to be subjected to analysis. Transcriptions are then used to focus on particular aspects of this data. For example, Figure 7.2 shows an aerial re-presentation of the section of the photo shown in the square. The analysis here concerns the ways in which the people are managed by the staff within this section of the queue, and the ways that devices such as bag searching tables and fences are used to display and control interactional boundaries. The re-presentation depicts a part of the photo and illustrates how this piece of data relates to the other unseen parts of the interaction that are happening behind the small fence that can be seen in the foreground of Figure 7.1.

The re-presentation shown in Figure 7.2 performs the two roles of transcription that we discussed earlier, as it serves as both a 'guide' and 'analysis'.

As a guide, the transcription draws attention to particular features of the data. In this case, the transcript focuses on the spatial organization of members of the public in relation to objects and institutional staff. Secondly, the transcription imposes categories or 'analytic concepts' that divide up or 'give analytic sense to' the data. Here, the categories of 'members of the public' and 'institutional staff' as well as 'fence', 'building' and 'bag searching tables' (the latter three being part of the more general category of 'objects') are used as ways of separating out the things that are of interest for the analysis.

In what follows we focus our attention on the transcription of audio forms of data. This is by no means intended to privilege these forms of data but is merely a way of rather arbitrarily dividing up our discussion. Other chapters of this book deal in much more detail with the analysis of photographic data (Chapter 9) and video (Chapter 10).

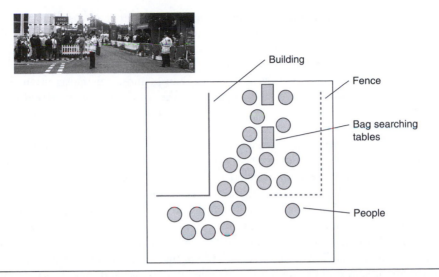

Figure 7.2   Re-presentation of queuing behaviour

Forms of transcription

Transcripts are produced so that the data can be represented in ways that are appropriate to the specific interests of the researcher. When researchers transcribe they do so in such a way as to enable them to *focus* on the data in some way or another. There are many ways in which researchers can represent their data, many of which, as with Figure 7.2, are only relevant to specific analytic questions. Researchers may create their own modes of transcription and representation in response to a particular question. In this way, transcription and re-presentation is not a matter of simply following techniques, but is a creative process that entails trying to work through a particular set of analytic concerns in relation to specific research interests. In this section, we discuss three general approaches to transcribing audio data. However, it should be emphasized from the outset that these are merely intended as quite general ways of thinking about forms of data representation.

Box 7.2   Three general types of transcription

Indexical transcription involves producing some form of *index* of a given data set in relation to a timeline or some other indexical dimension.

Unfocused transcription involves creating a record of 'what happened' within a given recording of speech or action. Typically, the entire data set will be transcribed in the unfocused approach as there is no specific analytic focus.

Focused transcription involves generating a detailed outline of 'what was said or done' in a recording that emphasizes particular features of that behaviour.

The first common approach to transcribing that we want to discuss here involves a concern with creating a very general overview of the contents of a recording. We call this approach **indexical transcription**, and it entails creating an index of the data. The second approach we address also involves a concern with providing an overview of data, but in slightly more detail than in indexical transcription. This entails writing down 'what is said', i.e. to write the words that were uttered in an interview, or to outline the actions that occurred in a video observation. These sorts of transcription are sometimes referred to as 'broad' transcriptions (perhaps because they offer a 'broad overview' of what occurred – see Gee, 1999). We will use the term **unfocused** for this mode of transcription because the analysis does not involve focusing on particular sections or interactional aspects of the data, but is simply concerned with providing a general overview of the entire data set.

There is a very thin line between indexical and unfocused transcription and one can quickly merge into the other. An index may provide an overview of a given data set in much the same way as unfocused transcription, and an unfocused transcript may well include an 'index' that indicates where that data is to be found. The point of this discussion is not to set out firm dividing lines between different sets of practices, but to reflect on different ways of conceiving representation.

In contrast to these two approaches, **focused** transcription (which is sometimes referred to as 'narrow' transcription – see Gee, 1999), involves a concern with *how* things were said or done within the data. In this approach to transcription there is usually an analytic commitment to examining *how* things are said or enacted by illustrating, for example, how talk overlaps or the relevance of a particular voice intonation. Typically, focused transcripts are only produced for particular sections of the data, rather than for an entire data set. We will address each of these forms in turn.

Indexical transcription

In this approach, the concern is with mapping out the contents of a set of data in very general terms and outlining the 'locations' at which they can be found. With text-based data, the index may look something like an index to a book, with a system used to represent the location in a document where relevant data sections are to be found. With photographic data, researchers may construct a grid with numbered x and y axes that are used to highlight the points in the photo that are particularly relevant. In audio or video forms of data, the transcription usually takes the form of a timeline, indicating the point in the recording where the relevant feature occurred. In this section we are particularly concerned with timeline indexes.

Timeline transcription

The choice of how to set out a timeline is really pretty arbitrary. A researcher may decide to run a timeline horizontally and represent particular events underneath it, or to run it vertically and display the events along the side. Whatever mode of representation is chosen, the aim is to be able to map a recording as a visually represented overview of events. Extract 1 shows a very short timeline analysis of a professional evaluation between two teachers. The teachers are watching a video together, and producing comments as they go along. Jill (or J) is the teacher in the video being evaluated and Fiona (or F) is the professional mentor helping to provide the evaluation. Here, the times are shown running down the page, with quite brief descriptions of the actions that occurred at those points next to them.

(1) Timeline transcription of a teacher evaluation

00.24	J identifies a problem 'I thought my pace was too slow', and F disagrees
00.38	J and F interrogate the activity together (the aims and structure of the activity)
02.17	J raises a concern 'I am not really confident in my questions'
02.43	F suggests a way of dealing with the problem
03.03	J asks if she thought the activity was effective and F says that it was
03.36	J comments that all the students had their attention focused on the activity
03.46	F compliments J on how she went into character within the drama activity
04.17	J comments on the difficulty of getting students to imagine (this observation is made in relation to an activity they were watching)
04.47	F observes that the children are getting very involved in the activity
05.00	J makes an observation about a particular student (which seems to be picking up on F's previous point).
05.17	J provides an assessment of the students' general behaviour
05.25	F says that she thought the students were very focused on the activity being conducted

This mode of representing data is very good as an index of events as, at a glance, researchers can see what happened at a given point in time within the data. Compared to other modes, these forms of transcription are quite quick to produce. However, they may still require the researcher to work through the data several times before they can decide which parts of the recording are relevant. There are three important issues to bear in mind when producing indexical transcripts:

Standardization – The descriptors used in the index should be standardized across the different parts of the data. For example, if a researcher has 15 interviews, each timeline for each interview should use the same terminology, vocabulary and indexing system.

Regular reviewing – The index should be reviewed periodically to make sure that it is relevant to any emerging interests. As analysis is always iterative, the indexes will commonly need to be updated to take account of newly developed analytic foci.

Precision – Researchers need to make sure that the descriptors and descriptions that they use in the indexes are intelligible and sufficiently precise. As the index is a guide to the data, words and phrases need to be selected so that they accurately represent the analytic issues that they reference.

All forms of indexical transcription are produced in orientation to the analytic concerns of the researcher. Indexical transcription involves producing an outline of analytically relevant points within a data set. It is not a 'neutral' guide to data (in fact, the word 'neutrality' has no place in descriptions of transcription), but an analytically instructive re-presentation of the data. This type of analysis can be a good alternative to transcribing large data fragments, and may work as an overview and in conjuncture with other transcription modes, such as focused or unfocused transcription. An index acts as a kind of 'first order' analysis and as a precursor to more detailed forms of interrogation.

Unfocused transcription

Unfocused transcription involves outlining the basic 'intended meaning' of a recording of speech or action without attempting to represent its detailed contextual or interactional characteristics. This mode of representation does not involve a concern with illustrating nuances of speech or action such as the intonation of voices, overlap in talk or non-verbal forms of communication like gestures or gazes, but simply attempts to characterize what was meant within a given piece of data. Extract (2) provides a very brief example of a piece of unfocused transcription.

(2) A transcription of some friends talking

MARY:	What did John say he was doing?
SUE:	Oh, I didn't really understand it. Something about picking up music.
MARY:	Well I wish he would tell me when he was coming home late.
SUE:	'Cos Mike was going too, but I guess he didn't tell you that either.

The transcription provided here involves an identification of the people who are speaking (in this instance the speakers names are anonymized by using pseudonyms) and the basic sense of what was said. The transcript also includes a small representation of a colloquialism, such as the '*cos*' in the last line being used instead of '*because*', and the use of punctuation, such as commas, question marks and full stops.

Through teaching on postgraduate courses on qualitative analysis for many years, we have found that when students are asked to produce a transcript of a piece of talk they will typically include things like colloquialisms and punctuation as shown in the above extract, and that they will do so without really reflecting on the ways that such indicators give meaning to the text. It seems to be quite natural for a lot of researchers that these forms of speech should be represented, and that things like question marks, commas and full stops are obvious ways to represent them. There is, of course, nothing wrong with using such representational devices, which, after all, carry important information about the data – and a casual consultation of published research that includes these kinds of transcription will show that it is certainly normal practice – but it is very instructive to reflect on the reasons for, and the implications behind, these forms of representation.

A key question to reflect on when producing and reviewing transcripts is:

Q – What are the implications behind the punctuation that is being used and its relation to the meaning of the discourse?

Box 7.3 provides an example of critical reflection in relation to extract (2).

Box 7.3   An interrogation of the representation features used in extract (2)

Colloquialisms – We might ask why the 'because' in line 4 of extract (2) is represented as a colloquialism and why no other aspects of the talk are? In this instance, the 'what' at the beginning of the first line could have been shown as 'wha', as the 't' at the end was not enunciated, but this was not indicated in the transcription. Similarly, the 'well' at the beginning of line 3 was actually pronounced 'wew', but this was not displayed on the transcription either. There is a lack of consistency in the use of these colloquial features. One of the possible implications of this is that some participants may be represented as using colloquialisms more than others. Colloquialisms and accents carry social significance that may lead the researcher to interpret or make sense of the transcript in certain ways. Similarly, it may lead other people who read the transcript (e.g. in the final report or other dissemination methods) to interpret the participants in unintended ways. The general point is that there are implications behind the use of colloquialisms that need to be deliberated on. Representing such forms may or may not be relevant, but that really needs to be a deliberate decision rather than an unreflexive production.

Punctuation – the question mark at the end of line 1 is a clear sign that the utterance shown in the first line was formulated as a question. The question mark represents some probably quite complex voice intonation (like rising intonation at the end of the sentence). Similarly, the comma after the 'oh' in line 2 indicates that there was a break in the utterance, and the mode of representing here *implies* a particular intonation in the preceding 'oh,' and a slight gap between the following 'I didn't'.

(Continued)

(Continued)

The punctuation, then, is shorthand for complex features of the speech, but it is used very selectively as there are nuances of speech thoughout the data that are not indicated in the transcription: the speed, volume and pitch of the talk; the pauses, intakes of breath and utterances such as 'umm' and 'err'; the ways that non-verbal interaction was used to give emphasis to or alter verbal meanings – none of these aspects of the interaction, which were most certainly present within the encounter, were shown within the transcription.

Researchers need to be clear why they are representing some features of speech rather than others. As the intention is to represent the meaning of a given section of dialogue, certain gestural features may be necessary and others may be peripheral. It is imperative that researchers are aware of the implications behind the punctuation that they use.

As Box 7.3 implies, while the representation of the nuances of speech in unfocused transcription is less of an interest than in focused transcription, it is still an analytic concern because it bears on the matter of meaning, and the overall aim in the creation of an unfocused transcript is to end up with an accurate reflection of the meaning of the discourse as interpreted by the researcher.

However, in unfocused transcripts, 'accuracy' is a rather slippery issue as their production requires a certain degree of creative licence in order that as good a fit as possible can be made between the *representation* and the *data*. It may be necessary to add in or change some words, or to correct mistakes or confusions in the talk that may mislead the reader. The aim is not to show what was said, but what was meant by what was said, or perhaps *what the researcher interpreted in what was said* and, as such, some level of *alteration* is to be both expected and creatively embraced.

Meaning and 'misrepresentation' in focused transcription

Researchers should be aware that there is a very real possibility of changing meaning through their forms of representation, and a great deal of reflexivity and sensitivity is required in order to avoid *misrepresentation*. Precisely because the written representation of a transcript involves a form of *translation*, so it is possible that in producing that translation some of the contextual meanings and nuances may be lost and that new and unintended meanings and significances imposed.

Extracts (3) and (4) provide a very informative example of this issue. These transcripts come from a study of doctor–patient interaction within eye test consultations and offer two different representations of the same piece of dialogue. (Extract (3) uses an unfocused transcription, while extract (4) provides some representation of the intonation within the speech, including the overlap of the dialogue. In extract (3) the question in the fifth line appears as if the doctor is offering an alternative between two possibilities (i.e. 'reading' and 'distance'). However, the transcription offered in the second extract makes it clear that the intonation of the sentence (upward intonation, and the speed of connections between the words 'reading' and 'distance') was presenting an incomplete list of options, and that it would have been appropriate for the patient to add an alternative type of 'getting worse'.

The relevance of this is very significant in this instance as the analytic concern here is with the ways in which doctors enquire about the subjective experiences of vision from patients. Thus, while the sentence shown in the first extract was indeed a question, the inclusion of the question mark makes it look like a closed question whereas, in fact, it was presented as an open set of possibilities. An alternative way of representing this may have been to put a series of three dots within square brackets to show that this was not a completed sentence (e.g. [...]).

(3) Unfocused transcription of doctor–patient interaction

D: Any difficulties or problems at all with your vision or your eyes?
P: The right eye has gotten worse
D: The right eye feels a little weaker
P: Yes
D: When you say a little worse, is this general vision or would you say specifically more the difficulty is with reading or in the distance?
P: In the distance
D: In the distance

(4) Focused transcription of doctor–patient interaction

1	D	any difficulties or problems at all with your vision or your eyes:
2	P	(.) er: [I
3	D	[inaudible]
4	P	I think (.) er: (.) the right eye has: (.) gotten worse
5	D	The right eye feels a little weaker
16	P	Yeah
17		(3.5)
18	P	The eyes h *h*ave been (.) quite different an
19		(2.0)
20	D	Right (.) [inward breath] dy r:m (1.0) when you say a little worse (.) is this
21		in general vision or would you: say specifically more (inward breath) the
22		difficulty is in readi::ng or in the distance↑:
23	P	in the distance
24	D	in the distan[ce
25	P	[m*h*m]

This example is not intended to suggest that all researchers should produce detailed and focused transcripts, but merely to illustrate some of the problems that can arise if researchers do not pay attention to the implications of the ways that they produce unfocused transcripts. While it is always advisable to work closely with data and transcripts, in practice it is very common for researchers to rely substantially on transcripts when they are conducting data work and not to regularly revisit the original data. It is extremely important, therefore, to double-check transcripts against the original recording in order to make sure that no misrepresentations have been produced in creating the unfocused transcription. It can be helpful to wait a few days between producing an initial transcription and checking through it. It is also very beneficial to invite others to check transcripts against data, as it is common for listeners to pick up on different things. These sorts of approaches can help to minimize the difficulties of either mis-hearing or misrepresenting data.

Focused transcription

Focused transcription involves a commitment to representing some of the details of speech in order to show *how* something was said rather than simply *what* was said. Researchers who use these types of intricate approach do so because the details are important for their analysis. Undertaking detailed transcription does not mean that the researcher attempts to represent *all* the features of a given section of speech, but that some specific elements of how something was said are relevant to them. As Gee (1999) has commented, transcriptions are as detailed as they need to be for the analytic purposes of the researcher. As with all modes of transcription, when undertaking focused transcription there is *selectivity* in deciding what is to be re-presented.

There are a wide variety of conventions for using symbols to represent particular features of talk. Box 7.4 provides a list of some of the more frequent ones. This is taken from a review of transcription systems undertaken by Richard Dressler and Roger Kruez (2000), who compiled some of the more common approaches to representing verbal discourse. Another popular system has been developed by researchers interested in children's speech (the Child Language Data Exchange System – CHILDES: see MacWhinney (1996), for more information on this system). To reiterate, it is not the case that researchers have to use all of the forms of representation within a given transcription system, but that these are some of the things that researchers may choose to represent in their transcriptions.

Box 7.4   Dressler and Kruez's (2000) transcription system

?	=	Rising intonation at end of sentence
.	=	Falling intonation at end of sentence
/ \	=	Rising and falling intonation within text
,	=	Continuing intonation (like in a list)
CAPS	=	Stress or emphasis in the text
(0.5)	=	Pause in tenths of a second
...	=	Short untimed pause
< >	=	Talk spoken slowly
> <	=	Talk spoken rapidly
:	=	Lengthened syllable
–	=	Word cut off (abrupt self-termination)
=	=	Latched talk (no gap between two speakers)

[ ]	=	Overlap speech
{ }	=	Backchannel talk (someone who is not being transcribed)
? ?	=	Spoken softly
ITALICS	=	Spoken loudly
H	=	Audible breath
.h	=	Inward breath
h	=	Outward breath
(( ))	=	Paralinguistic behaviour
( )	=	Unclear or unintelligible speech

An interesting way to approach this form of transcription is to imagine that any word or phrase that is written and that doesn't contain any of the above notations is to be heard as a monotonal sound. Researchers can then think about the ways in which the actual data differs from that representation and reflect on the aspects of those differences that are relevant to their analysis. Undertaking focused transcriptions is extremely time consuming (it takes something like one hour to transcribe one minute of talk, depending on the speed of the interaction and the amount of detail that a researcher needs to represent). It is usually therefore impractical to transcribe large sections of talk in this manner.

Selecting which features of talk to pay attention to is analytically driven, but it may not be apparent from the outset which aspects these are. Researchers, therefore, may need to work with a section of data for quite some time before they realize what it is that they want to represent and how they want to represent it. In the process of working through data, researchers may also create multiple transcriptions of the same data segment, each one focusing on a different aspect of the data.

Extract (5) is an extract from the very beginning of the conversation between the two teachers transcribed in extract (1) (time 00.24 and 00.38). This is an extract from a 42 line **stanza** or *transcription segment*. The transcription uses slightly different symbols from Dressler and Kreuz's system (e.g. the use of arrows for falling intonation – see the descriptors at the bottom of the transcript). The analysis of this text concerns the ways in which the speakers managed the production of criticism within the talk. The aim of their activity was to provide feedback to Jill. In the first version of this transcript, volume and speed of talk were not included in the segment. However, repeated listening showed that the subtleties of volume and speed were important features of how the speakers designed their utterances. For example, the drop in volume from '↑*while I was watching this*' to 'I thought my pace was to <slow>)↓' in lines 3 and 4 of the transcript, and the decrease in speed of the '<slow>↓' served to mark out the topic under discussion as not being about 'while I was watching this' but about the pace of the activity being slow. They also help to indicate that this is a question being directed to Fiona, rather than simply a statement of 'fact' and that there is a preference from Jill that Fiona addresses this point in her next comment. Similarly, the slower speed and higher volume of '<*they we:re:*>' in line 6 helped to signal out the students as being at fault and not Jill. In the first transcription, the absence of an inclusion of speed and volume made this less clear.

(5)

1	J	oka:y (1.5) I <↑don't thin:k> (.) you had come in then↓ (.)
2	F	no:
3	J	>you hancome in yetst ↓< (2.5) but ↑*while I was watching*
4		*this*:: (3.0) I thought my pace was too <slow>↓
4		(2.5)
5	F	(.h) I think your pace was led by the chil↓dren (1.5) and
6		<↑*they wer:e:*> (.) maybe a bit sl↓ow: (0.5) >what they doing
7		writing the learning obj[ectives<
8	J	[>they were just ↑ryin' to write the
9		learning objective ↓< (.) and trying to get them all together
10	F	(2.) (h.) Do they↑need↓to write the learning objectives.
11		(2.0)
12	J	er:m (2.0) for writing in their book they do↑: (2.5) and
13		*having evidence*: (1.0) especially with your table that one
14		{you were working at?}

Transcription symbols:

Time in tenths of a second

(.)	Micro-pause
><	Text spoken quickly
<>	Text spoken slowly
↑	Rising intonation
↓	Falling intonation
italics	Spoken loudly
[]	Overlapping talk
:	Elongated sound
{?}	Unclear speech

By using these forms of representation, researchers are able to examine in great detail the particular ways in which talk is created and managed by participants. One of the challenges that analysts face is in working out the particular aspects that are analytically relevant or interesting. While on some occasions an analytic focus may be quite apparent, in other instances it may not, and the researcher may need to create various transcriptions of the same piece of talk in the process of figuring that out.

Technology and transcription

Trends in recording technology come and go. Until the late 1990s the tape recorder was one of the most popular modes of capturing sound. Researchers could use tape recorders not only to record interviews but also to make audio copies of their data, or to record their own fieldnotes, often through smaller, portable and less intrusive tape formats such as dictaphones. Through the use of transcription machines, the tape format becomes a very quick and easy technology to transcribe. **Transcription machines** are tape players that are controlled by foot peddles, which enable the user to play, stop and rewind a tape using the feet, leaving the hands free to type or write out the transcript. Transcription machines make the cumbersome business of transcription much easier.

In the late 1990s and early 2000s, mini-disks became a very popular alternative to tape recorders. Mini-disks use a digital diskette instead of a conventional tape to record, and this results in a very high quality of sound and replayable recordings that don't diminish with use (which was a common problem with conventional tapes). However, researchers need to convert the format of the recording over to tape in order to use a transcription machine, and this often reduces the quality of the recording.

More recently, digital recorders have become standard equipment for many researchers. With the exception of quite expensive professional devices, these recorders are generally not as good quality as mini-disks, but they do not require researchers to carry around other tapes or disks as the recordings are usually saved on to the recorder's own in-built memory (although some use 'flash cards' as forms of data storage). There are good reasons why digital recorders are becoming so popular. Digital recorders are designed to enable users to store their data on a computer where the data can be edited or analyzed with CAQDAS (computer assisted qualitative data analysis software). While in theory mini-disks and conventional tapes can also be moved over to a computer, in practice this is not at all straightforward to do (see Gibson et al., 2005 for a discussion this process). The newer digital recorders can record many hours of talk, and often have an external microphone slot to help produce better quality sound. Many of them also come with their own software, which can be used to edit the files by, for example, cutting sections, inserting sound or converting the file format. Some of the bigger companies, such as Panasonic, also produce digital transcription hardware and software, which include peddles that plug into the computer to replicate the functionality of tape-transcription machines.

There is now a range of software available that can automatically transcribe audio recordings. Since such software programs typically work by training the software application to recognize a voice (and usually just one voice) these sorts of package are currently only useful for transcribing things like audio fieldnotes rather than interviews (the software will not be able to transcribe voices that it has not been trained to recognize). New versions of qualitative data analysis software, such as Atlas.ti and NVivo, can now be used to analyze digital audio and video. This means that researchers can use the original data recordings instead of, or as well as, transcripts of those recordings. As we show in our later discussion of CAQDAS, the ability to analyze such data in audio form does not mean that transcription is no longer relevant. While there are some interesting possibilities that can come from the direct analysis of audio-visual data, transcriptions still have a very important role to play in the analysis process because transcription comprises the generation of analytic focus.

Transcription and epistemology

We have argued throughout this chapter that transcription is best thought of as the *re-presentation* and the *rendering* of data into new form. Transcription *could* be seen,

Table 7.1 Advantages and disadvantages of recording technology

	Advantages	Disadvantages	Particularly good roducts
Tape	Easy to transcribe using a transcription machines	Hard to move the recordings over to a computer for analysis with software	None recommended
Digital recorder	Easy to move recordings over to a computer Some companies produce transcription machines that work with their recorders	Recording quality generally not as good as with mini-disks	Zoom Digital Recorder
Mini-disk	Very good quality recordings	With some proprietary recording formats it can be hard to move the recordings over to a computer and to convert them to appropriate file formats	Sony MZ RH1

then, as the nexus between data and data work; as the point at which the researchers' interpretations replace or *do something to* the actual data that was generated in the research. In such a view, questions inevitably arise about the relationship between the data and its representation. For example:

Q – Is the transcript showing 'what actually happened' or 'a reading of what actually happened'?
Q – Does data represent 'the reality of the situation' and the transcript 'an interpretation of that event'?
Q – Is the transcript simply 'what the researcher saw in the data' and, if so, what does that imply for the reliability of that interpretation?
Q – Would another researcher have transcribed the same data in the same way, and does it matter if they wouldn't have?

But such questions implicitly fetishize data, and ignore the ways in which the processes of data generation *themselves* create analytic focus. In this chapter we have described data forms such as photographs, audio recordings of interviews, fieldnotes, and video observations. All of these forms are partial and produced in relation to particular analytic issues. A photograph of someone doing something is not a neutral object, but a snapshot of interaction that decontextualizes a moment of activity from the flow of actions which gives it its sense. An audio recording of an interview is a partial rendering of what happened, which ignores the non-verbal cues or structure of the environment that may be important features of the interaction. Even a video is shot from a particular angle that does not capture the broader periphery of the setting, and contains start, end and sometimes edit points that frame that data. The very process of data 'gathering', it must be accepted, is interventionist and has a bearing on the outcome of the products that comes to be called 'data'. Transcription, then, is not in fact the first nexus of interpretation, and 'the world' as the data itself is already a mediated construct. Rather, transcription is perhaps best thought of as a *re-mediation* of a mediated view.

To make this point, though, is not to belittle the issues that arise from the interpretive nature of research. Just because 'interpretation' cannot be easily pinned down to a particular research 'stage' does not mean that it is any less of a concern for researchers. The famous metaphor of researchers layering interpretation on interpretation demonstrates the ubiquitous nature of interpretive practice. A key strategy used to orientate to this interpretive nature is *subjective reflexivity*, where researchers reflect on the ways in which their distinctive motivations, taken-for-granted assumptions and interventions act on the research process (see Davies et al., 2004 for discussion of these issues). The 'layering metaphor' helps us to see that there is nothing particularly special about researchers' confrontation with such issues at the point of transcription. Transcription is a mediated practice, but then so is every aspect of research, and the strong reflexivity that is required to effectively take account of this is as necessary during transcription as it is in any other research practice.

Concluding remarks

The transcription of data is not an antecedent to analysis, but is a central aspect of the ways that researchers analytically orientate to data. The precise way in which transcription takes place is formulated through reflection on the nature of the data required to answer the research questions. Very often, working out how best to transcribe data will be an iterative process, with each rendering of transcription leading researchers to ask other questions that require different transcription foci. In this chapter we outlined three general approaches to transcription, each of which involves using different representational features and implies specific analytic challenges. However, transcription, as with all data work, is ultimately a matter of experimentation, so these representational forms should not be regarded as enshrined practices, but simply as possible analytic strategies.

Recommended further reading

There are surprisingly few texts that deal directly with transcription. Most qualitative research textbooks will have some brief discussion of the issue, but this is unlikely to be more detailed than the discussion we have provided here. However, there are some interesting readings available on the epistemological and political aspects of transcription:

Bucholtz, M. (2000) 'The politics of transcription'. *Journal of Pragmatics* 32: 1439–65. A thought-provoking consideration of the political implications of transcription.

Vigouroux, C.B. (2007) 'Transscription as a social activity: an ethnographic approach'. *Ethnography* 8(1): 61–97. A nuanced discussion of the methodological issues involved in transcription in social research.

8

Identifying themes, codes and hypotheses

This chapter discusses the following issues:

- Concepts in thematic analysis
- Coding
- Code families and relationships
- Hypotheses
- Hierarchies

Introduction

The analysis of 'themes' in relation to data, such as interview transcripts, observation schedules, fieldnotes, photographs, and so on, is often one of the first things students refer to when they are asked to describe what qualitative analysis means. Indeed, the reader may recall the definition of 'analysis' provided by Marshall and Rossman (2006) that we presented in Chapter 1. In this definition, 'themes' were offered as a key aspect of qualitative analysis. As we use it here, the term **thematic analysis** refers to the process of analyzing data according to commonalities, relationships and differences across a data set. The word 'thematic' relates to the aim of searching for aggregated *themes* within data.

As we hope to have shown in this book, analysis is very varied and might not include this type of thematic work, but there is no doubt that many approaches to analysis do involve some interest in themes. Some of the most influential qualitative analysis texts deal in a significant way with this type of analysis. Miles and Huberman's 'cross-case' analysis involves, in essence, a description of how to code and analyze themes across *cases* of data (Miles and Huberman, 1994). Narrative analysis is directed towards working out and working through discursive themes across interviews (see, for example, Mishler, 1999; Emerson and Frosh, 2004; although see also Riessman (1993) on the limitations of approaching narratives 'thematically'). To take a final example, hermeneutic 'genre analysis' is orientated towards the comparison of data sources, with the aim of comparing communicative actions and the basic structures of social action (see Knoblauch and Luckman (2004) for some description of this form of analysis and Hitzler (2005) for a discussion of its relation to other 'hermeneutic' orientations to analysis). The general interest in 'themes' is one of the few things that these approaches have in common, though, as they come from very different analytic starting points and have distinctive aims and disciplinary affiliations. The point we wish to make is that thematic work, in some form or other, is a very common aspect of qualitative enquiry. The discussion of thematic work that we provide in this chapter draws heavily on grounded theory and cross-case analysis, as these are particularly well known and explicit examples of thematic techniques.

It is extremely important to emphasize that while a textbook such as this one may provide some indications of how thematic work might proceed (and this is indeed the aim of the chapter), no text could ever provide a good definition of why or how such themes should be created in the first place. As Henn et al. comment, 'coding is a process for which there are no rules, merely guidelines' (2006: 202). In other words, the reader of this chapter will not learn how to thematically analyze their data, but will simply gain some ideas about the types of procedure they might think about using when doing so. This is because the thematic organization of data is not simply a technical matter, but a theoretical and conceptual issue that cannot be codified or abstracted into concrete rules of practice.

We have already briefly discussed some of the issues that we will be dealing with in this chapter under our discussion of grounded theory (see Chapter 2). We also deal with some of these matters in our discussion of analysis software in Chapter 11. Indeed, the use of software has very much become standard practice in many forms of thematic analysis. The value of software for thematic work comes from the simple fact that in these types of analysis, researchers often handle large amounts of data and generate quite complex analytic frameworks that are much easier to work through and explore using computers. The basic *procedures* of such analysis, however, are not contingent on computers and so our discussion here does not make much reference to them.

The concept of 'thematic analysis'

There are three general sets of aims in thematic analysis: the examination of commonalities, the examination of differences and the examination of relationships.

Examining commonality – A key feature of thematic analysis is the examination of commonalities in the data. This typically involves finding ways to pool together all the examples from across a data set that can be categorized as 'an example of x'. These commonalities are then subjected to further analysis and subdivision.

Examining differences – In addition to similarities, researchers also look at the distinctive features across a data set. The aim here is to find and analyze the peculiarities and contrasts within a given data set, and to examine their potential relevance for the specific issue being explored.

Examining relationships – Finally, researchers examine the relationships between the various elements of their analysis. This may mean looking at the ways in which different code categories relate to each other, or how particular individual characteristics or differences relate to general themes.

In this chapter, we explore these broad aims in relation to the more specific techniques of data exploration.

Critiques of thematic analysis

Van Manen (1998) offers a phenomenological discussion of the notion of 'thematic analysis' and shows that, from a phenomenological perspective, themes can be viewed as a poor substitute for the lived experiences to which they refer. A 'theme' is a generalized and decontextualized category of contextually specific aspects of social life that become treated as 'of a generalized type' in order to compare them with other instances of data that are labelled in the same way. To give an example, a researcher who conducts interviews with 20 different doctors on their experiences of administering treatment to physically abusive patients may produce answers that are thematically similar on topics such as 'reasons for abuse', 'responses to abuse', 'professional discretion', and so on. However, in using these categories the researcher invariably brackets out the details of the experiences to which those accounts relate. By creating a generalized 'set' of data that speaks to a range of participants' experiences, researchers lose focus on the particularities of the cases being examined. This process can result in an impoverished view of complex lived features of social life as the categories can potentially *hide* rather than *reveal*.

However, this phenomenological observation need not imply that categorization is not valuable. Analysis is, in many respects, about storytelling and as any novelist will attest, themes are a useful device for narrative construction. Van Manen describes a theme as '…like knots in the webs of our experiences, around which certain lived experiences are spun' (1998: 90). In this view, a theme provides a way of linking diverse experiences or ideas together, and of juxtaposing and interrelating different examples and features of data. The themes do re-present and recontextualize the data to which they relate, but this can be of value in creating new readings and renderings of that data. Furthermore, it is not always the case that the themes are directed to merely showing the similarities across cases: narrative analysis is a good example of the ways in which the *differences* across data cases are as much a concern as the *similarities* between cases (see, for example, Mishler, 1999: 9–17). The phenomenological critique serves more as a kind of health warning for the pitfalls of incautious analysis than it does as a suggestion that thematic work is not valuable.

There are two particularly important implications of this 'health warning' that we would like to emphasize here: the relevance of **context** and **sampling**. As a theme is a generalized feature of a data set, an important part of the work of the analysis must involve working out the relevance of the context of a given piece of data to its membership of a category or categories. This involves attempting to answer the general question:

Q: What is distinctive about this piece of data and why might that matter in relation to this category?

To return to our example of interviewing doctors, it is incumbent on the researcher to think about how the context of a doctor's experiences might relate to the conceptual configuration of a category. So, if one general practitioner says that they have lots of experience of working with 'abusive patients', and another says that they don't, it is important to reflect on the broader contexts of their work in order to hypothesize possible reasons for 'why' that difference might exist (e.g. because of the socio-economic context of the doctor's patients and the types of treatment that they are seeking).

This reflection on the context requires researchers to think about how, through sampling, the categories might be explored further. If it turns out that one doctor has a very specific set of experiences, how can a reflection on the general question outlined above help us to think about other people who could be involved in the study? Are there other doctors who work in a similar, or indeed very different, setting that it would be interesting to include? This process of developing samples through their conceptual relevance to a study is referred to in grounded theory as theoretical sampling. While it is not always possible to iteratively develop samples in research, and while not all researchers would (or should) categorize their work as involving grounded theory, it is very instructive to think about the implications of ongoing analysis for possible samples. Even if that sample is not actually developed, having a sense of potential conceptual interests/limitations can be just as important as exploring those as a means of delineating the limits of one's interests.

Distinctive features and resources in thematic analysis

In this section we outline some of the central tools and analytic resources that are often used in thematic analysis. We do not suggest that researchers need to use all of these, but merely that they represent a range of possible ways of moving forward in analysis. Table 8.1 provides a list of some of the central concepts that we will be discussing below.

Code

The concept 'code', as used in relation to qualitative research, is said to have originated in Howard Becker's work (see Fielding and Lee, 1998), and has become a standard apparatus in discussions of qualitative research. To **code** is to create a category that is used to describe a general feature of data; a category that pertains to a range of data examples. In this respect, a code draws attention to a **commonality** within a data set. We can distinguish two types of code: apriori codes and empirical codes. **Apriori codes** are defined prior to the examination of data, while **empirical codes** are generated through the examination of the data itself.

Table 8.1 Key features of thematic analysis

Feature	Definition
Code	A label that describes some general category of data
Code family	A collection of codes that can be regarded as belonging together in some way
Sub code	A subdivision of a code
Property	A defining feature of a code
Super code	A higher order code that describes some relationship between two or more codes
Hypothesis	A relationship between two or more features of an analytic framework that can be empirically tested
Negative case	A feature of an analytic framework that is regarded as distinct in some way

Coding and data

It is common for researchers to associate coding with interview methods but this is a very restricted conception. A code is simply a conceptual device for the description of commonalities in data, and the processes of creating and applying codes in the above ways is relevant to a wide variety of data forms, including interviews, observations, visual and textual data. Box 8.1 provides a brief example of coding in relation to observational fieldwork. The point to emphasize is that any data form may be worked through using the processes of thematic comparison, and using any of the tools and concepts we outline in this chapter.

Box 8.1   An example of thematic organization in fieldnotes

Becker et al. (1997: 34-38) provide quite a rare insight into the process of creating codes and the thematic organization of fieldnotes. While they do not use the term 'coding' in their descriptions, the approach that they use does involve bringing together pieces of data with common characteristics in the ways that we describe above. Becker et al.'s aim was to create a description of the 'perspectives' of students in a medical school. In this instance, perspective refers to 'patterns of thought and action which have grown up in response to a specific set of institutional pressures and serve as a solution to the problems those pressures create' (1997: 36). Their data comprised fieldnotes produced by the researchers that documented their observations of students in particular contexts. The processes of thematized comparison that the authors describe involved:

(Continued)

(Continued)

- Creating fieldnotes comprising key observations of students' practices

- Generating a global index of all the fieldnotes that were created.

'Each entry in the index summarized some observed statement or action of one or more students. Each entry was put in as many categories as it seemed to be relevant' (Becker et al., 1997: 37).

Through this process, the researchers moved from closed, individualized observations of particular students, through to general categories that were indexed to particular instances in those observations. This facilitated comparison between cases or instances of data and between participants.

Apriori and empirical codes

In general, **apriori codes** are created to categorize aspects of a more general prespecified interest. All research is **motivated** in some way or other – i.e. it is directed towards exploring a particular issue, often (although by no means always) formulated in the form of a research question. Apriori codes are categories that relate firmly to these interests. To give an example, a researcher interested in the exploitation of immigrant labour in industrialized countries might begin their research with a categorization of forms of work (such as 'service industry', 'manual labour', 'hospitality', 'skilled professional', and so on) as a means of separating or partitioning domains of experience. The research design would, of course, be developed in such a way that data could be generated from each of these occupational sectors, perhaps in the form of interviews with people who work in those sectors (although a workable design would be *much* more specific and detailed than this very vague formulation). The researchers might be particularly interested in the relationship between the work expectations of the immigrants before arriving in the host country and their experiences once they arrived. The researcher might begin by outlining a range of interests that might, in the first instance, look something like the following:

- Motivations for emigration
- Qualifications and work experience/skills of the workers
- Knowledge of immigrant work rules in host country
- Expectations about the process of securing work in the host country
- Familial and friendship support networks in the host country
- Experiences of job seeking upon arrival.

Each of these interests forms an area of concern within the broader topic of 'expectations and experiences'. It may be that interviews with personnel in these sectors is the most appropriate mode of generating data, and that these themes are used to construct a detailed interview schedule. The interview schedule would involve mapping specific questions on to the areas of interest outlined above. A central aspect of the analysis of the data produced through the interviews will involve considering these prespecified themes of interest. This will involve indexing the data across the interviewees according to these general apriori themes.

Apriori codes serve as general categories that derive from one's research interests, and form a basic skeleton outline for preliminary categorization in order to begin the exploration of the data. This exploration may reveal that some of the categories are not relevant, not particularly revealing, hard to gather data on, or simply not interesting. In other words, the very early examination of data through apriori coding may show that important changes need to be made to the research design in order that different or more specific topical areas can be explored.

Empirical codes emerge through the exploration of data. They may be a derivative of an apriori category or something entirely new that was not foreseen in the original research formulation. To continue with the above example, it could be that the data produced through the interviews reveals a number of sub-categories within the general area of 'motivations for emigration' (e.g. economics, political/social persecution, desires for upward social mobility, education, to be with family or friends). Empirical codes may also emerge as distinct interests that were unforeseen in the original formulation of interests. Perhaps a researcher exploring this topic discovers that access to healthcare provision is a particularly strong theme within the data, and one in which they had not originally been interested.

This relates to an important point: all codes are simply categories of data that represent a thematic concern. Where new thematic concerns emerge through data, researchers need to reflect on the relationship between that concern and the data they have generated/could generate. To explore our example further, the interest in access to healthcare may lead the researcher to want to look at workers' experiences of receiving healthcare, and to generate new samples of research participants that enable them to explore that thematic concern in directed ways. To put it another way, emergent code categories may hint at areas of interest that have not been systematically explored through the research design. An important aspect of thematic analysis, then, involves thinking about how emerging interests and findings of analysis may be taken forward through iterative research design (see Chapter 4 for more discussion on some of these issues).

Why and how do researchers develop codes?

This question is very common. While the general principles of coding that we outline above (and in more detail below) can be quite easily conceptualized, it can be difficult to understand when a code should be generated. Everything is categorizable in some way or other, so how do you know where to start? Other questions that relate to this general issue include:

- How many codes should I create?
- What counts as a good code?
- How do I know if a code is relevant or not?
- I have some codes, now what do I do?

In many respects, deciding which aspects of the data should be developed as a code involves 'following hunches'. *Hunches* are a very important, if rather ethereal, aspect of qualitative analysis. While the nature of the moments of inspiration that lie behind such *felt*, rather than rationalized inclinations is hard to speak of in certain terms, it is perhaps to be expected that the heavy emersion in data will lead to such inklings. The very fact of one's emersion in data as a qualitative researcher, and the richness of the experiences, mean that intuitions are almost bound to occur sooner or later. However, this kind of answer is of course not very comforting to researchers who would like to hear something a little more tangible than 'don't worry, it will come to you'.

Perhaps a better way to answer the question, then, is to outline some of the common reasons for creating codes. Such a list might include the following:

Something occurs more than once – When a researcher sees the same feature across the components of a data set (i.e. different interview transcripts or fieldnotes or texts or photographs), and where that feature is relevant to the research interests, then there may be a case of creating a code to categorize that commonality.

Something is said with intensity or strong emphasis – When dealing with talk, the use of emphatic speech or the presence of strong emotions can be an indication that something is particularly important to that individual/set of people and, therefore, may be relevant to the researcher as well.

Parties in a conversation very readily agree on something or **something goes uncommented or unnoticed** – Ready agreement or a lack of reflection can indicate that some aspect of behaviour is taken for granted, and taken-for-granted procedures are very often key resources for understanding how/why people do what they do.

People disagree – Disagreement is often a useful sign that an aspect is an area of conflict or negotiation and, as such, is an issue for participants. Where that issue is also of concern to the researcher, this may be an interesting area to code.

Mistakes occur – Mistakes are interesting not just in themselves, but in the way that they are resolved. Resolution often betrays the priorities and contingencies of people, and this can be of great value to researchers in trying to understand social worlds.

These small strategies are, of course, not exhaustive or universally applicable – *their relevance will be dictated by the research questions being asked and by the contexts of data being dealt with*. Pointing to these kinds of strategies may be a slight improvement on the 'it will come to you' answer, but it is still far too general to be of much value. A better response to the questions is, we think, to suggest that the questions are substituted for new and far more productive ones:

- Instead of 'How and why do researchers develop codes?' try 'What are my main areas of interest, or themes?'
- Instead of 'How many codes should I create?' how about 'What kind of picture am I developing through my categories and codes?'
- Instead of 'What counts as a good code?' or 'How do I know if a code is relevant or not?' ask 'What is the relevance of this code to my research question?' or 'What analytic work does this code do that that one doesn't?' or 'What is the relationship of this code to my initial conceptualization of the phenomenon I am exploring and how does it help me to understand what I am seeing?'

These sorts of questions are all about the relationship between initial analytic concepts (or theory), data and research interests, which is the concern that should drive analysis. They are far more useful than the very abstract questions about coding provided at the beginning of this section.

Basic coding procedures

In this section we outline some key ideas that can be very usefully kept in mind when undertaking thematic forms of analysis.

Creating and managing the code definitions

When a code is generated it is extremely useful to specify a definition of it. Box 8.2 provides some examples of code definitions in relation to a number of research projects that we have conducted. The definition needs to outline the central defining feature of that code. One way to create a definition is by outlining a basic rule that needs to be fulfilled in order for a code to be applicable to a piece of data. While some apriori categories of interest may be specified in advance of the analysis of data, most codes will be defined iteratively, and even apriori codes are very likely to evolve as data is produced and examined.

As we have seen, a part of the purpose of creating and using a code is to work out its analytic relevance. Specifying the defining features of the category, then, is an ongoing part of the analysis.

Box 8.2   Examples of code definitions

Mistake – Where some intended outcome during a musical performance is not achieved because of a personal failing of technique, memory or other individual characteristic. *(This code was used to characterize a range of data, including observations of performance, reflections on personal performance, interview conversations and documentary data.)*

(Continued)

(Continued)

Direct question response – Where a piece of educational dialogue is directed towards answering a directly preceding question (i.e. in the immediately preceding turn). *(This code was used to categorize recordings of speech in educational settings.)*

Inadequate training – Where a student does not have the knowledge to be able to carry out some professional task. *(This code was used in the analysis of interview data.)*

Because code definitions are iterative, applying codes is often cyclical rather than linear. As a code evolves, it may be useful to revisit the data that has previously been indexed with that code in order to examine the impact of the newly conceived definition. If a code becomes more focused, then this greater specificity might imply that previously coded data are now no longer relevant. Of course, if a code is broadened in its scope, then it may be that there are now relevant data that were previously *excluded* from the code. For this reason, it can be useful sometimes to revisit one's transcripts and other data sources in order to check the relevance of altered code definitions to non-coded data.

The iterative nature of coding means that it is an extremely time-consuming and messy process, which is why it is almost impossible to know in advance how long the process will take. We have found that coding can sometimes become something of an obsession too, with the increasingly complex puzzles of the relationship between codes and data becoming, on occasion, unproductive. One of the tricks to efficient and effective analysis is to be able to keep one's eye on the bigger picture of the research, and remember that the details of coding are only relevant and useful as far as they help the researcher to deal with their research issues.

Splitting codes

A code may be split into two or more distinct elements as a means of segmenting out particular aspects of it. It is common for codes to quickly become rather complex, and separating them out is a useful way of creating more refined distinctions within a given analytic concept. Conversely, it is also common for researchers to want to bring more than one analytic category together by **merging codes**. It may be that two potentially interesting and closely connected themes prove not to be prominent features on their own but are, together, quite significant. Equally, it may be that two themes become increasingly intertwined and difficult to distinguish. Whatever the reason, when two or more codes are merged it is important to redefine the properties and boundaries of the newly merged code and to check that it fits all instances of the data to which it is being applied.

Deleting or discontinuing codes

In empirical coding, a code category is created because it is thought that it *might* be analytically relevant, but there are no guarantees that such assumptions are going to prove to be correct or appropriate. Particularly important instances in which the relevance of a given code may need to be reconsidered are when the categorization that it offers doesn't help make sense of the phenomenon or when the categorization is not obviously related to the research question. When using analysis software (see Chapter 11), it is actually possible to delete a code from the records of the analysis. Usually, however, 'deleting' is too radical an option, as it permanently removes the analysis. By discontinuing a code, researchers simply stop using it in their analytical work, but can always return to it later on.

Code properties

In Chapter 2 we raised the issue of code properties, as conceptualized in grounded theory. In their work, Glaser and Strauss (1999 [1967]) and Strauss and Corbin (1990) regard a property as a feature of a code that varies along a sliding scale. A code property is a way of comparing data that have been categorized as a member of a code according to a constitutive sliding scale. While this approach may be relevant in some instances (and we gave one example in Chapter 2), there is some difficulty in this concept as it implies that such variations should be 'measurable' in a definable way, but many of the issues that qualitative researchers deal with do not have this characteristic. That said, there is value in the subdivision or inter-classification of data within a given code, and this need not necessarily require 'scalic' analyses. Researchers can simply create particular categories that exist within the code in order to subdivide the code. We discuss this approach in more detail below in the section on 'sub-codes'.

Keeping a code log

Given the very complex nature of coding, it is very important that researchers keep a code log of all the processes that they undertake when coding. A code log is simply an index of all the coding decisions that are made in a project. A code log does not need to include a record of every instance in which a code is applied as it functions as a global index of the key coding events and changes. A log might simply be a chronological list that indicates when codes were created, altered, merged, deleted, etc., or it may constitute a number of themetized lists (e.g. a list of the codes created or a list of the codes that have been merged).

Having retrospective access to the decisions that were made in the process of coding is very useful. Because coding is complicated, lengthy and subject to much variation, it is easy to forget why a particular change in a coding structure was made (or even *that* it was made). Code logs help to keep track of all the changes made and provide useful guides for reflecting on the development of a coding system.

Moving beyond individual codes: relational analysis

The creation and manipulation of codes is only one part of the process of thematically analyzing data. A significant part of the aims of thematized analysis involve working out the relationships *between* code categories, and the significance of such relationships for the development of theoretical conceptions and statements.

Code family

The term **code family** refers to a collection of two or more codes that are regarded as being related to each other in a significant way. Unlike code merging, where the codes are simply amalgamated, code families involve maintaining the original codes as distinct features of analysis, but drawing attention to some important relationships between the codes. A family is a group of codes that bear some 'family resemblance' in a way defined by the researcher. As with codes, it is important to define very clearly the conditions on which a code may be regarded as a member of the family grouping. While there is no upper limit on how many codes can be included in a family, there is perhaps a case for arguing that the more codes there are, the less value there is in the grouping as its constituent feature(s) become more and more diluted.

An example of a code family comes from Gibson's (2006) study of jazz performance. The code 'mistake', included in Box 8.2, was one of a number of codes that related to a failure to fulfil an intended musical outcome. The two other codes in this family were 'mistake by others' and 'unusual interventions by others' (see Box 8.3 for more details). The family to which these codes belonged was called 'Change of plan', and the key conceptual aim behind the family was to draw attention to the ways in which some source of trouble might have prevented a musical outcome from being achieved.

Box 8.3   An example of a code family: 'Change of plan'

Code family: 'Change of plan'.

Code members: 'Mistake'; 'Mistake by others'; 'Unusual interventions by others'.

Membership rules: Each code provides a reason for why a given plan of action may have been altered in response to some trouble or other.

Notes: The reasons for alteration can come from oneself (as with 'mistakes' or 'changes of mind') or from others as with 'mistakes by others' or 'unusual intervention by others'.

The issue of 'trouble' is important here. The code 'changes of mind' is not included in this family as it does not typically create problems (although it can do sometimes).

Of course, codes may be members of more than one family. For example, the code 'Mistakes by others' is also part of another family called 'knowledge of other performers' (see Box 8.4). The cross-membership to different families creates an interesting way to think about the relationship between codes. Codes can be thought of as directly related to one another, but also as having a wider familial relationship through indirect association.

Box 8.4   Example of a code family: 'Knowledge of other performers'

Code family: 'Knowledge of other performers'.

Code members: 'Mistake by others'; 'Others' preferences'; 'Predictable things'; 'Past experiences with others'; 'Making decisions'.

Membership rules: Each code relates to the knowledge that a musician has about other members of the group being performed with.

Notes: People build up a stock of knowledge about their colleagues and know how they are likely to react to certain situations, and what their stylistic preferences are. This knowledge is, in part, used to identify when someone makes a mistake (although there are other ways to do this, related to knowledge of generalized conventions of practice).

Knowledge of others' performances is also used to make decisions about what to do next – knowing what someone else is likely to do helps to decide how to formulate a strategy for one's own interjections.

One way to think about a code family is simply as a way of drawing together a set of codes in the form of a meta-description. This meta-description involves conceptually grouping together the abstracted categories that characterize a data set.

Hypotheses

As conceptualized in some forms of 'quantitative enquiry', an hypothesis involves stipulating a relationship between two or more variables. This conceptualization can fit somewhat uneasily with qualitative enquiry, where the aim is not to think in polarized ways about the relationship between variables, but to interrogate the character and complex interrelational nature between intricately specified and defined phenomena. Similarly, as Werner Meinefeld (2004) notes, researchers in qualitative approaches often wish to escape from being tied down to a preformulated hypothetical statement. However, there is an alternative conceptualization of hypotheses, very much related to Glaser and Strauss's (1999 [1967]) uses of the term, that involves regarding them as *a way of postulating the relation between different aspects of an analytic framework*. The following is a useful definition of a hypothesis for the purposes of thematic forms of analysis:

Hypothesis: a conceptual relation between two or more aspects of a given analytic framework.

In this definition, a hypothesis is simply a way of exploring interrelationships between analytic elements. Hypotheses are generated to test a relationship between some people, events, practices, attitudes, and so on. In grounded theory, the data that is generated is used to construct these hypotheses. As more data are produced, they are explored (tested) in relation to hypotheses, which are, in turn, amended where necessary so that they fit with the data, and so that they provide an adequate conceptual analysis of the data. Indeed, this notion of conceptual analysis is key to grounded theory, as it is these more abstract expressions of relationships that are seen as representing *theoretical* rather than *descriptive* accounts.

The constituent features of an hypothesis might be any of the features outlined in Table 8.1 (see p. 131). Below, we discuss some of the ways in which these aspects may be combined and explored in the context of hypotheses.

Cause and causality

Causality is an expression of a deterministic relation between the variables in an hypothesis; to say that a variable causes another is to state that *it always does so* under the specified conditions. Clearly, and as we outlined above, there are problems with this notion in relation to qualitative research. Indeed, demonstrating causality, which can only effectively be achieved through an experimental form of design (in which the exploration of the relationship between a dependent and independent variable, while controlling for other variables, can be designed into an empirical investigation), is problematic in the social sciences more generally as the required level of manipulation is practically and ethically difficult to achieve. However, there is still potential in the use of this notion to reflect on one's analytic framework.

Karl Popper's (1959) famous notion of **falsification** involved suggesting that a useful way for researchers to proceed is by looking for the instances in which a proposed hypothesis does not pertain. To put the matter very simply, Popper suggested that researchers ought to direct their efforts towards finding the things that would prove a hypothesis to be *wrong* rather than the things that would prove it to be *right*. In this view, any amount of 'proof data' does not actually prove a theory – it merely shows that evidence has been found that accords with that theory, leaving a residual scepticism that there may be some as yet undiscovered evidence that disproves it. In 'scientistic' research approaches, Popper's model is used as a way to make sure that any specified causal relation is actually correct – i.e. the aim, in the end, is to gain security in a specified causal relationship. Falsification is a useful tool in qualitative research too. By postulating a causal relationship, researchers specify a simplistic and unidirectional relationship, and can then set out to prove why this characterization is inadequate. Causal relationships, then, can be seen as *tricks* that are designed to focus analytic attention on complexity.

An interesting way to start to explore relationships between analytic elements is to develop an hypothesis that specifies a clear causal relationship between those elements. To reiterate, the purpose of doing so is to find out all the ways in which such a specification might be defective. The following is an example of an hypothesis taken from Gibson et al.'s (2001) study of the professional training of pharmacy students. The research was particularly concerned with the fit between university training and pharmacy practice.

> **Hypothesis:** When pharmacists do not have the knowledge that a particular activity is reliant on, they are unable to carry it out.

The hypothesis suggests that where pharmacy professionals have not been given training in a particular area of professional practice, they will not be able to operate in that area. This hypothesis was investigated by looking at the various codes and data examples that related to professional practice and education. This exploration showed that pharmacists have a lot of resources at their disposal that are not related to their educational training and which are also very valuable aids to effective practice. This, in turn, helped to show that the notion that academic training was a necessary condition for effective work may be misconceived, and that actually, the academic training is just one set of resources that pharmacists require in order to undertake an activity.

A causal, and testable, hypothesis, then, serves to direct attention towards a possible relationship and as such is a valuable resource for researchers. In the context of exploring such relationships, researchers are likely to find all kinds of interesting relational features that their original formulation had ignored.

Contradictions and inconsistencies

In simple terms, the idea of a contradiction is to set up an inconsistency of some kind between two aspects of an analytic framework. We can distinguish at least two forms of contradiction (although there are assuredly other nuances of distinction here too): **polar opposition**, where the contradiction represents something that is 'the opposite of' something else, and **inconsistency**, where two or more features are 'not consistent with each other'.

Polar oppositions are always an interesting relationship, wherever they occur. An interviewer may find that two interviewees provide directly opposing views on the same issue or that two codes provide opposite characterizations of some phenomenon. One way to approach contradictions is to look for the reasons why the opposition exists: to try to explain how the two oppositional characteristics may exist in the same empirical space. This may be quite straightforward and simply involve characterizing the different contingencies and perspectives that different people have, but it can also be a very involved exercise of trying to come up with a more abstract account of why or how these differences can be accommodated.

An example of the discovery of an apparent opposition comes from the analysis of pharmacy practice. When analyzing the code for 'relevant pharmacy training', it was found that some students working in shops regarded a particular aspect of their training as highly relevant while other students regarded it as irrelevant. This was confusing because the students were conducting the same activities in apparently very similar conditions. While, initially, the differences were dismissed as simply 'a matter of personal opinion', further investigation revealed that those students who regarded their training as irrelevant were being supervised by people who had no understanding of their educational background, while those who saw the relevance were being supervised by people who continued to have involvement in the educational training programme. The ability of some students to see relevance came from the fact that they were working with people who operated informally as mentors to their work.

Inconsistencies between analytic objects are also very insightful and can constitute the nitty-gritty detail that comprise analysis – the working out of how slight differences and distinctions can be incorporated into a system of explanation and understanding. Coding is, in essence, a matter of creating generalities, but it is common for some of the data that are included within codes to have some distinctive properties that remain analytically relevant, in spite of (or in addition to) their relevance as a generalized member of that category. A particular research participant may be categorized in a generalized way, but have a unique aspect that is, itself, relevant to the analysis. Exploring 'inconsistencies' in these kinds of ways can be valuable for gaining insight into the relational character of categorical data.

Sub-codes and parent codes

The creation of subdivisions within codes is a way of generating further nuances within a given code structure. Very often, by interrogating the constituent data of a code, researchers will find that there are themes within the theme that can be categorized in new ways. Rather than separating these out as new codes, these can become *sub-codes* that are treated as subsidiary features of the existing 'parent' code. This is sometimes referred to as the creation of a **coding tree**, with relational branches specifying the linkages between the codes.

Subdivisions can also work backwards. A researcher may start with a code and subsequently realize that that code would be usefully subsumed along with other codes under a more general code category. The code 'mistakes' shown in Boxes 8.2 and 8.3 was the first of a number of codes relating to 'mistakes in performance' to be created (including 'mistakes by others', 'habitual mistakes', 'technical mistakes', and 'problems with technology'). In the end, it was realized that the more general issue of mistakes was relevant to the research and that it had value as a code in its own right. All the instances that had been coded with the code categories outlined above were therefore given the additional code 'problems' (as a descriptor for this generalized issue).

And this brings us to an important point: any code, code subdivision or parent code should only be created if there is a potential purpose to the creation. Possible divisions will be visible in all kinds of features of the data, but it is only appropriate to create a functional representation of that division where it is supposed to be relevant. Of course, it may be that there is a supposed purpose or relevance that turns out to be misplaced. While such false moves are inevitable, the important thing is that there is an initial rationale for a given code.

Super codes

A **super code** is one that is created to describe a piece of data that has been coded with a combination of existing codes. Super codes are usually generated by asking questions about the relationship between codes using Boolean search terms AND, OR, NOT, AND/OR. So, for example, a researcher using a form of analysis software may run a search using the AND function to find all the instances in the data where two different codes occur together, or where two different codes do NOT occur together. Similarly, a researcher may use the AND/OR function to see the relation between three codes. For example:

When code X is present do either (AND/OR) codes Y and Z occur?

Equally, strings of Boolean search terms can be used to create more complex searches of one's data. For example:

When code A is present and code B is NOT present, do either (AND/OR) code C or code D occur?

When a search such as those outlined is conducted and the data are shown to have a particular relevance, then a new code can be created that is used to categorize that relationship. This new code is called a super code. A super code is different from a 'parent code' because not all the instances of data related to the constituent codes will be relevant to the super code; only those that are used in a defined combination with other codes will be coded in this way.

Concluding remarks

In this chapter we have outlined some of the central principles, procedures and concepts involved in the thematized organization and exploration of data. These procedures are generalized processes of thematic organization and relational analysis that draw particularly on grounded theory and on cross-case analysis. The three basic procedures that are present in these procedures involve examining commonality, differences and relationships within the aspects of a given analytic framework (i.e. within the codes, the people, and the constitutive data that relate to those).

There are very many specific analytic frames that might well orientate towards some of these procedures without describing themselves as involving 'thematic analysis'. The phrase 'thematic analysis' should not be seen as delineating a particular approach, but is rather a way of describing the organization of data into themes. As we stated in the introduction, these types of organizational principle are by no means 'all there is' to analysis, but are merely some of the key ways that a researcher might think about organizing and working through their data.

Recommended further reading

Boyatzis, R.E. (2008) *Transforming Qualitative Information: Thematic Analysis and Code Development*. Thousand Oaks, CA: Sage. A thoughtful approach to thematic work that provides a detailed inspection of the uses of themes in qualitative enquiry.

Miles, M. and Huberman, M. (1994) *Qualitative Data Analysis: An Expanded Sourcebook*. Thousand Oaks, CA: Sage. A detailed exploration of the principles and procedures of thematic work.

Strauss, A. and Corbin, J. (1990) *Basics of Qualitative Research: Grounded Theory, Procedures and Techniques*. London: Sage. A practical guide of how to use the procedures outlined in this chapter using the framework of grounded theory.

9 Images and texts

This chapter discusses the following issues:

- Practical issues in the uses of images in social research
- Social semiotics and textual analysis
- Rhetorical analysis and textual analysis

Introduction

This chapter is concerned with exploring the ways in which social researchers can analyze textual resources, including images. In Chapter 5 we discussed some of the potential uses of documentary forms, and we now turn more focused attention to approaches analyzing certain forms of text. The chapter is organized into two sections: the first part explores the analysis of pictorial texts (i.e. images of various kinds), and the second part looks at the analysis of written texts. Our discussion of these issues uses forms of semiotic analysis to exemplify the ways in which analytic frames can be used to foreground relevant features of certain kinds of data. We have focused our discussion around semiotic approaches because they are particularly common strategies for interrogating images and texts, but they are by no means the only approaches available. In addition to outlining the distinctive features of these approaches, this chapter builds on the discussion we provided in Chapter 2 by exemplifying further the ways in which conceptual resources work to make data *speak*. At the end of this chapter we broaden our discussion of analysis to consider the ways in which other analytic approaches might also be adopted to explore pictorial and written textual forms.

Analyzing images: semiotic analysis

The examples of approaches to analysis that we discuss in this chapter all draw on semiotics.

Semiotic analysis (or *semiotics*) involves the investigation of the meaning-making systems that are at work within language, texts, photographs, and other signifying systems. **Signifying** refers to the structures of meaning that are implicated within a given object, text, language, etc., and **semiotic analysis** refers to a set of approaches to investigating such meaning. Semiotic analysis involves using a preformulated set of concepts to help categorize and describe the processes of meaning making. Historically, two of the most dominant theorists in this area have been Ferdinand de Saussure and Charles Peirce. Both Saussure and Peirce provide elaborate systems and formulations for analyzing meaning in visual signs that have become significant not only in their own right, but also in how they have been taken forward by other authors (see Table 9.1). To note that these authors worked in the same 'tradition' is not to claim that they were necessarily in agreement with each other, or that there is absolute consistency with their ideas. It merely points to quite loose similarities and elegances that are relevant for understanding something of the development of the perspectives.

Table 9.1 Authors using Peircian and Saussurian semiotics

Influential authors working in the Peircian tradition	Influential authors working the Saussurian tradition
Charles Ogden	Claude Lèvi-Strauss
Thomas Sebeok	Mikhail Bakhtin
Max Harold Fisch	Julia Kristeva
Ivor Armstrong Richards	Roland Barthes

For the purposes of this discussion, we will focus our attention on a Saussurian analytic tradition. Saussure proposed that language can be analyzed as a system of signs. A **sign** is comprised of two component parts, signifiers and signifieds. **Signifiers** are the words in language (literally, the collection of letters used for representing sounds as well as the sounds themselves), and the **signifieds** are the concepts to which those words (sounds and letters) refer. **Signs** are the relation between signifiers and signifieds. Figure 9.1 provides a frequently used pictorial outline of the relationship between these three aspects.

Figure 9.1 Saussure's sign system

Roland Barthes took this idea forward through his notion of myths. A myth is a *message*, or a system of communication. Any object, idea, concept, thought or form/system of representation can be expressed through myth, but the myth, like Saussure's concept of 'sign', is distinct from the object, idea, concept, thought, etc. upon which it plays. Myth is a manifestation of socio-historically organized systems of meaning and *signification* about things in the world. Myths are not just expressed by speech, but through written or pictorial discourse as well as through gesture, movement, music, soundscapes, architecture, objects, fashion, and so on. Barthes makes clear that signifiers are not necessarily *words* or *letters* but any mode of expression that represent the signifieds – the concepts to which those signifiers relate. Again, the *sign* is the totality of the meaning of these signifiers and signifieds. Myths are a '*second order signifying system*' (Barthes, 1993: 114, emphasis added) that build on existing sign systems.

The details of these theoretical accounts do not concern us here, as their relevance is merely in providing a context for our more focused discussion of approaches to analysis. Our interest is in exploring practical ways in which these approaches to conceptualizing meaning can be taken forward as strategies of analysis. However, while a detailed discussion of the theoretical ideas underpinning this form of analysis is not necessary, some basic familiarity with key concepts is useful in order that the process of analysis can be demonstrated.

Key concepts in 'Saussurian' semiotic analysis

Table 9.2 provides an outline of some of the key concepts we wish to use here.

A key distinction is to be made between *denotive* meaning and *connotive* meaning. **Denotations** refer to obvious readings within a given image or picture, while **connotations** describe the particular cultural significations and implications associated with an image. The most revealing way to explore this mode of analysis is through an example.

Figure 9.2 shows a poster that was used as an advertisement for an academic conference on tourism in Asia. Obvious denotive meanings associated with the image (rather than the text) might include: beach, man, lying down/propped up, waves,

Table 9.2 Descriptions of concepts in social semiotics

Concept	Description
Motivated signs	Signifieds that can easily be read from the signifier
Unmotivated signs	Understanding of signification that requires detailed and specific cultural knowledge
Denotation	The direct, immediate and obvious meaning in a sign
Connotation	The implied, culturally specific meaning in a sign
Difference (forms of difference include):	The relationship between elements of a message
Repetition	Repeated messages
Similarity	Similar signifying practices
Accumulation	The number of times a practice is signified
Opposition	The contradiction of meaning between signs
Metaphor	A sign as metaphorically standing for a particular set of meanings

Figure 9.2   Conference poster (this is included here with kind permission from Dr Tim Winter, the University of Sydney)

swimming trunks, forest. These denotations are, however, signifiers that can be mapped on to complex cultural meanings. Such mapping involves expanding the 'literalist' denotive meanings to include cultural connotive significances. Table 9.3 provides an outline of some of the ways in which some of the denotations in this picture may be mapped on to cultural connotations.

One of the quite evident points that the analysis provided in Table 9.3 helps to demonstrate is that the 'individual' denotive signs within a given image always reference and play off each other. It is extremely difficult to treat a given sign as isolated within an image because its significance is far more than the sum of its parts and is very much constituted in the interplay that it generates with other signs. Many of the concepts outlined in Table 9.2 are useful for working through the relational significance within a given text. Below we provide a brief outline of some of the ways that such concepts can be seen to be present in the analysis offered in Figure 9.2.

Repetition: the beach, trunks, body posture, sea, bright colours, the apparent emptiness of the beach – all of these are signifiers that play through the trope of 'holidays as relaxation'. The 'signs' can be seen to repeat and restate the association, and to almost coerce the viewer into an imperative reading of this notion. This restatement of meaning through multiple signification results in something like an **accumulation** of significance, where the 'obviousness' of the association is made clear. There are strong associative **metaphors** at work here too: the man/posture/tan/trunks speak of tourism – they *represent* and re-present notions of 'tourist practice' which, through the imperative clause of the poster title, direct the reader to work through the significance of this implied theme for the advertised conference. The **oppositions** here are not between the signifiers in this image but related to the sets of signifieds or connotations that they implicate: Asian, sexuality, tourism – all become relational tropes that jostle for priority and force the reader to shuffle and reshuffle their signification and interpretation.

The approach to analysis exemplified in the above discussion involves attempting to explore the ways in which potential meaning is produced through signification. It focuses on the production of meaning and the *relationality* of potential meaning-making aspects. Of course, this form of analysis is not restricted to photographs, but also to less 'motivated' sign systems, such as paintings.

Table 9.3   Denotations and connotations of symbolism in a conference advertisement

Denotations	Connotations
Beach	Apart from the man, the beach appears to be empty and there is nobody in the sea. This gives a sense of the ideational character of beaches as represented in western tourism, as sites of 'escape' and places to be 'alone', to 'relax', to be 'contemplative', and to reverse the 'normal' character of everyday Westernized/post-industrial societies as busy, populated, non-relaxing, non-contemplative. The beach therefore speaks not only of itself, but also of the promise that it offers as an opposition to the 'everydayness' of the tourists' ordinary life. The beach, as with the tourism, is the 'other' to the tourists' everyday life experience – it is the second (and preferable?) half of an implied dichotomy.
Man	The man is of Asian descent, probably Japanese. The title of the poster and the use of the phrase 'Of Asian Origin' topicalize this characteristic of the man as part of the subject of the image. The positioning of the text in relation to the man enhances this sense, as the man is positioned in the same reading line as 'Of Asian Origin'. However, the 'Of Asian Origin' also describes the topic of 'tourism' – the tourism of Asians and the tourism *in* Asia. An uncertainty arises here: is the man to be seen *as* an Asian tourist or as *the site of or attraction for* Asian tourism? But the matter is more complex still. Another characteristic of the man is that he is highly sexualized: the exposed flesh and the posture of the body offered up to the voyeuristic gaze. This sexualization creates some further ambiguity, very deliberately it would seem, about the relationship between the implied concepts of tourism, Asians and sexualization. The relation between these concepts becomes an illusive trope, an ambiguous object that shifts from one reading to another, never quite managing to maintain a distinct character.
Trunks	The white trunks contrast strongly with the man's tan, emphasizing the notion of tourism as 'sun-soaking'. The strong western cultural association of 'holidays' and 'tans' is not a universalistic one, and is not a typical association in Asian notions of tourism. The word 'rethinking' in the poster title helps suggests that new practices in Asian tourism, such as tanning, may be emerging and directs the reader to interrogate this association. That *the genre* of this text as an academic conference poster implies some preferences for topical themes that may emerge from such interrogation – the globalization of cultural practices, being a particularly striking theme.

(Continued)

Table 9.3   (Continued)

Denotations	Connotations
	The trunks are also part of another signification – that of gender and gender preferences and performance. The masculinized body form, with the flamboyance of a performative posture and a sexualization of the self, all implicate notions of homosexuality and, in so doing, twist the tropes of 'tourism' and 'Asian' in yet more complex relations. The opening of the gender category raises the inquisitor's curiosity, who poses the question 'why a man?' Were the focal object of this image a woman, the signification would be all too conventional and the 'rethinking' in the subtitle of the poster would fit uneasily. It is the *rethinking* that pushes the interlocutor to examine in new ways and to interrogate the relationality of the imagery in a manner that privileges the non-conventional.
Sea	The sea contains movement and displays strength, but the gentle breaking waves and the bubbling surf show this as a usable beach for tourists, a fun environment with enough movement of swell to be enjoyed, but not enough to be dangerous. The sea signifies itself as a feature of the tourist experience in Asia. It speaks not just of itself but acts as a metaphor for an exciting but caring industry that offers fun, but with the promise of protection, and the attitude of subservience and service.

Critiques of semiotic forms of analysis

Meaning and cultural context

One of the criticisms that has been commonly made of this mode of analysis is that it is overly deterministic in its account of how meaning is created. There is an implication that a sign must mean what the semiotician says it does. Some approaches to semiotics, particularly in the field of **social semiotics**, emphasize that signs are merely *resources* that can be used to create *potential meanings* (Jewitt and Oyama, 2001). Meaning is contextual, and the contexts in which meaning is *constructed* (rather than the contexts in which it is reconstituted by the analyst) are fundamental in formulating analyses of what a particular meaning might be. The construction of an interpretation is not a universal phenomenon that everyone will undertake in the same way, but nor is it an entirely individualistic one. People operate in various communities (families, friendship groups, work cultures, national cultures, local communities), each of which comprises particular ways of being in and seeing the world, and distinctive practices and interpretive frames. Meaning is culturally organized and often experienced as imperative rather than negotiable (Fish, 1978).

In the case of the conference poster in Figure 9.2, the *reading* provided is made from the point of view of an academic who might be interested in the conference: a reading which, in this case, probably tallies reasonably closely with the author of the poster's intended significations. Most certainly, however, members of different communities will achieve different readings of the poster. Indeed, one of the interesting features of this image was the reaction that it caused when it was posted up in university campuses in Singapore. The poster was variously covered up, ripped down and defaced by viewers who, for one reason or another, objected to it. We can surmise from this that some people's interpretations of the connotations were somewhat different from the rather 'detached', academicized, Western reading that we have provided here, and by reflecting on some of the dominant cultural practices and values in Singapore it is not all that difficult to imagine what such interpretations might have been. The idea of signs as *resources* draws attention to the ways that cultural groups might mobilize particular ways of being in or seeing the world as frames for building particular connotive associations.

Meaning and local context

A further criticism of semiotic analysis is that the practices of meaning making that it is concerned with are *assumed* rather than *demonstrated*. The analysis proposes a potential meaning and reading of textual objects, but does not examine the processes by which such readings might be achieved. Studies in interactional sociology have emphasized the ways in which meaning is not only created in relation to cultural frames of understanding, but is also made in relation to particular circumstances of reading and social practice (Garfinkel, 1967). People are doing things when they make meaning, and the things that they are doing, and the various communicative and collaborative resources that they bring to bear in doing them, might be just as important for the construction of meaning as more generalized cultural understandings are. In this view, then, the notion of 'meaning' might be far too vague a concept to capture the very broad ways in which people might make sense of or use images and texts.

Many forms of analysis are particularly concerned with examining the construction of meaning in images in the broader contexts and communicative practices. Multimodal analysis, for example, involves looking at the ways in which meaning is made in the interaction between various signifying forms, including images, gesture, talk, movement and gaze. Similarly, conversation analysis and ethnomethodology both use a concern with *how* people achieve meaning as a lens for investigating social practices. Chapter 10 looks in detail at some of these approaches to analysis.

Analyzing written texts: rhetorical analysis

Semiotic modes of analysis have used the same concerns with social position and forms of representation to analyze written texts (e.g. van Leeuwen, 2005). In such analysis, the interest is in the ways in which concepts, ideas, arguments and points of view are positioned in relation to each other through the voice of a particular author in the creation of specific and preferred readings of a text. Many of the ideas and concepts used above can also be used to look at other forms of written texts. In the interests of variation, however, we would like to discuss an alternative approach to the analysis of text, called **rhetorical analysis**. To reiterate, our use of this approach is to exemplify how particular elements and concepts in a given approach to analysis can be used to make sense of textual data.

Rhetorical analysis is derived from the ancient Greek concern with the rhetorical structure of arguments, and the concepts that are used for analysis which are derived from Aristotle's work. Rhetorical analysis is concerned with the processes of constructing arguments and has much in common with semiotic approaches to analyzing meaning. Both are interested in the creation of readable patterns of meaning in text and the use of concepts to foreground such meanings. Rhetorical analysis is not only useful for analyzing texts, however, as it can equally be applied to the enacted speech (e.g. conversations, public presentations, arguments). In this discussion, however, we will focus our concern on how to use these concepts to look at written texts.

Key concepts in rhetorical analysis

Rhetorical analysis is directed towards the persuasiveness of a given discourse, and there are a range of concepts that can be applied to these ends. Table 9.4 describes some of the main concepts in this approach to analysis. In what follows we provide a brief outline of each of these concepts and their relevance for the analysis of text.

Table 9.4   Key concepts in rhetorical analysis

Concept	Description
Exigence	The context of a discourse event
Ethos	The credibility of an author or a text
Pathos	The emotionality of a text
Logos	The logic of an argument within a text
Genre	The social conventions surrounding the production of a particular text
Cultural memory	The cultural assumptions that are used in a text or that are necessary for interpreting a text

Exigence

Exigence focuses attention on the contexts in which a given discursive event is situated. The analysis of a political speech, for example, may begin by working out how the contents of that speech relate to other similar discourses. In interpreting the speech, a researcher may ask: is the speech reporting on some policy initiative or responding to a policy move by a rival party or reacting to some form of criticism of the political party? The analysis of a set of minutes from a meeting may begin by examining the institutional context in which the meeting functions, or by looking at notes from other, previous meetings as a means of *situating* the text into a broader context. The analysis of such context often includes an outline of how the text relates temporally to other discursive practices, and how it fits with them. Building up an understanding of the context of a story enables the researcher to understand something of the motivations that may underlie the text, and also helps to bring to the surface some of the resources that the text author and text interpreter (i.e. the reader, viewer or listener) may be using to make sense of the discourse.

Very often, the texts themselves will include rhetorical strategies that indicate how they are related to previous discourse events. As such, the texts can reveal quite a lot about how they are to be understood and what is to be counted as 'the context of their interpretation'. This is useful, of course, because 'building the context of discourse' is a potentially limitless task. The aim is to gain enough information to be able to make sense of the contents of the discourse.

Newspaper headlines provide an instructive example of how texts can *reference* their own context. Reports of breaking news (i.e. new stories) will use a different language from stories that are a continuation of an existing news story. Consider the following headline:

'Calif. Firefighters make progress against flames' in *The Washington Post*, 25 October 2007.

This headline can be read as a continuation of a story about wild fires in California that began a few days previously. The term 'make progress' indicates that the story is a report on a continuing event rather than on a new story.

This helps to raise an important point: producing rhetorical analysis in this way demands that the analyst is familiar with the genre of documentation that they are examining. The obviousness of the function of the news headline above comes from the fact that 'everybody knows' what newspaper headlines look like. This 'everybody' is, of course, a very crude gloss for 'people who are familiar with the discourse of newspapers'. It is extremely difficult to make sense of unfamiliar texts because the cultural resources that are used to construct the text are, to some extent, the same resources that the analyst uses to read the text. We will come back to this point shortly. The main question to be addressed when examining the 'exigence' of a text is:

Q – What is the context of the text's production and how does it relate to other, similar discursive events and practices?

Ethos

Ethos refers to the credibility that an author may have in relation to the text they produce. This does not involve trying to identify whether or not a given author is socially credible, but is rather a matter of attempting to establish how the author of the text builds credibility into their account through particular discursive strategies. Such strategies are likely to be implicit rather than involving direct appeals to a particular status or authority, but the impact of such implicit moves is, ultimately, regarded as discursively equivalent to explicit claims.

An example of this form of analysis can be found in Ken Hyland's (2005) examination of academic argument. Hyland uses the concepts of 'hedges' and 'boosters' to explore the role of *ethos* in the presentation of arguments in published academic work. **Hedges** are aspects of discourse that illustrate caution or uncertainty within a given argument (e.g. 'it may be that' or 'it could be argued' or 'perhaps'). **Boosters** are words or phrases that provide an imperative behind the presentation of an idea (e.g. 'it must be concluded that' or 'we cannot escape the fact that' or 'undoubtedly'). Hyland uses these two concepts to examine Charles Darwin's authorial style in the *Origin of the Species*, and argues that these twin strategies of tentativeness and assertiveness are used by Darwin to display both his sensitivity towards appropriate claims and his assuredness in relation to ideas that he wished to evidence.

Pathos

Pathos describes the appeal made to the emotions through discourse. Here, analysis concerns the way that phraseology is used to stir up particular feelings. An interesting example of how pathos may be analyzed comes from a speech by George W. Bush on 12 September 2002 to the United Nations General Assembly in New York:

> Mr. Secretary General, Mr. President, distinguished delegates, and ladies and gentlemen: We meet one year and one day after a terrorist attack brought grief to my country, and brought grief to many citizens of our world. Yesterday, we remembered the innocent lives taken that terrible morning. Today, we turn to the urgent duty of protecting other lives, without illusion and without fear.

> We've accomplished much in the last year – in Afghanistan and beyond. We have much yet to do – in Afghanistan and beyond. Many nations represented here have joined in the fight against global terror, and the people of the United States are grateful.

These two brief paragraphs include expressions of emotion (e.g. grief, fear, terror), moral principles (e.g. innocence, protection), and moral judgements (e.g. terrible, urgent, global terror). Words and phrases can carry an 'appeal' to emotions and implicitly invoke them through quite 'direct' expression (as in 'after a terrorist attack brought grief to my country') and through implication, such as the suggestion of moral imperatives (e.g. 'joined the fight against global terror').

There are other aspects to the analysis of pathos, though, which is invoked not just explicitly, but also through narrative structure. For example, in the above speech, the formality of the discourse is clearly signified in the formal means of address in the opening phrase ('Mr. Secretary General, Mr. President, distinguished delegates, and ladies and gentlemen'). The *formality* here is related to the emotional tone of the speech as it signals the seriousness of the topic to be discussed. The second line begins with a classic oratorical opening ('We meet one year and one day after…') that both implicates commonly played out story-telling tropes (e.g. 'a long, long time ago' or 'once upon a time') and references a period of time that has had significant mythical, legal and religious connotations throughout history. (In Great Britain, up until 1995 if 'one year and one day' passed between an act and a death to which that act was said to be related, then that act could not be regarded as murder. For example, should a person be injured in a road traffic accident and die a year and a day after the accident, no person associated with that accident could be charged with murder.)

The phrase at once reinforces the serious business at hand and implicates the speech as itself potentially *classic* and *mythical.* The phrase 'brought grief to my country' displays the institutional position and power of the president, and implicates his sense of *ownership* over the country and that the incident was both an attack on a nation and an attack on him personally. The focus on the notion of pathos, then, is not simply a matter of paying attention to explicit emotional words, but to possible discursive moves that implicate emotions within a given text.

Logos

Logos refers to the internal logic of a given text and the way in which sets of propositions are related to each other. For example, in the above speech we may say that the chronology from 'Yesterday, we remembered the innocent lives taken that terrible morning' to 'Today, we turn to the urgent duty of protecting other lives …' creates a conceptual link between the act of protection and the processes that caused the deaths, implying that protection is the logical step needed to stop a similar loss of life. The text itself, or, more accurately, the orator of the text, makes these links seem inescapably obvious, and treats them as inescapable truths. For the purposes of analysis, the idea is to investigate such points of connection and to try to analyze any possible implications arising from them. For example:

- What is the author trying to tell us by making this connection?
- What is the author trying *not* to tell us by making this connection?
- How does this form of connection relate to other discourses on the same topic?

These types of question help to focus the attention on the implications of conceptual connections.

Genre

As we have already seen, genre is a commonly used concept that describes the conventions of production surrounding a given text. In the speech presented above we can identify the following discourse strategies:

- The use of formal means of address
- A description of the context of the discourse
- The reference to things that have been achieved and things yet to be accomplished
- The stating of imperatives of action and responsibility.

All of these manoeuvres are analyzable as normal aspects of a political speech, and as the sorts of things that many, if not *most*, political speeches might display.

The concept of genre is frequently used in the teaching and study of academic writing as a way of analyzing and explaining the common approaches to presenting ideas and arguments in academia (see, for example, Belcher and Braine, 1995). This same approach is used in rhetorical analysis to provide a description of the ordinary stylistic parameters and structures of a given text. Examining genre, then, involves trying to identify the aspects of a given text that make it identifiable as part of a particular genre. For example, what is it about *this* book that makes it recognizable as a textbook, or about the picture in Figure 9.2 that makes it readable as a conference advertisement?

While texts do very often explicitly label themselves (as in Figure 9.2), such labels are frequently not needed to figure out what they are. When researchers are investigating genre, one useful approach is to examine the relationship between a text and the common practices of its genre. This is important because, very often, texts use strategies that breech, manipulate or 'play with' genre conventions. We might say of the poster in Figure 9.2 that the rather arresting picture is not typical of many academic conference posters, and that this peculiarity is one of the key rhetorical devices of the picture – i.e. to breach conventions of representation. Genre, then, refers to the 'language of convention' implied by a given text, and the way in which 'language' is *used* in the creation and manipulation of meaning.

Cultural memory

This term draws attention to the cultural *assumptions* implicit within a given text. Returning to the example of the newspaper headline in the *Washington Post* presented above, Box 9.1 outlines some of the basic ideas that are implied/not implied by the headline. While such ideas may very often seem obvious and self-evident, analyzing cultural assumptions in this way draws attention to the common-sense and everyday knowledge by which discourse is structured, and which are a *requirement* for the discourse to be made sense of in the ways intended by the authors. The analysis of cultural memory can therefore be very useful for bringing to the fore the basic ideas on which a given text is trading.

Box 9.1 Cultural assumptions surrounding a newspaper heading: 'Calif. Firefighters make progress against flames'

- Calif. refers to a place – specifically, the state of California on the west coast of the USA.
- That 'Firefighters' and 'flames' are not football or other sports teams.
- That the firefighters are professionals and not just ordinary people engaged in the act of fighting fires.
- That 'flames' refers to 'the wild fires in California' and not to fires anywhere else.
- That the fire implied by 'flames' is a serious fire and not a small event.
- That 'make progress' describes the process of trying to put the fire out rather than trying to get past the fire or get somewhere before the fire.

Critiques of rhetorical analysis

As we have already seen, successfully undertaking rhetorical analysis is dependant on having knowledge of the genre being examined. As a result, it is very difficult to analyze anything that is not already somehow familiar to the researcher. This same limitation can be levelled at very many forms of qualitative analysis, as a central aim behind much analysis is to 'see from the insider's point of view'.

As with semiotic approaches, rhetorical analysis does not look at the ways in which meaning is created in social contexts and treats meaning as a rather abstract entity. However, it would be slightly unfair to portray this as a 'limitation' of the analysis, which is perhaps more accurately described as a *characteristic*.

Other forms of textual analysis

Textual analysis in the form of social semiotics and rhetorical analysis constitute approaches for interrogating the 'signifying systems' and 'rhetorical strategies' by which authors create preferred meaning. They can be used to reflect on the cultural practices and assumptions through which texts are put to use as rhetorically functional devices. These forms of analysis help researchers to prise open the authorial methods used to create texts, and to relate these methods to the wider cultural knowledge and practices in which they are situated.

As we stated at the beginning of this chapter, the 'analysis' of texts, as with the analysis of any form of data, is *contextual*: it is related to a very particular set of aims, interests, methods and data. The particular aims and interests of semiotic forms of analysis are not *generalizable* to all research projects. The purpose of including these semiotic examples is not only to demonstrate the particular aspects of these approaches, but also to illustrate further how theoretical positions and concepts work as tools for analysis. While the tools themselves may change, the general character as resources for analysis does not. Of course, this 'general character' is *far too general* to be of much practical use to researchers, which is why our discussions of analysis are grounded in exemplars. The point we wish to emphasize, however, is that by using these examples we do not suggest that 'this is how pictures and texts should be analyzed', but simply that *this is what analysis looks like when using these perspectives*. Different approaches will bring different analyses and result in distinct methods for *making the data speak*.

Table 9.5 shows the ways in which different analytic frames might lead researchers to orientate to the analysis of images and texts. Through distinctive theoretical positions and/or specific concepts, each approach involves a particular set of aims and methodologic strategies:

Critical discourse analysis – As we saw in Chapter 2, critical discourse analysis (CDA) is directed to exploring the relationship between ideology and language, and the ways in which linguistic practices come to embody particular ideological positions. In relation

Table 9.5   Some alternative approaches to analyzing images and texts

Analytic approach	Examples of strategies for foci of analysis
Critical discourse analysis	The *display* and *enactment* of ideology through image and text The interaction of text and image as ideological reinforcements
Thematic analysis	Coding images and text according to apriori and empirical themes Examining how particular aspects or uses of images and tests compare
Ethnomethodology	The methods by which social actors put images and texts to work in particular social contexts The negotiated achievement of textual readings
Narrative analysis	The uses of images and texts in the telling of life histories and personal biographies The construction and reflection on notions of identity through the interrogation of texts and images

to images and texts, CDA involves applying this same concern with the ideological character of discourse in relation to the structures of visual and written modes rather than spoken modes.

Thematic analysis – The procedures of coding for data comparison that we explored in Chapter 8 can be used to thematically work through the relationships between data sets comprising images and texts. Thematic analysis is not a 'top-down' theory, such as CDA, rhetorical analysis or semiotics, so does not prespecify concepts for analysis, but merely offers some *methods* and *procedures* for data organization.

Ethnomethodology – Ethnomethodology's concern with the methods by which societal members work through social practices may be used to work out how texts and images are produced and used as interactional creations or resources. In ethnomethodology, the meaning and significance of texts is contextually located and negotiated, and so the interest in texts will be tied to empirical investigations of how they are situationally worked through and with.

Narrative analysis – Narrative analysis involves looking at the ways in which narratives are structured and organized. The aim is to understand how narratives are organized to construct particular identities. Images and texts may be examined as resources for the construction of narrative, and the ways in which identities use or orientate to particular textual forms.

Concluding remarks

The relevance of images and texts in research, and the specific approach taken to their analysis is a contextual matter. The examples of semiotic modes offered in this chapter involves exploring the ways in which cultural knowledge is used as an authorial and interpretative device to *give sense to* and to *make sense of* images and written texts. The shorter examples at the end of this chapter illustrate how particular analytic frames may be used to make sense to textual resources. The relevance of these approaches to particular research projects needs to be worked out in the context of the aims and contingencies of those projects. In the next chapter we move to look at strategies for making sense of audio and video data.

Recommended further reading

Grbich, C. (2007) *Qualitative Data Analysis: An Introduction*. London: Sage. This rich book deals with an interesting range of issues in qualitative research and contains a useful chapter on analyzing visual data.

Leach, J. (2000) 'Rhetorical analysis', in M. Bauer and G. Gaskell (eds), *Qualitative Researching with Text, Image and Sound: A Practical Handbook*. London: Sage. A useful and concise guide to key concepts in rhetorical approaches to analysis.

Pink, S. (2001) *Doing Visual Ethnography: Images, Media and Representations in Research*. London: Sage. A thorough overview of the issues, practices and procedures involved in visual research.

van Leeuwen, T. and Jewitt, C. (2001) *Handbook of Visual Analysis*. London: Sage. A semiotically situated examination of approaches to analyzing visual data.

10 Video and audio data

This chapter discusses the following issues:

- The characteristics of audio and video data
- The analysis of conversation
- Practicalities in collecting and analyzing video data

Introduction

Our central aim in this chapter is to give examples of the ways in which researchers might work with video and audio data. The examples we provide involve using the perspective of conversation analysis (CA). In doing so, our overall intention is to display how a focus on the minutia of social practice can sharpen a researcher's sense of their data. As we work through the examples provided here, we will also discuss some of the basic features of CA. Following these examples, we will discuss the practicalities that researchers face when collecting audio and video data. Before we move to the first of these aims, it is useful to reflect more generally on the character of audio and video data forms.

The character of audio and video data

Audio and video materials are used in a wide variety of approaches to social research. They provide resources for recording a range of data types, including observations, interviews, focus groups and fieldnotes. Table 10.1 provides an outline of the relevance, advantages and limitations of these data forms for these various functional roles. In general terms, audio data is appropriate where the analysis is concentrating particularly on verbal conversation, and where the non-verbal features of interaction

Table 10.1 Advantages and limitations of audio- and video-recorded data

	Audio recording	**Video recording**
One-to-one interviews	Audio recorders are often felt to be less intrusive than video cameras and are in many cases 'good enough' for the analysis of one-to-one dialogue. However, where non-verbal aspects of communication are a component of the analysis, audio data is clearly limited	Video provides an accurate and re-accessible record of the events of an interview and can be particularly useful for interpreting dialogue that the interviewer was not involved in (e.g. an interview conducted by somebody else). Because videos record from a particular angle, the interpretation is still restricted
Focus groups	It is difficult to analyze multiple speakers in conversations from audio data because the absence of non-verbal information makes it hard to understand the negotiations in the dialogue or to identify speakers	Video makes it easier to identify speakers and the non-verbal characteristics of the conversation. The value of the data, though, is very much dependent on the positioning of the camera, which needs to capture all of the participants, including the facilitator
Observations of practice	Audio data has a limited value because as an observational tool it is restricted to verbal activity, which is a small aspect of social practice that is often contingent for its meaning on non-verbal features	Video is the best mode for recording observations of practice, but is still only partial as it is always taken from a particular point of view
Fieldnote (as an analytic record of what happened in a given setting)	Although quicker to produce than written versions, audio fieldnotes require the development of either an effective indexing system and/or a form of written transcript for them to be used effectively	Video has no analytic benefit over audio as a record of analytic reflection on observations

are not relevant and are not required to make sense of the dialogue. Where those features are important, however, video is a more appropriate tool.

The decisions about which recording form to employ are not made simply on the basis of their analytic utility, but also on the ethical and practical issues involved in their use. Both audio and video data forms are extremely intrusive because they record, in detail, the performances or practices of the research participants. While both forms of data can be anonymized in a written transcript for the purposes of presenting data, video is often usefully transcribed using still-screen shots that are mapped to the spoken dialogue. These are harder to anonymize. In their analysis, Charles and Marjorie Goodwin often use drawings of the video in place of video stills which make anonymity a little easier (see, for example, Goodwin, 2000). Both data forms can be hard to anonymize prior to analysis as the masking of voices and faces is potentially complicated and, more importantly, can make the data hard to understand during analysis. Furthermore, there are significant practical challenges in using these forms, which require particular conditions at the time of recording for the data to be usable. Even quite small background noises, such as the sounds of cars driving outside a building, or the tapping of a foot on a table leg can make a recording hard to interpret as they can mask the relevant sounds. Static interference from lamps, mobile phones, image projectors and so on, banging doors, ringing telephones – all of these constitute real obstructions to the collection of data, and many of them are hard or impossible to control for.

When to use audio and video data

Of course, no data form is *inherently* better than another. The relevance of audio of video materials comes from a reflection on the research topic and the constraints and possibilities of the research setting. The most important starting point for thinking about data should be questions like:

Q – What kind of data do I need to be able to address my research question?
Q – What are the practical challenges faced in generating it?

For some research questions, the details of how a particular activity was enacted as displayed through a video recording will be irrelevant, while in others it will be centrally important. As we stated in Chapter 4, when designing research it can be very useful to reflect on the ways in which different data collection methods can be used to produce data for dealing with a given question. A part of such interrogation involves reflection on the character of the data, and how that may relate to the research being conducted. The purpose of this chapter is to discuss some of the key issues involved in the analysis of audio video data, and to give some examples of their comparative value and of how they can be put to work.

Analyzing audio and video recordings

Many of the approaches to analysis discussed in this book *can* be used to analyze audio data, e.g. grounded theory, thematic analysis, critical discourse analysis, semiotic analysis and narrative analysis. Just as reflections regarding the kind of data that may be relevant for answering a particular research question are contextual, so the decisions about which analytic approach to use should be made in relation to the analytic commitments of a project. Furthermore, it is not necessarily the case that a formalized and enshrined 'approach' is required at all. As we argue throughout this book, the explication of 'what counts as analysis' is a contextual matter that is very hard to discuss in abstraction from particular examples.

Furthermore, the depiction of the orientation to an analytic method as being a matter of 'free choice' is something of a misrepresentation. Researchers very often have pre-established analytic interests that lead them to have general preferences regarding analytic approaches, rather than contextually specific ones. In other words, it is not common for researchers to approach each research project they undertake with the question 'Which analytic method shall I use?', as they tend to have well established preferences and expertise that are used to frame the questions they ask.

Given all of this, the question 'How do you analyze audio and video data?' would be a strange one for us to pose or, indeed, to try to answer. Instead, our aim is to exemplify a particular form of analysis (namely, conversation analysis), and to show some of the affordances of audio and video data forms for this approach. Different analytic approaches will potentially present different issues, and a part of the challenge during analysis is to work through such issues. Before we move to look at the uses of conversation analysis it is important to discuss some of the basic features of the approach.

Ethnomethodology and conversation analysis

In the previous chapter we outlined a number of approaches to the analysis of texts that could be usefully employed to examine textual meaning. The two main examples we used, semiotic analysis and rhetorical analysis, involved an attempt to investigate the encoding and decoding of signification, and to reflect on the use of texts as 'meaning resources'. In all of the examples that we gave, the resources (texts) and the approach to investigating their potential and preferred significances were considered in isolation from other social practices. The analysis did not look at how texts were 'put to use' or their meaning was *negotiated* in particular settings; the *meaning* was treated as an analytic problem to be addressed by the researcher rather than as a problem for real 'social actors' in real social settings.

Ethnomethodology (EM) and conversation analysis (CA) are both forms of sociology that are interested in the methods through which people achieve recognizable practices. Actually, to put the matter like this is a little misleading as EM and CA are diametrically opposed to other forms of sociology. Researchers interested in CA or EM are well advised to pay close attention to the debates regarding this relationship, as the debates about what EM and CA are and their relation to other sociological approaches are fundamental for understanding the motives underlying the perspectives (see Sharrock and Anderson (1986) for a clear introduction to these issues). It is best not to think of CA or EM as 'research methods', but as particular and distinctive approaches to the examination of social practice.

In contrast to forms of semiotic analysis, EM and CA are not concerned with meaning as an abstract issue, but are instead interested in how the participants of social action negotiate 'what is to count as meaning and representation' (see Goodwin, 2001). Harold Garfinkel, the 'founding father' of ethnomethodology, proposed a particular notion of **social facts** (i.e. the observable characteristics of social life) as local achievements that are 'recognizable as facts' because of the particular strategies that people employ to produce them. For example, a doctor–patient consultation is recognizable as such because of the practices that the members of that encounter *produce* collaboratively. These are that both parties have very specific roles in the setting; that doctors have certain interactional rights that patients don't, and that participants routinely display these rights in the ways in which they organize their conversations; that the 'business at hand' is concerned with dealing with medical problems (see Robinson 1998 and 2001 for examples of this approach to medical practice). In EM, the analytic interest is in how these 'social facts' are worked out in practice.

Box 10.1   Ethnomethodology and Conversation Analysis

Harold Garfinkel (1967) developed ethnomethodology as a means of investigating the *constitutive* procedures and practices of social life. The central aim of the discipline is to understand the *methods* through which ordinary members of society do the things they do. Garfinkel regarded these methods as the principal data for understanding how society works. **Harvey Sacks'** (1995) conversation analysis shared these general aims, but with a particular focus on the ways in which conversation functioned as a site of social action and practice.

It is simplistic to describe ethnomethodology and conversation analysis as unified disciplines, either internally or in relation to each other, as there are divisions within these loose communities of researchers (see Cuff et al., 1990, for discussion of these differences). Such divisions do not concern us here, however, as our interest is in the ways in which their shared concern with the methods through which social practices are negotiated is taken forward through the examination of talk.

Conversation analysis shares ethnomethodology's broad concerns, but is particularly interested in how conversation operates as a site for the constitution and negotiation of social facts and practices. Harvey Sacks, who was a colleague and student with Garfinkel and the founder of CA, argued that conversation can be seen as a principal mechanism (or 'site') through which social practices get done. Sacks was clear, however, that conversation itself was only ever of interest to him as far as it enabled him to comment on the organization of social practices through social members' *methods*. As Livingston (2008) has commented, there is nothing particularly special about conversation as a site of social action, apart from that it is easy to capture and inspect; it is possible to 'witness' the social in any cultural artifact or social setting.

Sacks' writing on CA came at a time when the technology for producing audio recordings was becoming more and more affordable. Sacks commented that this technology was an extremely valuable resource for researchers as it enables them to replay and reconstruct the detailed and nuanced conversational practices that constitute a key aspect of people's ordinary methods for producing a sense of social facts.

The technology facilitated the production of detailed analyses of conversation, which was, Sacks argued, fundamental to adequately explore the procedures of social practice. The focus of 'traditional' CA has often been on conversation in abstraction from other features of interaction, such as body movement, gaze, gesture and the use of objects. This has changed somewhat over the last two decades as the use of video data has become more and more affordable for academic researchers. In what follows we offer a closer look at the ways in which audio and video data can be used in relation to the forms of analysis offered by EM and CA.

Conversation analysis and the analysis of audio data

In this brief section we will give an example of this form of analysis in relation to data recorded as part of a teacher's professional evaluation. A key analytic concern in conversation analysis is with the sequential organization of talk. This is of interest because it is of recognizable concern to the parties in conversation. As Emanuel Schegloff and Harvey Sacks (1973: 299) famously put it, the question 'why that now?' is a key resource for participants in trying to work out *why* someone said something in the way they have at the particular point that they did. We use this basic maxim as a mechanism for working through the exemplar presented below.

Exemplar: the evaluation of the professional practice of primary school teachers

Extract (1) shows a part of a conversation that we looked at in Chapter 7. The extract is taken from a video recording of two primary school teachers (i.e. teachers who teach students between 5 and 11 years old) undertaking an evaluation of professional practice. In this extract, J is the teacher being evaluated and F is the more experienced teacher helping to provide the evaluation. The two teachers are sitting in front of a video recording of a class that J taught.

(1)   Opening sequence in a teacher professional evaluation

1	J	oka:y↓ (1.5) I <↑don't thin:k> (.) you hadn come in then↓ (.)
2	F	no:
3	J	>you hancome in yetst↓< (2.5) but ↑*while I was watching*
4		this:: (3.0) I thought my pace was too <slow>↓ (2.5)
5	F	(.h) I think your pace was led by the chil↓dren (1.5) and
6		<↑they wer:e:> (.) maybe a bit sl↓ow: (0.5) >what they doing
7		writing the learning obj[ectives<
8	J	[>they were just ↑tryin' to write the
9		learning objective↓< (.) and trying to get them all together

(Continued)

(Continued)

10		(2.0)
11	F	(h.) Do they ↑*need*↓to write the learning objectives.
11		(2.0)
12	J	er:m (2.0) for writing in their book they do↑ :: (2.5) and
13		*having evidence*: (1.0) especially with your table that one
14		{you were working at?}
15		(0.5)
16	F	Yeah bu (.) couldn't (2.0)
17	J	C[ouldn't they] do it later::
18	F	[er:;m]
19	F	a learnin support system do it (.) or: Y ↑eah:
20		cos: (.) w↑ot are they getting from it (.) A<part fro:m::>
21		copying off the board
22		(1.0)
23	J	Just getting ready for the work they have to d[o.
24	F	[Yeah I mean (.)
25		theyre not ↑learning <anything>
26	J	N[o:
27	F	[or] being (.) ↑all theyre learning is: . I can copy that of the board

The transcript is produced according to some of the conventions of transcribing that we described in Chapter 7. Simply as an example of the type of interest that CA has, let us start by asking the following question: Why does the 'oka:y [1.5]' in line 1 take the form that it does, and what are its interactional consequences? The 'oka:y' and the pause following it can be heard (and read) as marking the beginning of a new **topical sequence**. It demonstrates something like 'we are now going to talk about something' and, more specifically, 'we are now going to talk about the thing we are supposed to be talking about'. One of CA's interests is in understanding how this quite complicated 'meaning' or *interactional achievement* is carried out. There are some basic things that we can point to in hinting at a preliminary answer to this. Note, for example, the elongated 'a' sound at the end of the word. This marks out the 'ok' as of a particular type – it is not a question (as in 'are you ok?') because an 'ok' that is a question would probably have an upward intonation at the end, and this one is downward. It is not an 'agreement' to anything because there is nothing preceding it in the transcript for it to be an agreement to. So part of the reason why it can be heard as an 'ok' of the type described above is because it isn't obviously any other kind of 'ok'. Another way to think of this 'ok' is 'as a way of starting off', which of course is a part of it being about a new topic. Along with other **discourse markers**, such as 'right', 'now', 'so', 'well', 'oks' are ways of starting off a conversational turn – they are common things that conversational participants use to get things going.

So, with these very simple points we can see that this 'ok' is a really complicated thing. With this example we want to show something of the interest of CA. Its concern is with understanding the structures of conversation – with why they take the forms that they do, their interactional achievements and consequences. We will move on now to say something a bit more general about the organization of this particular conversation.

Two basic conversational maxims

We are going to introduce two maxims that can be seen, Sacks (1995) suggests, as principles for the accomplishment of conversations. One of the basic features of conversation is that it is organized through turns, i.e. that speakers take it in turns to speak. That is our first maxim. The second is that people do this with the general preference that those conversational turns do not overlap. Together, these two maxims form a basic principle for how conversations work. This does not mean that it is never the case that speakers speak more than one at a time, or that talk never overlaps, but that in all kinds of contexts (although not *all* contexts) these operate as basic organization *preferences*.

The implication of both these maxims is that participants in conversations have to cooperate to produce recognizable turns such that they can accomplish 'one person speaks at a time with no overlaps'. This becomes more and more complicated to negotiate as the number of participants in a conversation increase. One way this is achieved is by participants listening out for points at which they might take a turn, i.e. trying to spot conversation transition points. In the conversation between F and J, the 'oka:y (1.5)' can be heard as a possible transition point, a point at which a next speaker (F) may take a turn. In this instance, F does not interject and J continues to speak. This shows that at a transition point two things can happen. A transition can be made or the original speaker can carry on.

Turns are structurally organized in other ways too. One way is in what have been called 'adjacency pairs' – pairs of utterances or turns that are tied to each other. 'Question–answer', 'greeting–greeting', 'request–response' are all examples of adjacency pairs, where the first part of the pair calls forth the second part of the pair. Not all utterances take this form (the 'oka:y' doesn't, for example), but they are one common organizational feature in talk. In this sequence we can see a number of question–answer sequences. For example:

Q – >what they doing writing the learning obj[ectives< (lines 6–7)
A – [>they were just tryin' to write the learning objective↓< (.) (lines 8–9)
Q – (h.) Do they need↓to write the learning objectives. (line 11)
A – er:m (2.0) for writing in their book they do :: (2.5) (line 12)

In both of these examples the questions *call forth* an answer – they imply that the next turn is the next speaker and that that turn should be used to provide an answer to the question. It does this in an imperative fashion, with the recipient of the question being *impelled* to answer (which doesn't mean that they *have to* or *will* do so, but that there is an observable moral imperative emerging from a question). In these ways, the adjacency pair sequence is a powerful mechanism in talk that interactionally directs the next turn utterance in very constrained ways.

But these kinds of sequences do not always work in such neat ways. Conversations are routine, but they are also improvised, and one of the consequences of this is that conventional order does break down from time to time. In such instances, conversation analysis is interested in looking at the restoration of order or *how people work through the problems*.

Lines 16–19 of the transcript are very interesting in this respect. At line 16, F starts to ask a question. 'Yeah bu (.) couldn't (2.0)'. J treats this as a turn transition point and provides a turn that completes the question 'C[ouldn't they] do it later::' (line 17). This creates difficulties, and the maxim 'next turn speaker answers the question' becomes ambiguous, as F is the next speaker, not J. We might say that the imperative for 'next turn' shifts to F. F's next turn 'a learnin support system do it (.) or: Y eah:' (line 19) completes her question but then ends with a response to J's part of the initiated question 'or: Y eah:'. The 'Y eah' structurally 'answers' or perhaps 'deals with', but most certainly *relates to* J's utterance in line 17. In the loosest of terms, then, we can say that this section of dialogue displays a concern with providing a question and answer, and the turns are organized to achieve that, even though the maxims of 'how turns are typically organized' have been breached.

It may be useful to clarify some points at this stage. CA's concern is not with specifying meta-rules that are said to control conversation, but with trying to work out how conversation comes to take the form that it does, and how it is ordered in particular settings. The 'rules' and maxims' are something like 'hypotheses that are then explored in relation to wider data examples'. So, one of the classic early papers in CA by Sacks, Schegloff and Jefferson (1974) used multiple examples of data to explore the basic organization of turn-taking sequences that we have been discussing. These maxims can then be used to look at how conversations work in different settings and how conversations come to have particular structural outcomes. This concern is not with the psychological character or the motives of the speakers who speak those acts: it is not typically interested in finding out how those speakers felt, or why they said what they did. Rather, as Sharrock and Anderson put it: 'conversation analysis is more concerned with utterances than speakers, being concerned with the ways in which utterances can combine themselves into unified, internally organized, developing exchanges' (1986: 69). However, we *can* inspect the interactional consequences of the utterances, and we can examine conversations to see how people *showed* that they understood something or how they *displayed* an intention. In these sorts of ways, conversation can allow us to see how talk, as a site of interaction, functions in particular settings and in general.

The organization of topics

Another organizational feature of conversations is that the *topics* or *conversational issues* are brought up in quite particular ways. There is an order to the ways in which matters are brought up and finished. So, to take an example, the '< don't thin:k> (.) you hadn come in then↓ (.)' following the 'ok' in line 1 introduces a potential topic. This topic can be understood as what has been described as a **preliminary matter** (Button and Casey, 1984) that is used as a device to bring around the main topic of conversation, which is the 'pace' of the activity (line 4). Incidentally, it is interesting to note that F's 'no' in line 2 can be heard as an agreement rather than a denial (i.e. it means something like 'no, I hadn't come in' and not 'no, I *had* come in). Structurally speaking, we might say that the 'no' acts as what Jefferson (2002) has called a **response token** that glosses an 'elaborated meaning' and is 'hearable' as agreement precisely because it does not elaborate a meaning. There is, Sacks suggests, a preference that contradictions are not glossed but are elaborated on. In other words, if a speaker disagrees, there is a preference that they provide some detailed elaboration for why they disagree.

This 'no' is part of the sequence of turns that is used to move to what Button and Casey have called the **business at hand**, the central conversational topics to be dealt with (i.e. pace). So, again, this 'trivial' business of *bringing up a topic* involves some very complex interactional exchanges. Importantly, we can see and read these exchanges and we can see quite clearly and unequivocally that 'pace' is the matter to be dealt with, not the presence or absence of F. Indeed, F's next turn topically deals with exactly this issue, using the same descriptor 'pace' that helps to topically tie the turn to J's topic opening in line 4.

The process of analysis

The detailed analysis of data in these kinds of ways through approaches like conversation analysis demands a high level of detail in one's observation. The focus on the moment-by-moment working out of talk in social interaction requires the production of detailed transcripts from audio or audio-visual recordings, such that the necessary details of 'how' can be explicated and worked through. The transcript is, as we saw in Chapter 7, a resource for analysis and not an outcome from it (or a precursor to it). The transcript can only be produced in the necessary detail if the researcher has a sufficiently detailed recording from which to produce it.

Analysis typically involves looking in very close detail at some particular example of data, and then moving to see if the specific mechanisms or 'machinery', as Sacks (1995) calls it, can also be identified in other data examples (see Maiwald, 2005, for a description of this general feature of analysis). Maiwald (2005) suggests that conversation analysis typically proceeds in three phases:

Phase one: work utterance by utterance (or 'turn' by 'turn') answering questions such as 'How does turn "x" relate to the preceding one?' and 'Why was it undertaken *like this* rather than *like that*?'
Phase two: to figure out the implications of the turn by trying to answer questions such as 'What turn options are implied by it, and why/how does it make such implications?'
Phase three: examining the ways that the utterances were dealt with by subsequent speakers.

This analytic process is very time consuming. Sacks famously commented in various places in his writings that he often spent many years working through small fragments of data, trying to find the 'machinery' that would explain why it took the form that it did (Sacks, 1995). Within CA, there are a wide range of concepts and ideas that can be used as resources in analysis. Some of the central concepts are outlined in Table 10.2.

Table 10.2   Concepts in conversation analysis

Concept	Definition	Exemplar references
Sequentiality	The turn-by-turn organization of talk in social interaction	See particularly Schegloff (2007)
Topicality	The organization of topics in conversation	Button and Casey (1984)
Adjacency pairs	The pairing of utterances within sequences of talk	Schegloff (2007)
Membership categories	The use and organization of social types and categories within conversation	See particularly Hester and Eglin's short collection (1997)
Response tokens	The uses of mechanisms such as 'uhu' and 'mmm' as organizational principles in talk	For an interesting example of early writing in this area see Schegloff (1968) and, more recently, Jefferson (2002)
Preference Organization	The organization of talk around preferred and alternative actions	

A critique of conversation analysis

One of the limitations of this mode of analysis is that the conversational practices are treated as purely linguistic phenomena, rather than as *bodily practices*. By concentrating simply on the *talk* rather than on other features of the interaction environment (such as body movement or the role of objects in the encounter) the analysis is potentially impoverished (see Heath and Hindmarsh, 2002). As we saw earlier, Sacks' enthusiasm for CA came from the observation that audio technology enabled him to replay the activities of conversation in order to explore in detail the mechanisms of social production. However, Sacks emphasized that, in the abstract, it may be that other mechanisms, such as bodily movement, may turn out to be just as important for the analysis as the verbal conversation itself (see Silverman, 1998).

Since Sacks' early and highly influential writings, video has become a standard and readily affordable means of data collection, and just as audio data influenced Sacks' work, so video has shifted the professional gaze of conversation analysts to the role of the visual as a feature of social interaction. The visual refers to a variety of features of interaction, including movement, gesture, gaze, touch, the use of objects, and so on. It is the interplay between such aspects of interaction and the way they are contextually used and worked out that characterizes the ethnomethodological and conversation analytic concern with visuality. In the following analysis we explore how these broader concerns can help to shape the analysis of the data fragment presented in extract (1).

Gesture and the contextualization of talk

Extract (2) is a transcript that re-presents the beginning part of the talk shown in extract (1), but with additional information regarding physical movements. The movements are represented with text in square brackets [J] and curly brackets {F} under the discourse. The open bracket indicates the start of the movement and the close bracket indicates its end point.

We can see here that at line 1 J's 'oka:y (1.5)', which was identified as signifying the beginning of the activity, is also accompanied by her moving to sit down on to her chair and by her looking at the TV. As the purpose of the activity was to discuss the video recording, these combination of actions along with the 'oka:y (0.5)' indicate that the movement to a new topic is likely to be 'about the thing we are looking at on the TV'. The gesture is fundamental to the creation of a sense of the discursive context as it indicates not only that a new conversational topic is about to occur, and that 'this activity is now beginning', but also that 'what I am about to say relates to the video recorder and the purpose of the activity'.

(2)   Gestural features of interaction in the professional evaluation of a teacher

1	J	oka:y (1.5) I ↑don't thin:k (.) you had come in then↓ (.)
		[Sitting down]
		{looking at TV..}
		[pointing at TV with remote control]
2	F	No:
		[looking at TV]
3	J	>you hancome in yetst↓< (2.5) but *while* I was watching
		[bends down and picks up pen..
4		this:: (3.0) I thought my pace was too slow↓
		.....] [leans forward] [turns to face F]
4		(2.5)
5	F	(.h) I think your pace was led by the chil↓dren (1.5) and
		[J picks up writing pad from floor and put it on knee
6		<↑*they wer:e:*> (.) maybe a bit sl↓ow: (0.5) >what they doing
		....]
		[......... F turns head towards J
		[F turns to face TV
7		writing the learning obj[ectives<
8	J	[>they were just tryin' to write the
		....]
9		learning objective↓< (.) and trying to get them all together
		....}
		[J opens book]
10	F	(2.) (h.) Do they ↑*need*↓to write the learning objectives.
		{turns head to face J....................}
11		(2.0)

The movement of pointing to the TV while saying 'I ↑don't thin:k (.) you had come in then↓ (.)' can be seen to give some specification to the 'then' which, in the absence of this gesture, is a somewhat ambiguous mode of reference. In other words, the gesture defines what 'then' refers to.

J's motion of picking up the pen from the floor is part of a broader action (which continues until the end of line 9) of preparing the notebook on her lap ready to write. The turning of her head to F indicates that the '*I thought my pace was too* slow↓' emphasizes the turn selection point and that the matter of 'pace' was a topic to be treated as 'the issue under discussion'. The readiness of the pen also shows that the topic is one that can be treated as 'the kind of thing one might take notes on' and therefore 'part of the business at hand of undertaking an evaluation'. The move to dealing with *the business at hand*, then, is not just a linguistic matter, but is also a gestural accomplishment, which is worked and displayed through the use of gaze, bodily orientation, and the positioning and use of physical objects.

F's turn of the head at line 6 during the pause after her utterance may be taken to indicate that this also was treated as a potential turn transition point but which was not taken up by J; when F turned to face J, J was in the process of picking up the notebook from the floor and not looking at F. When F asks 'do they ↑*need*↓to write the learning objectives' she turns her head to face J, again repeating the observed pattern that on potential or intended turn change points the gaze is redirected towards the other participant.

Implications of the analysis of gesture and other modes of communication

One of the points that this discussion serves to highlight is that transcription is made in relation to analytic interests. As we say in Chapter 7, transcripts are not 'neutral', but are focused renderings of practice. Thus, transcription is produced to display what the researcher regards as relevant and interesting, rather than to represent all of the interactive features of a setting. Indeed, any transcript that did try to represent 'everything' that occurred, would likely be extremely inaccessible. It is interesting that the transcriptions are really quite difficult to read, let alone produce. The accurate representation of gesture and talk in sufficient detail and in such a manner that they can be easily understood is no easy task. Norris (2002) has argued that the representation of interaction in transcripts is often more effective where it uses pictures, screen shots, and other visual add-ins to illustrate the different 'modes' of communication and interaction. Norris takes examples of interaction among children with computers and televisions and shows how the analysis benefits from non-linguistic transcription techniques. Textual renderings such as those provided above are often harder to interpret than more visual modes.

More generally, however, the analysis provided here is intended to show that:

- Gesture contextualizes discourse and provides an important resource for understanding why discourse takes the form that it does
- Gesture comprises a distinct communicative mode that has significance and interactional consequences that will go unnoticed if researchers concentrate solely on spoken discourse.

These observations may or may not have any particular relevance to a given research project. There is nothing *generic* about analytic relevance, so it certainly cannot be claimed that these observations will be of value to all researchers in all settings. What is of value, however, is that the analysis of video is usually conducted because, for one reason or another, the above observations regarding gesture *are* of relevance. In other words, where researchers are using video, it is normally because there is some reason why gesture (or movement or position or the use of artifacts or other physical aspects of interaction, communication or social practice) will be useful to them. This may not be in the form of an analytic focus on such features. It may simply be that they need to see the participants in order to understand 'who said or did what'. However, this section has aimed to show how questions about 'who said what, why and how?' can be given more depth through analytic frames such as conversation analysis. What we hope to have demonstrated here is that the very specific interests of this form of analysis are useful for bringing to the fore some of the taken-for-granted or glossed features of the production of recognizable social practices.

Practicalities in the analysis of social interaction through video

Repeated listening – Analyzing data in these kinds of detailed ways can be a very slow process. Researchers frequently have to watch a section of video or listen to a recording many times over in order to understand it fully, or to discover something new or analytically profitable about the way in which the activity was undertaken. The process of listening, transcribing and writing is an iterative and cyclical one, and the analytic output is the result of moving backwards and forwards between these activities.

Transcription – A part of the process of listening involves the production of transcripts to help identify and focus on particular aspects of the data. Researchers may use different transcripts to concentrate on distinct features of the interaction and may produce a number of transcripts during the analysis. However, some software enables researchers to produce annotations of their video materials in electronic form, and to index them to the video, which can be a very convenient device (see Loehr and Harper, 2003).

Collaborative analysis – Conducting analysis in groups is often more productive than on one's own. Jordan and Henderson (1995) describe an approach to collaboratively analyzing video data in collective data sessions, where a multidisciplinary team interrogates data together, raising points in relation to the data as it is being watched. The multiplicity of perspectives and viewpoints can help to create a much more nuanced exploration of data. This is particularly noticeable where professionals who are familiar with the settings being investigated are present during data analysis sessions. In these kinds of ways, researchers are able to expand the range of insights that they can get about data by including professional knowledge and skills that is outside their area of expertise.

Presence – A key issue for researchers using these forms of technology is whether or not they need to be present during data capture. It may be necessary to move the camera or audio recording device during the session (e.g. if the participants move around). Similarly, it may be necessary to use more than one device in order to capture different visual perspectives. However, the presence of the researcher may make the data collection more intrusive.

Microphones – Built-in microphones in recording devices like digital audio recorders and video recorders are often of a poor quality that may not pick up conversation that is far away from the device or that is competing with other background noises. It is very often advisable to use a recording device that has an external microphone input so that better quality sound can be recorded.

Length of recording time – It is important to consider how much data will be required in a given recording session and whether or not the device being used is capable of holding that amount of data. Just as audio recording formats have proliferated over recent years (see our discussion of this in Chapter 7), so researchers can choose to record video direct to a built-in hard drive, a DVD or a mini DV cassette tape. In all cases, there is of course a limit to how much data can be recorded. When using a mini DV, it is often better to use 'top loading' recorders that can have the tape changed without removal from a tripod. Hard-drive cameras that record straight to an internal disk can be awkward as the data needs to be transferred to a computer or external hard drive once the device is full.

Placement – The placement of the recording device is, of course, crucial. If an audio recording device is placed on a table, it is likely to pick up the small knocks and taps that participants sitting at the table may make. Cups or plates being moved around, feet knocking against chairs or tables, people fiddling with, tapping, banging or brushing against microphones, and static interference from mobile phones, lights, computers and other electronic devices can all be significant problems that can dramatically alter the quality of one's data.

Box 10.2 provides a checklist of questions that can be useful to reflect on when beginning any data recording session.

Box 10.2 Key considerations when conducting audio or video recordings

- Will the recording device(s) need to be moved during the recording process?
- Is more than one device required?
- Is an external mirophone needed? If so, what kind of microphone? A tie clip mic? A floor mic? Stereo mics? A surround sound mic?
- Where is the device going to be placed? On a chair, plinth, tripod, wall, table?
- Where should the microphone be directed?
- Are the lighting conditions sufficient or is extra lighting required?
- How much data is required and now much data can be recorded on the device?
- Does the recording device need a direct power source? If so, what is the proximity of that power source to the placement of the device?

- Does the device require an operator or can it be left to record automatically/ controlled by remote control?
- Are there any noises external to the recording environment that may interfere with the quality of the data (e.g. cars going past the window, noisy adjacent rooms or hallways?)
- What factors in the recording environment may interfere with the quality of the recording? Mobile phone interference? Static interference from lights or computers? Doors that may open and close? Telephones that may ring?

Concluding remarks

Audio and video data are important resources in social research that enable researchers to inspect, repeatedly and in fine detail, the settings to which such data pertains. Audio data is a far more common research resource than video data and is often the default form for interviews or focus groups. Video data is a more specialized resource in qualitative research, but one that can be just as valuable in interview or focus group research as it can be in observational work. In general terms, the advantage of video data is that it contains information about the gestures of the interaction that can be useful for making sense of the talk. However, such devices are often felt to be more intrusive than audio recording devices. Working through the relevance of these different forms of data and the particular ways they are to be used in a project is very much a contextual matter for researchers.

Recommended further reading

Heath, C. and Hindmarsh, J. (2002) 'Analyzing interaction: video, ethnography and situated conduct', in T. May (ed.), *Qualitative Research in Action*. London, Sage. A practical guide to the analysis of video and social interaction.

Schegloff, E. (2007) *Sequence Organization in Interaction: A Primer in Conversation Analysis*. Cambridge: Cambridge University Press. An overview of issues in conversation analysis from one of its most outspoken practitioners.

Silverman, D. (1998) *Harvey Sacks: Social Science and Conversation Analysis*. New York: Oxford University Press. A detailed introduction to Sacks' work, key concepts, and the debates and divergent practices to which it has led.

ten Have, P. (1999) *Doing Conversation Analysis: A Practical Guide*. London: Sage. A thorough and accessible introduction to CA with some interesting activities and a good overview of key ideas.

11 Using technology

This chapter discusses the following issues:

- Qualitative analysis software
- Collaborative analysis and technology
- Hypermedia and analysis

Introduction

There is a simple truism that is very useful to keep in mind when thinking about the role of computers in research: computers and computer programs do not analyze data, researchers do. The computer and qualitative analysis packages are merely tools that assist researchers in their data work. Bearing this point in mind is important for helping to focus on the ways in which the various possibilities that technology may offer relate to the specific interests of a research project.

Not all analysis packages are relevant to all analytic approaches. Just as research design is developed in relation to particular research interests and the data requirements implied by them, so the technologies used during data work are selected and put to work according to the objectives of the analysis. Technology should never be used 'for the sake of it', and should only be employed if it can facilitate some of the work that researchers need to undertake. As we shall show in the discussion below, some qualitative analysis software products are orientated towards particular analytic approaches and agendas, and so researchers need to be aware of how their own interests fit with these design parameters.

This chapter aims to help researchers in these considerations by outlining some of the key analytic processes that qualitative analytic software facilitate, and by exploring the methodological issues surrounding them. In brief, computer software has become a standard feature of work with qualitative data. Since the 1980s academics have been commenting on the potential benefits of computers for managing the large amounts of data that qualitative researchers so often accumulate (for interesting examples of these discussions, see Sproull and Sproull, 1982; Podolefsky and McCarty, 1983; Becker, 1984; Brent, 1984; Anderson, 1989; Tesch, 1990). Since these early discussions, debate has shuttled between enthusiasm for the potentially revolutionary effect of such technologies on the practices of researchers, to scepticism that they may represent either nothing more than a bit of a gimmick or, more ominously, an additional and potentially unnecessary step in the research process that may itself effect the outcome of analysis. In the second part of this chapter we look at some of the specific manifestations of these debates by examining a number of the concerns that have been levelled at Computer Assisted Qualitative Data Analysis Software (CAQDAS), paying particular attention to debates around:

- the convergence on particular modes of analysis
- the ways in which such technologies may encourage the removal of data from context
- the potential problems with 'automated' coding.

Before we do this, however, we will look at some of the key ways that CAQDAS packages may be used by researchers to help them organize their analysis.

Box 11.1   CAQDAS

CAQDAS stands for Computer Assisted Qualitative Data Analysis Software and refers to specialist programs that are designed to aid the process of analysis. In general, these programs act as databases that enable researchers to label and index their data and, in the case of theory-building packages, to conduct meta-analysis of the codes that they create.

CAQDAS

There is an increasingly wide range of products available to help researchers in their data work. There are a number of texts and web resources that provide detailed overviews of these types of technology (see, for example, Lewins and Silver, 2007, and the Web links at the end of this chapter). We do not wish to repeat this work here, but merely to provide a brief overview of some of the key concepts and distinctions in CAQDAS.

Three very popular programs used to analyze qualitative data are **Atlas.ti**, **NVivo**, and **HyperRESEARCH**. With all of these programs researchers can develop and apply codes to data and run queries about potential code relationships in their coding schemes. These tools also provide quantitative outputs of one's coding, visual mindmaps for conceptualizing coding work and memo functions for recording notes on the analysis. Another increasingly popular package is **MAXQDA**. This package has much of the functionality of other programs, in terms of the coding of data, the use of written analysis through memos, the production of quantitative *descriptive* statistics of coding work, and the facilitation of collaborative and group analysis. Atlas.ti and HyperRESEARCH both support the analysis of text, video-audio data and still images. Other programs that are useful for analyzing multimedia formats include **Transana**, **Qualrus** and **Anvil**. These programs are all designed to perform versions of thematic analysis, as outlined in Chapter 8.

CLAN is a program that is designed for the analysis of talk in interaction. The name of this program is an acronym for *Computerized Language Analysis*, and uses a conventional system of discourse transcription called **CHAT** (see MacWhinney, 1996, for a discussion of this system). Through CLAN researchers are able to link transcripts to audio files and to perform analysis with the software by creating codes to categorize particular aspects of speech for subsequent retrieval by the software. This system facilitates the fine-grain analysis of data and the comparison of data exemplars. The CLAN program and the CHAT transcription and analysis system are part of a corpora-sharing project, one of the aims of which is to facilitate the development of shared data and analytic tools.

Code and retrieve functions

The term 'code and retrieve' has been used to describe the process of applying categories to sections of data and then collating the instances of those categories (e.g. Richards and Richards, 1991, 1995; Weitzman and Miles, 1995; Coffey et al., 1996). Most CAQDAS packages facilitate this basic database function, which is an extremely useful way to manage data. Instead of struggling with negotiating multiple documents and manually searching for relevant sections, researchers can view all the parts of a given data set (like a group of interviews or a set of fieldnotes) that have been coded in a particular way by simply clicking a few buttons in a given CAQDAS package. This provides an easy way to compare the data that has been used in a code.

Comparative coding involves the comparison of data within a given code in order to refine and develop that code. Examples of the sorts of things that may be constitutive of comparative coding work can be found in Box 11.3. The general procedures for undertaking this form of comparative coding are outlined in earlier chapters of this book (particularly Chapter 8), so we will not discuss this issue any further here.

In addition to this kind of thematic coding, code and retrieve tools may also facilitate other forms of analysis, such as forms of discourse analysis. For example, extract (1) is a section of dialogue from a doctor–patient consultation and eye examination. The extract comes from a study of ophthalmology practices that employed conversation analysis to look at the achievement of diagnoses within the consultation. An aspect of the analysis involved comparing the ways in which ophthalmologists organized the routines of a consultation. In the extract, the coding simply involved labelling the function of this aspect of discourse. In this study, Atlas.ti was simply used as a database to facilitate the easy retrieval of data for subsequent analysis.

(1) A consultation opening in an eye examination

1	D	owe kaay (.) now er:m (.) I can see your obviously wearing glasses: er:m
2		(.) how long have you had your (0.5) current (0.3) prescription here your
3		current the lenses that your wear[ing
4	P	[abou:t two years]
5	D	About two years
6		(3.5)
7	D	an (.) I'll take a measurement of those at the end and we'll [(.) compare as to
8	P	[alright]
9	D	any d[ifference that we might find today er:m (.) [inward breath]
10	P	[yeah]

Consultation Opening

Similarly, **content analysis** may be conducted very easily with these sorts of packages, as many of the product market leaders, such as Atlas.ti and NVivo, contain features that enable researchers to search for particular words within the texts being analyzed and to automatically count how often particular words occur within the texts. Combined with coding functions, these packages are very useful ways of applying categories to particular words and phrases. Researchers are able to search for words and to then code specific instances of their use for subsequent retrieval, comparison and analysis. The automated nature of this process in a CAQDAS package significantly reduces the labour of this form of analysis.

Box 11.2   Content Analysis

Content analysis is sometimes regarded as a quantitative rather than qualitative method of analysis (see, for example, Berelson, 1952; Weber, 1985) because it involves a largely numeric approach to examining written discourse (e.g. counting the frequencies of words or phrases). However, to reiterate the argument made in Chapter 1, the distinction between qualitative and quantitative research needs to be treated with some caution. There are forms of content analysis that display the kind of reflexive stance towards the production of meaning that is often associated with more 'qualitative' approaches (see Krippendorff, 2003, for a discussion of this issue).

Many of the programs that support code and retrieve types of analysis also provide further functions for dealing with data. These sorts of 'advanced' functions are often described as facilitating the development of theory. Unlike this basic code and retrieve resource, these mechanisms tend to be designed for particular modes of analysis, notably for grounded theory (Coffey et al., 1996).

Theory-building functions

Theory building within CAQDAS entails the development of theoretical frameworks through the examination of coding schemes and, in this respect, follow and use principles within grounded theory. CAQDAS can be used to explore the ways in which codes are developing in relation to a given data set.

In addition to interrogating the data related to an individual code through comparative coding, researchers can enquire as to the relationships between different codes. For example, such computer packages enable researchers to conduct Boolean searches in order to explore the relationships between codes; to display the frequencies in which codes have been used; to build hierarchies of codes; and to develop relationships within those hierarchies.

The functionality of computers means that the process of running queries about, say, how often two particular codes occur at a given time, or displaying all the quotations within a given code, are very quick to perform. The basic processes of how such coding work is conducted, however, are no different from how it would be conducted without such software. None of these functions is exclusive to computers as all of them can be carried out by hand. CAQDAS simply make the exploration of coded data much easier.

Box 11.3   Examples of basic code work that can be facilitated by CAQDAS

- Creating and applying codes
- Compiling and comparing the instances (data) of codes
- Searching data for key words and phrases
- Exploring the relations between codes
- Creating meta-codes (super codes) to describe the relations between codes
- Creating and exploring hypotheses
- Attaching definitions to codes
- Making notes about coding work
- Displaying the frequencies with which codes have been used

Note: See Chapter 8 for further discussion of these practices.

An example of theory building

The following example of theory building expands on the exemplar we gave in Chapter 2 of the study of pharmacy practice work. The research (Gibson et al., 2001) was interested in examining the ways in which different types of professional pharmacy role for postgraduate placement students drew upon the skills and knowledge that they had learnt in their university course. One of the key coding structures was the role itself. Codes were developed for the three areas in which students worked:

- Industry work
- Hospital work
- Community (shop) work

Another set of codes pertained to the types of role that students would be employing during their work placements. Two of the key features of the work of interest related to interaction with other healthcare professionals and the interaction with patients in relation to their illnesses. Two codes were developed to categorize these interests:

- Interaction with profs
- Interaction with patients

Both of these codes were divided into sub-categories that captured the type of interaction that was being undertaken. Two of the most important sub-categories are shown below for each of the two 'parent' codes:

Interaction with profs

- Advising on conditions or drug options
- Consulting on patient medical history

Interaction with patients

- Consulting and advising about drug interactions
- Consulting about medical history

After the interviews had been conducted and transcripts had been produced, the researchers developed a suspicion that there was a relationship between the type of role that students had and the level of professional involvement that they experienced (as described by the above categories). This hunch was taken forward by coding the data according to these categories (which was only a small part of a much wider coding structure), and then running queries to display instances in which the codes appeared together. For example, the researchers ran a search to find all the instances in which *hospital work* (code title: 'hsp wk') and *advising on conditions and drug interactions* (code title: 'adv drg int') occurred together. Similarly, the researchers ran a query on the coincidence of *community work* (code title: 'com wk') and *advising on conditions and drug interactions*. The results of these queries were then compared. This comparison substantiated the suspicion and led to the finding that there was significant variation within the placement settings in terms of the types of work the students undertook and the extent to which they drew on their of university training.

It may be a little grandiose to describe the above example as constituting the development of a *theory* as such, but it is quite a clear illustration of how the functionality of 'theory-building' tools in CAQDAS can be put to work in order to explore the relations between codes within a given coding structure.

Technology and collaborative analysis

In addition to facilitating integrated analytic platforms, CAQDAS packages provide a useful aid to the collaborative analysis of data. While it is not always possible, analysis between groups of researchers is often very productive. It is common for different researchers to pick up on distinct features of data or to interpret data in different ways, so having more than one input on a data set is a useful way of creating more ideas to take forward. There are also good methodological reasons for using more than one researcher. It has been argued that teams of researchers can increase the **internal reliability** of analysis by checking the interpretation of an individual researcher against their colleagues (e.g. LeCompte and Goetz, 1982). Internal reliability here refers to the testing of the use of a given coding scheme between different researchers within the same research team as a way of ascertaining the degree of consistency within the study of processes, measurements, interpretations, and so on.

However, the issue of reliability in qualitative research is often far more complex than simply checking the consistency of procedures and judgements between researchers. LeCompte and Goetz (1982), for example, argue that in ethnographic research, *reliability* can be established through adequate description by the researcher of the process by which they gathered their data. By demonstrating clearly the types of construct that are being used to make sense of data, the sources of data (e.g. the social groups that were involved in its construction or the locations in which research was undertaken) and the processes of its production (e.g. the role of the researcher in generating data, or the relationship of the researcher to the researched), other researchers (either internal or external ones) are in a better position to make sense of how the ideas presented in a given project were arrived at and the extent to which these can be considered to be 'reliable'.

Box 11.4   Reliability

Internal reliability in qualitative research can refer to the extent to which researchers on a given team may agree about the 'trustworthiness' of processes and the resulting analysis. **External reliability** could, in these terms, be taken to describe the extent of agreement of researchers not involved in the research. However, the notion of reliability is contested in qualitative research because the commitment to understanding the processes of meaning construction often entail a detailed reflection on the role of the researcher in that process. A concern with inter-rater reliability (i.e. the consistency by which a system of coding is applied by different researchers), then, may be less interesting than a detailed reflection on why and how particular code categories are developed and the conceptual role they may play. Given this, some authors have suggested that other concepts, such as **credibility**, **trustworthiness** and **consistency**, may be more useful terms (see Guba and Lincoln, 1982; Katz, 1983; Mishler, 1990).

The difficulty of bringing sets of analysis together mean that it can be hard for groups of researchers to coordinate analysis. An analogy is two people co-authoring a document: if those two people work on different versions of the document there may be a problem in subsequently combining them. The same is true of analysis. CAQDAS packages provide a unified platform where analysis can be undertaken. Some of these types of software enable researchers to filter the analysis that is displayed, e.g. to see only the analysis undertaken by a particular person or the analysis undertaken on a given day.

CAQDAS provides useful tools to help researchers coordinate their analysis and to create integrated research databases that contain not only the coding of data (where such an approach is taken), but also all of the notes related to a given project, which explicate the complexities of how data was collected, the types of data source that were used, and the ways in which constructs were arrived at, defined and modified. By using CAQDAS, such professional sharing and collaboration becomes a much more straightforward proposition.

Box 11.5   Social networking software

Web 2.0 social networking software, such as wikis and blogs, provide very interesting resources to aid the collaborative and distributed analysis of data. These sorts of tools can help researchers to move away from very private forms of work, and to open their data and its interpretation up to wider communities. This work might include not just detailed outlines of the analysis itself, but also logs of the development of the analysis. Clearly, there are very important ethical considerations in such practices, which need to be given serious thought before any data is made public. In particular, it is important to think about how the opening of data to the wider community may impact on the research participants, and how the conditions of their consent to participate may or may not be compromised.

CAQDAS packages are not the only ways of organizing such analysis, however. Wikis, for example, are an increasingly popular means of undertaking collaborative work. A wiki is essentially a website that can be edited by multiple users. While wikis often use some form of technical markup language to do that editing (e.g. using symbols such as asterisks or colons in the text to indicate particular kinds of formatting, like bold or italic text), this language is reasonably quick to learn. Within wikis, users can create and edit web pages, and link them to pages within the wiki or to other external websites. From the point of view of analysis, wikis represent a very useful way to coordinate the analysis of data. There are two features of wikis that are particularly interesting. First, users can collaborate in the production of a given web page. In the context of analysis this web page may be the analysis of a given interview, interview section, observation, piece of text, and so on. Individual users can add to that page at any point, and gradually accumulate a piece of written analysis. This, of course, is not very different from how people might work collaboratively on the creation of a document. There is now a range of web-based collaborative writing software that would facilitate this type of work at a distance. Even quite 'mundane' technologies, such as email and word-processing packages, can be very effectively used to coordinate collaborative work. However, the second interesting aspect of wikis is the ways in which pages can be linked together in the creation of alternative analytic structures and reading paths. We discuss the benefits of hyperlinking as an analytic form in the following section.

Hypermedia and qualitative analysis

Hypermedia refers to the linking of data and documents through hyperlinks. This mode of organization facilitates the creation of multiple pathways through data, offering users dynamic strategies for moving between and representing texts and other data sources (see Fielding and Lee, 1995; Dicks and Mason, 1998; Gibson et al., 2005). Hypermedia offers researchers novel ways of both analyzing and presenting (or 'writing up') their data, and gives researchers the ability to use and make available to readers multiple forms of data, including text, video, audio and still pictures.

Hypermedia does not really represent a distinctive technology, but is a description of a way of moving between things. Hypermedia links are used in CAQDAS software to move from, say, a code category to the instances of that code within the data. Hyperlinks can also be used in many other types of web-based and desktop-based technology. Users can link from one type of software to another and can link between different types of document (such as text-based Microsoft Word document to an audio Windows Media Player file). Web-based platforms also use hyperlinks. Collaborative workspaces, such as wikis for example, use hyperlinks to move between user-created pages within the wiki, or from 'internal' to 'external' pages.

It has been suggested that hyperlinking is distinct from coding in that codes simply represent ways of categorizing aspects of data of a particular type, whereas hyperlinks offer researchers the possibility of specifying relationships between particular parts of data. For example, 'this' part of the transcript is a function of 'that' part (see the Cardiff research group discussion of this at http://www.cf.ac.uk/socsi/hyper/index.html). The idea here is that hyperlinking can involve creating pathways between data instances and can entail the specification of the functional relations between those instances, rather than simply providing pathways from a category to the instances of that category. However, as many of the CAQDAS packages that offer tools for coding also include features that enable researchers to specify relations between parts of the data, perhaps the distinction is a little forced. It is more useful simply to think of hyperlinking as a way of relating things to each other. We will discuss four ways in which hypermedia can be used within qualitative work: linking different data representations; linking ideas; creating alternative narrative routes; and data integration and corpus sharing.

Box 11.6   Hyperlinks

Hyperlinks can be valuable for linking:

- different modes of transcription (e.g. an indexical transcript to a more detailed and *focused* transcript). Similarly, researchers may produce two different types of transcription of the same phenomenon and link these to each other to provide alternative readings or versions of a given data section.
- one data form to another (e.g. an interview with a video observation). Here, researchers might provide a hyperlink between an interview and particular parts of an observation. These links might help researchers to juxtapose the ideas explored in interviews with particular ideas seen in practice.

- transcripts to data (e.g. from a transcription to an audio interview). A researcher might link from particular parts of a given interview to the actual recording of that interview saved as a file on a computer. This helps the researcher to keep the actual data central to the analysis and prevents over-reliance on data re-descriptions.

Linking different data representations

As we discussed in Chapter 7, the presentation and representation of data is a significant concern for researchers – particular modes of transcription, for example, involve imposing a particular view on 'what is of interest'. Through hyperlinking, researchers are able to move between different forms of presentation of the same data set. This may involve moving between different forms of transcription (e.g. between a focused transcription to a timeline transcription), or between a transcription and a recording of the data. In either case, the combination of modes of presentation through hyperlinks is potentially both analytically insightful and practically useful. By producing transcripts that show different features of the same data set, researchers can 'bracket out' different things and shift between different ways of seeing. The ability to compare alternative presentational forms of data means that researchers can operate with more than one form of analytic gaze.

When dealing with audio or audiovisual data, hyperlinks provide an extremely useful way to move from one genre or data type to another (Dicks and Mason, 1998). In their project examining nurse education, Gibson et al. (2005) used audio files and transcripts to analyze the production of meaning in postgraduate seminars. One of the approaches taken to the analysis involved using basic audio editing software to cut up the audio recording and to store these locally on a hard drive. Typed transcripts of these segments were then produced and the two documents linked together through hyperlinks. This enabled the researchers to compare transcripts with the actual data to which they pertained. The transcribed sections could be read while listening to the original recording, and corrections could be made to the transcripts as they were being played.

Dicks et al. (2006) outline the ways in which different media forms may offer very distinctive analytic frames, and have pointed to the value of being able to move from one modality of representation to another. Dicks et al. argue that the semiotic affordances of media types, and the ease of movement between such forms of meaning may create new analytic possibilities. The authors show how media such as writing and photography, to pick just one of their examples, trade on different semiotic structures, and suggest that the creation of linkages between such different forms generates new ways of juxtaposing meaning (see also Lemke, 2002, on this idea). The exploration of the semiotic implications of multimedia hyperlinking is beyond the scope of our discussion here. We simply wish to draw attention to the possibilities that researchers can open up by linking different modes of representation through hypermedia.

Linking ideas

Hyperlinking is not just a useful way of dealing with data, but also provides interesting possibilities for managing the writing and reflection on that data. We have already talked about the important role of memos in grounded theory and thematic analysis (see Chapters 2 and 8). In both approaches, the interlinking of memos is an important aspect of theory development. Hyperlinking through CAQDAS programs, online writing environments like blogs or wikis, or through standard word-processing utilities provides a means of joining up those various thoughts. For example, by inserting hyperlinks within a document to another document or to another part of the same document, researchers are able to create flexible reading paths through their notes and memos, and to generate clusters of ideas that relate to each other. Hyperlinking becomes a means of moving between ideas, and of creating meaning structures within one's writing. One of the challenges that hyperlink writing structures present is the maintenance of order within the specified links. Hyperlink writing can be usefully combined with forms of visual mapping that show the unfolding system of links in a pictographic form. Mindmapping or concept mapping software is now available as freeware, and helps researchers to maintain a sense of their developing analytic structures.

Creating alternative narrative routes

Hyperlinking is also potentially a valuable method for writing up and presenting one's analysis. Instead of being tied to linear narratives, researchers are able to create different pathways through texts. While links are still defined and created by the author, following them is a matter of reader choice, so authors can create different systems of potential movement through a narrative instead of providing one linear structure of a set of topics or ideas. This mode of organization has been used in fiction writing even before the use of computers, but the World Wide Web is increasing the range of poetry, fiction, graphic novels, and so on that are using hyperlinks as a modality of storytelling.

Social researchers are beginning to reflect more on the ways in which they may use hyperlink narrative structures in the context of their own writing (see Dicks and Mason, 1998). The ideas of using this form of research have been nicely explored by the Hypermedia and Qualitative Research team at Cardiff University, UK (see http://www.cf.ac.uk/socsi/hyper/index.html). The authors of these projects show how hyperlinks can be used to illustrate alternative perspectives or voices within research and to generate circular detours for readers to follow. However, actual experiments with the use of hypertext to author academic output are few and far between. Academic conventions of presentation are still strongly orientated to linearity, even within online publications (see Dicks and Mason, 1998).

Data integration and corpus sharing

Another potential area of value to qualitative researchers that hypermedia may provide is the linking to data sources. Currently, the dominant practice within qualitative research writing is for researchers to provide extracts of their data within the text of their writing. Quotations from interview transcripts, screen shots from videos or still photographs are typically included as exemplars, with narratives written around them. Electronic publication media, including online publications, facilitate the use of hypermedia to link to the data corpus itself. So, for example, instead of simply including a transcription of an interview, researchers can provide a hyperlink to that section of the interview so that readers can see the context in which an interview comment was made. This has even greater utility for video data, where researchers can provide a link to the video itself rather than relying on a small number of screen shots and annotations.

In addition to the obvious advantages of providing richer forms of data, this also gives researchers the ability to include multiple links to data extracts. The limitations on word counts that authors face when writing for journals, for instance, means that, typically, data is limited to the use of a small number of examples. Through hyperlinking, researchers can include multiple examples without increasing the size of their article. The methodological benefits of this are easy to see: researchers can create more substantive sets of evidence to support their narratives, and can use their data in its original form, without transforming it into textual representations. Also, researchers can quite easily make their data corpus and even their analytic strategy available to readers through such hyperlinking functions. In terms of transparency, researchers can, in the abstract, make their work a public resource.

However, there are also serious issues with this sort of approach. The ethical implications of using data in such an identifiable form are potentially quite complex as, among other things, ensuring anonymity becomes a lot harder when one is providing direct access to examples of participant speaking or interacting. Perhaps for these kinds of reasons it is still comparatively unusual to find examples of researchers using their data in these sorts of ways, in spite of the increasing use of online publishing media.

Concerns and debates in relation to technology and qualitative research

The range of CAQDAS packages, web-based collaborative technologies, and hyperauthoring tools that can be used in the context of qualitative research make these exciting times for researchers. These tools can help to take much of the labour out of dealing with data and can offer very interesting resources for representing, organizing, integrating and sharing data. However, this excitement should be situated in the context of continuing debates about the role of computing technologies in qualitative research.

The convergence on grounded theory

Some authors have pointed to what they see as a convergence on a particular approach to analysis within the various software packages (Lonikila, 1995; Coffey et al., 1996).

Lonikila (1995) suggests that two of the dominant analysis packages at the time of writing, Atlas.ti and NUD*IST, were both based on the idea of applying codes. The same point can be made in relation to lots of packages, including NVivo, HyperRESEARCH and Qualrus. While coding may be a significant aspect of qualitative research, it is, as we have shown in this book, far from being the beginning and the end of analytic options. Forms of discourse analysis, for example, rely more on the fine-grained analysis of discourse rather than on the production of categories and the application of codes.

The convergence on a code-based approach to analysis within computer software is held by some to exemplify a general enshrinement of the use of grounded theory in qualitative analysis technologies (Coffey et al., 1996). In some cases, such as Atlas.ti, software companies are quite explicit that they have based their programs on these sorts of methodological strategies. Atlas.ti's architecture reflects the processes outlined by Glaser and Strauss (1999 [1967]). The terminology used in the program, such as 'memos', 'codes', 'quotations', 'families' and 'nodes', are all derived from grounded theory. Other programs, such as NVivo and HyperRESEARCH, while not using the same labels for their software functions, essentially facilitate the same analytic processes.

However, other authors have suggested that claims of a general move to grounded theory approaches in CAQDAS programs are overstated. Lee and Fielding (1996) point to the different uses to which analytic tools may be put, and suggest that the basic functionality of a given program can give rise to quite different practices of use (see also Fielding and Lee, 1998). This is an important point. As our example of the use of code and retrieve software in discourse analysis is intended to highlight (see extract (1)), the use of technology may facilitate all kinds of practices, some of which may have nothing to do with the design intentions of that technology. However, it is nonetheless evident that certain forms of software are designed with particular types of usage in mind, and the undertaking of grounded theory/thematic analysis through the application and exploration of codes is one of the dominant methods.

The removal of context

A related concern within the qualitative analysis community is the idea that CAQDAS packages encourage the analysis of texts by removing sections of data from their wider contexts. As Fielding and Lee have put it, this form of coding analysis 'fragments the text, seeking segments of transcribed speech that can be lifted out of their original context to be compared with other segments similarly obtained' (1998: 47). Through code and retrieve procedures, researchers are able to create lists of data chunks for comparison. While such data is usually indexed to its point of origin and therefore to its context, many software packages are designed to aid the comparison of those *extracts* by, for example, enabling researchers to create files that contain only the extracted segments.

The central concern here is that the removal of context may transform the meaning of a piece of text. As studies of the organization of discourse have shown, people's contributions to conversations are designed very carefully to display understanding of the specific demands of the context in which they are speaking (e.g. Sacks, 1995). To put it another way, the contexts in which people speak are fundamental to the meaning which they are creating. By removing that context from the analysis, researchers remove the resources that would enable them to understand why the speakers said what they did or, perhaps more accurately, 'why they said it *how* they did'.

For example, extract (2) comes from an interview with a postgraduate pharmacist working in a shop as part of a project to evaluate the effectiveness of university training for pharmacy practice. One aspect of this training involved undertaking a practical project. In this extract, the researcher asks the interviewee whether they found this a useful aspect of their work. The response 'what do you think?' in the fourth conversational turn may be taken as a heavily sarcastic remark, indicating a negative experience. However, the response is related to an earlier part of the conversation where the researcher and interviewer had been talking about the practice of doing research and working individually. The respondent had been saying how difficult they found self-motivated study to be and the researcher's question in the extract 'and did you find doing the project useful or enjoyable?' (the third conversational turn) contains a sarcastic intonation that references this earlier discussion. By removing this extract from this broader context, it is easy to interpret the response in a very negative way, but the negativity is directed towards something quite specific that would be missing if the extract were decontextualized. One of the problems of CAQDAS 'code and retrieve' approaches is that they may encourage an insensitivity to the ways in which sections of talk are very often dependent for their sense on a much broader context.

(2) Postgraduate pharmacy interviews

RESEARCHER:	Ok, great. What did you do your fourth year project on?
RESPONDENT:	Let's get this right now because they were both research based. My fourth year project was about predicting in vivo interactions due to sips using in vitro analysis.
RESEARCHER:	And did you find doing the project useful or enjoyable?
RESPONDENT:	What do you think? The actual, the theory of it, knowing which drug, I mean because I only did sip to … gosh I nearly forgot then and the hours I spent on that, to … so there are certain drugs now that I know off the top of my head so that can be useful…

This caution regarding the potential danger of what is a very useful software function is important. Many postgraduate students have reported to us in our teaching sessions that the ability to extract examples of data under a given code quickly is one of the most useful features of CAQDAS software. While we share the enthusiasm for the potential time saving this may bring to managing data, it is important to work with these extracts in relation to the contexts in which they were produced, and in relation to other forms of analysis that may be undertaken.

Automated coding

Many CAQDAS packages provide mechanisms for automating the coding process. One of the most common of these is through the use of 'search and code' tools. One example of this is in Atlas.ti, where researchers can search the data to find out how different codes may relate to each other. A researcher may be interested in finding out the relationship between two codes (e.g. if the codes have been frequently applied to the same piece of text, or if they are never applied together). Through such queries, researchers can begin to build theories by exploring the structure of the coding of their data. In Atlas.ti, researchers can use Boolean search terms to examine such relationships. They may, for example, construct a search of their coding that looks for all the instances in which three separate codes have been applied to the same piece of data. They can then create a new code that the computer program automatically applies to these sections of the text.

Undoubtedly, this is a useful and time-saving mechanism that enables researchers to search very large amounts of data extremely quickly, and to easily perform coding operations. However, one of the concerns that has animated the qualitative research community is that such automated coding can remove the researcher from the interpretive process (e.g. see Roberts and Wilson, 2002). This echoes some of the concerns around the removal of context that we explored earlier. The specific point here, though, is that the software itself applies the codes to a range of instances that fit the specified criteria. As the allocation of a code to a part of the data can rarely be adequately codified in this way, the use of automated coding operations must come with a health warning and a reminder to pay attention to the details of the data and not to allow computers to tempt researchers away from the careful scrutiny of data.

Concluding remarks

Computers have impacted profoundly on almost every aspect of working with qualitative data, from the collection of information in libraries to the process of writing and publishing research reports. It is, of course, to be expected that there would be a similarly dramatic impact on the ways in which researchers use computers to manage, work with and analyze data. In qualitative research, the increasing range of software that is dedicated to the analysis of data, and the variety of resources available to help researchers to organize, categorize, share, present, represent, integrate and write about their data, has fundamentally changed the landscape of professional work for qualitative researchers. While the excitement this has generated within the community is entirely understandable and to be encouraged, there is value, we suggest, in paying attention to the sceptics too. The value is in helping to encourage methodological reflection, and to help keep one's focus on the specifics of one's interests, rather than get carried away by the potential of a given technology.

Websites for prominent CAQDAS programs
Atlas.ti – http://www.atlasti.com/
NVivo – http://www.qsrinternational.com/products_nvivo.aspx
HyperRESEARCH – http://www.researchware.com/hr/index.html
Qualrus – http://www.ideaworks.com/qualrus/index.html
MAXQDA – http://www.maxqda.com/
CHILDES – http://childes.psy.cmu.edu/

Online resources

http://caqdas.soc.surrey.ac.uk/ – A research and teaching unit based at the University of Surrey, UK, that runs courses, collects and disseminates resources, and conducts research on CAQDAS.

http://onlineqda.hud.ac.uk/Intro_CAQDAS/ – A set of online resources on using and comparing CAQDAS that was developed with funding from the UK's Economic and Social Research Council.

Recommended further reading

Lewins, A. and Silver, C. (2007) *Using Software in Qualitative Data Analysis: A Step-by-Step Guide*. London: Sage. A clear and accessible guide to CAQDAS.

Dicks, B., Mason, B. and Coffey, A.J. (2005) *Qualitative Research and Hypermedia: Ethnography for the Digital Age*. London: Sage. A fascinating account of the implications of digital technology for qualitative research practice.

12

Writing and presenting analysis

This chapter discusses the following issues

- Writing as analysis
- Research diaries
- Modes of presentation

Introduction

The aim of this chapter is to reflect on the ways in which writing and other forms of presentation can play a part in the process of working with qualitative data as well as acting as forms of dissemination of the outcomes of this process. It is common for people to talk about 'writing up' their research as if the process of writing is a neutral form of representing a completed process of analysis. While it is clearly essential to draw a line under the process of analyzing data at some point and to move on to represent the outcomes both in the form of text (a thesis or a journal article, for instance) and presentations (say, at a conference or seminar), it would be wrong to see writing and presentation as just a means of representation. During the process of analysis, writing can act as a way of exploring alternative interpretations, or of externalizing, formalizing and reflecting on emerging relationships or themes. This writing need not necessarily be solely in the form of words, but can also include or comprise diagrams or other kinds of image. In this way writing plays an active part in the process of organizing, working with and analyzing data. Likewise, presenting one's research to an audience can also play a formative part in the development of the research, both through the process of organizing the work into a clearly communicable form and through response to the feedback received from the audience.

Once the analysis is seen to be complete, writing and presentation continue to play an active role in the research. The process of presenting the outcomes of the research can lead to a researcher seeing these outcomes in a different light, can bring certain aspects to the fore or can draw attention to inconsistencies hitherto unnoticed. The process of presenting research can thus lead to new challenges, not least in making the research accessible to a variety of audiences. As with all other phases of the research process, this is an active and analytic process. 'Writing up' the research thus becomes so much more then mere representation. The account that is produced is more than a 'natural history' of the research or a statement of outcomes; it is a creative part of the overall project of doing research.

Presenting analysis

In our experience, presentations – be they written or spoken – usually offer some opportunities to think through one's analysis rather than to simply rehearse it. Where they involve active engagement with an audience, presentations can give researchers insights into their data from new perspectives. The opening up of analysis to others can be a rather uncomfortable experience, but the process of gaining insights from other points of view is nearly always analytically enriching.

The effective presentation of analysis is a very challenging enterprise for researchers. Whether in the context of a verbal conference presentation, a poster presentation, a written project report, a journal article, or an academic thesis, the creation of a coherent and persuasive story of analysis is an extremely difficult task. There are several reasons why this is the case:

- Researchers often deal with huge amounts of data and very complex analyses, and need to find ways to communicate that complexity effectively
- Analysis is a very personal act, to the extent that revealing one's data and analysis of it can feel like a rather intimate and exposing process
- Analysis can be highly theoretical, and involve explaining quite complex and detailed theoretical ideas. Talking about analysis potentially involves discussing every aspect of research (from question formulation to data gathering) and is therefore topically expansive.

In spite of these difficulties, though, the benefits of a disciplined and clear presentation of analysis, and the engagement by outsiders with the analysis are tangible. Through presentations, researchers are forced to pare down their analysis to a simple (although not *simplistic*) and *digestible* form. The experience of communicating with others necessitates clarity if the communication is to be successful. Clear communication requires, and often creates, clarity of thought. Being forced to present analysis frequently results in a clearer sense of one's ideas. Because of this, presentation should in no way be regarded as 'an optional extra' or 'an afterthought', but should simply be part of the process of doing research. In this chapter we discuss some basic principles and conventions that can be followed to make this process as profitable as possible.

Writing

The phrase 'writing up' is often used to refer to a stage 'post'-analysis in which researchers put their analysis on paper. However, we have yet to see an example of qualitative research in which this characterization accurately reflects the practice. 'Writing up' is nearly always intimately tied to the process of *doing* that analysis. Writing, more generally defined, is a means of thinking through one's ideas, of trying to set different formulations into a workable form that does justice to one's data work. Writing is a very personal matter, and every author has idiosyncrasies in terms of how they undertake the process. In this chapter, we are interested in exploring some of the issues that researchers face in working through analysis in the context of writing and other presentational forms.

The entire process of data analysis involves the production of writing: transcriptions, data notes, coding structures, concept maps and definitions, fieldnotes, interview sheets, data log books. All of these sources are written forms that constitute a part of the analysis process and which are likely to have some form of representation in the final written research. Writing up, then, can be characterized as a process of weaving existing writing together, of interlacing the various pieces of the analytic tapestry into place. But that process of stitching together is itself a creative one, where researchers try to find the right way of aligning these various ideas and shape and reshape those original pieces so that they conceptually marry and create a neat and coherent narrative.

Analysis is not analysis until it is written down

While it does perhaps unfairly privilege the written form over other modes of thought, there is something very focusing about the idea that only written work counts as 'analysis'. The process of putting something on paper and trying to logically connect or spell out ideas is very revealing, as misunderstandings and lack of clarity quickly show through. Writing is a means to thought, a way of crystallizing vague conceptions or of exploring ideas through the production and connection of otherwise loosely formulated notions. Writing qualitative analysis often involves working through concepts, rather than simply reporting on things that have been thought through and concluded. Even if some parts of an analytic framework have been well formulated and constructed, the process of writing about those ideas may well result in a development or alteration of them. Because writing has this character, it should not be regarded as something that researchers do at the end of their research, but should rather be treated as an integral feature of the ways in which researchers work.

Two ways of helping to develop clarity in one's analysis is to keep research diaries and to involve other people in the analysis.

Research diaries

Research diaries are a very useful way of helping to maintain a log of one's thoughts and analytic insights, and of both rehearsing and developing those ideas. Research diaries work in much the same way as ordinary diaries as they are organized by date and time. Some researchers like to organize their diaries thematically, with separate sections for different topical features, but this kind of organization can quickly become quite complicated. Using research diaries means that researchers become very familiar and comfortable with the process of writing, which helps both to increase the fluency of their writing and to create tangible written resources that can be used for more formal writing.

Research diaries give researchers the opportunity to connect different parts of their analytic work. To give some examples, researchers may use diaries to:

- *work out* how new concepts that are developing in the research relate to similar or contrasting concepts used in the literature
- *work through* the ways in which their research questions and focus is developing as data is produced
- *reflect on* the practices of data gathering and the issues that the strategies used may have on the data that is generated through those research interventions
- *think through* the relationship between epistemological orientations and more specific theoretical/analytic conceptions
- *make a note* of other possible lines of enquiry or potential topics for future projects arising from the research.

The research diary, then, is a basic **reflexive resource** *that helps researchers to think and work through the many issues that are encountered in research*. Research diaries are distinct from other written research documents, such as fieldnotes or interview analysis sheets (see below), as they are not restricted in their functional purpose. While they may be used to reflect on the processes of, say, writing fieldnotes, or on the content of particular fieldnotes, diaries should not be regarded as replacing them. Clearly, however, there is a potential overlap in the function and content of diaries and these other writing forms. This does not matter in the slightest as the main function of diaries is to act as a sort of 'thinking space'.

Collaborative writing and critique

Writing is often helped by the input of more than one perspective and critical insight. The inclusion of an editorial process, where other readers are invited to comment on one's work, is a very valuable means of ensuring that the goal of 'clarity' has been reached. Researchers who work as part of a team can make use of their colleagues as readers of their analysis. Of course, research students have supervisors or mentors who usually have some responsibility for reading materials, but they can also use their fellow students in this capacity.

However, outsiders to the research community can also be very valuable critics as the burden of clarity and simplicity of explanation and expression is usually much higher when aiming one's explanations to such people. The exercise of trying to explain research findings, processes and ideas to a layperson can help to minimize the over-reliance on jargon and specialized terminology. While it is inevitable that some specialist language will be used, there is also a danger that an over-reliance on technical terminology can make writing rather inaccessible. Outsiders are a very useful resource for minimizing this as they usually complain heavily when things become too loaded with jargon.

Presenting different forms of analysis

Different analytic genres present researchers with distinctive challenges in representing their analysis. In this section, we provide a brief outline of some of the key features that researchers may need to think about in relation to some of those analytic approaches.

Presenting thematic analysis

One of the difficulties of presenting thematic analysis is that the process involves selecting, from probably a large data set, key forms of and extracts from data to represent their analysis. The challenge that researchers face is in describing complex theoretical and conceptual relationships and in displaying how they relate to a large data set, in a very short amount of space. Typically, this works through **exemplification**, by showing the *type* of data that relates to a particular concept, code or category. As we noted in Chapter 11, online and hypertextual modes of publication may change this, as researchers may be able to place links in their data analysis to parts of the data contained in separate files. In conventional print publication formats, though, the issue remains a significant one.

Choosing the examples to use is to some extent arbitrary since the categories being represented can, by definition, be outlined with any of the data pertaining to that category. However, it is also often the case that some data is more 'vivid' or 'clear' than other data sections. One interviewee might be slightly more eloquent on a particular point than another, or give a particularly arresting example that highlights a concept or idea well. It is perfectly appropriate to select the data for the processes of exemplification on these rather 'unscientific' principles – i.e. on their aesthetic character – so long as they do conform to the principles being represented.

While the nature of the analysis and the way it was conducted will be the key referent in considering how to present the analysis, there are some commonly used approaches to organizing thematic work:

Structuring analysis around particular concepts – Researchers can use key themes within their analysis as a structural resource to help them 'tell the story' of their data. The analytic concepts may form section titles within a data discussion that are addressed independently of each other. For example, Darren Thiel's (2007) study of social class in the building sector in London involved using issues such as 'management and autonomy', 'physical culture' and 'hierarchical discourse' as thematic issues. Thiel's analysis is interesting because the dividing line between the discussion and the presentation of data and published discourse is blurred, with data used to corroborate or contrast with ideas presented in the literature. This is, however, a characteristic of the journal in which Thiel published his work. Many research publications require a much firmer divide between published discourse and data, with distinctive sections for each.

Analysis and cases – A 'case', in this instance, is a unit of study, such as an individual interviewee, a site of investigation, or a participatory research institution. Researchers may organize their analysis around these 'sites', comparing the findings, characteristics or analytic relevancies of the different cases they examine. They may, for example, compare the way in which different interviewees or different focus groups responded to or interpreted different issues. Equally, they may look at each case in turn, and *then* compare their discussion of the individuals. Both of these forms of organization can be particularly useful for creating clear contrasts between different positions and for teasing out the relevance of differences and similarities.

Organizing analysis around particular research questions – A very clear way to relate analysis to one's research questions is to use the questions themselves as the organizing principle of the analysis. Researchers may have their questions as particular subsections within the data analysis part of their report, and organize the data around answering those questions. This form of organization helps to create a very clear narrative as it is easy to map analysis on to research questions.

There are also examples of researchers choosing to organize their work around the questions that they asked in an interview, presenting and organizing their data in relation to the particular thematic issues dealt with in the interview questions. Normally, however, researchers are interested in gaining a level of analysis that goes beyond the actual questions they asked, and in exploring the underlying theoretical or conceptual issues to which those questions relate. It is important to keep in mind that the form of organization of material developed for the purposes of collecting and analyzing data may not be the most appropriate form in which to present the outcomes of the research. For instance, Trevor Walker (2007) organized the collection of his data, on the experiences of headteachers who were leading schools through a period of 'special measures' following school inspection, as six case studies. His initial presentation of the data analysis was a detailed description of each of the six cases, which were presented consecutively. This form of presentation made it difficult for a reader to grasp the key features of his analysis and to appreciate the analytic similarities and differences between the cases. In response to feedback on his work, he revised the text to produce a model of the process of working through stressful organizational change. Material from his case studies could then be used to support and exemplify aspects of his model, thus giving the reader a clearer sense of the analytic outcomes of his research, and how these might be applied to other settings and other phenomena, while also retaining the detail of the particular cases he had explored.

Presenting ethnographic analysis

In ethnographic work, data are often used to inform the production of narrative stories rather than as a form of 'evidence', as in thematic work. In such formats, the data are a resource for constructing a narrative in relation to the particular analytic issues, and are often used more sparingly in the actual text than in other genres. Ethnographic data are often quite varied, consisting of interviews, observation notes and pictures, but not all forms of data will necessarily appear on the written analysis. A striking example of this genre comes from Eva Bendix Peterson's (2007) short fictional story that depicts the working day of academics in a social science laboratory. The author uses her data and analysis to inform the development of what she describes as a 'plausible' account of a fictional day in the life of an academic. The data are entirely absent from the account.

This chronological storytelling narrative is also used in more conventional and straightforwardly empirical works. Sometimes authors use snippets of data narrative, such as short story narratives that are organized thematically, as in Matthew Desmond's (2006) ethnography of firefighting in the US forestry service. Desmond's account looks at the way that firefighters construct their own professional identity, and how they learn the practices, attitudes and identity characteristics of the trade. Desmond's analysis is based around certain analytic problems, including 'Why and how firefighters become involved in forestry firefighting?' and 'How firefighters learn to do what they do?', and he uses the intersection of theoretical concepts and ethnographic narratives as a resource for addressing these questions.

Images can play a particularly useful tool for ethnographic work as they can help to create a richer impression of the empirical domain being examined. Photographs, maps and drawings can all add to the sense of the place and the people in the study. See Chapter 5 for more detailed discussion of these issues.

Presenting discourse analysis

As we have said, the term 'discourse analysis' is extremely general and describes a wide range of analytic approaches. In this section, we use the term to distinguish the analysis of sections of focused transcript as opposed to forms of thematic analysis. Like thematic analysis, discourse analysis is typically selective in the data that it presents in accounts of the research, using particular sections of data to exemplify specific points. The sections of transcripts that are shown in the final data write-up may be simplified forms of the ones used in the actual analysis. Very detailed focused transcripts can be difficult to read for those not closely involved in the analysis, so it may be necessary to reduce some of the unnecessary complexity in the transcribed examples once the analysis has been completed.

In their written analysis researchers will typically refer to their transcripts by using the line numbers or symbols in the transcript as markers to point to particular features of the discourse. As the aim of discourse analysis is, loosely, to interrogate the minutiae of constructed meaning (although the specific aims of the analysis depend on the particular strategies being used), the analysis will normally work through the transcript line by line, and show the conceptual relevance of particular features of the discourse. The analysis of a very small amount of data can therefore generate a significant amount of written text, and it is very difficult indeed to fit such analysis into the constraints of short presentation formats, such as journal articles. This is particularly the case where researchers have multiple examples of the same phenomenon that they wish to reference. Usually, examples need to be used sparingly and are often selected with some of the rather imprecise criteria used in thematic analysis (see above).

Modes of presenting analysis

In addition to the specific issues faced by particular genres of analysis, different contexts for presentation also offer particular challenges and opportunities for researchers. In what follows, we undertake a brief review of some of the more common forms of presentation. There are, though, some key features of the presentation of qualitative analysis that are common to all modes. We have identified four that we feel are particularly important.

The reasons for the analysis – Why was the analysis undertaken? What questions was the analysis directed towards addressing? Why are these questions important?

The process of the analysis – How did the analysis occur? Were particular analytic perspectives or methods used? Did the focus of the analysis change? What procedures were used in the analysis? What problems were posed and how were they resolved or dealt with? Which apriori concepts were used in the analysis? How do the uses of those concepts differ from other published uses of those concepts?

The analysis itself – What are the key 'findings' of the analysis? What analytic claims, distinctions, categories, concepts are used? How are they defined/constituted? What do they show? Which data best represent them? How does the data relate to other data that are not included? How do the analytic concepts help to make sense of the data? What concepts emerged from the data?

The implications of analysis – How does the analysis relate to the questions being asked? Does the analysis answer the question? If so, how? How does the analysis contribute to existing understandings? How does it compare with other approaches to the same topic? What questions emerge from the analysis and how might they be taken forward by further research?

These four structural features are useful referents when thinking about the presentation of analysis. In some forms of presentation (e.g. Master's dissertations or PhD theses), a researcher will need to cover all of these in some detail. In others (e.g. professional reports or academic articles), they may need to cover them all, but with some sections being dealt with more briefly than others. For example, the *process* of analysis is typically far less important in professional reports than the findings and implications of the analysis. In other contexts, the researcher may focus on just one or two of these, as in conference presentations, where the time available to describe the detail of the research is limited.

Conferences

Because they are usually themed and topically focused, conferences offer great opportunities to discuss one's research with colleagues whose interests typically lie more or less in the same area. While there are exceptions to the rule, in most cases conferences are supportive environments. People are usually there to hear something interesting and to engage actively with other people's work, so there can be some very good opportunities for discussion with a genuinely interested and informed audience. Such interest is most effectively kindled by presenting analysis in accessible ways. There are some important rules of thumb that can help to make sure that the presentation is effective.

Keep to time – Even the most experienced presenters can overrun (and overrunning is far more common that underrunning). The way to avoid this is to *rehearse*. Practising the presentation, recording it, and listening back can help to make sure that it runs to time. Marking structural points on the presentation can also help to ensure that the time is appropriately managed and the delivery is well paced.

Have no more than three key points that you want to make – In most conferences, the members of the audience will listen to many speakers, so the more direct and coherent the presentation, the better. Audience members are not typically interested in getting into the details of a presenter's analysis, but usually want simply to hear about some of the key features of their project. Keeping the number of key points down to three helps both the presenter and the audience to focus on a manageable number of issues.

Pitch the presentation of your ideas to their expectations and knowledge level – If the audience are experts in the field being discussed, it is appropriate to make some assumptions about their level of knowledge and skip some of the basic details, like providing definitions of foundational concepts that would be common knowledge to those working in the area. If the audience is made up of 'outsiders', however, it may be necessary to be much more basic in the explanations that are given. The form and content of the entire presentation and the nature of the particular messages to be given need to be based on an analysis of the audience's background, needs and interests.

Importantly, the presentation and the discussion that it does (or does not) generate are not the 'be all and end all' of conferences. Far more interesting discussion often occurs over coffee or lunch, where there is more opportunity for focused discussion with people who you have identified, or who have identified you, as having shared interests or perspectives. Further, it is not only the presentation of one's own research that is of value. Hearing, listening to and engaging with other people's research is also useful for sparking one's own ideas and for self-reflection. While it is not always easy, the more communal one can be in research, the better. This is particularly true of analysis, which is, ironically, often one of the most insular parts of the research process. Seeing what other people do in the course of their analysis (which is best achieved by *talking to people about it*) is one of the best ways to learn about it, and getting other people's insights on a 'live' research project is invaluable.

Journal articles

One of the main difficulties for qualitative researchers in presenting their data and their analysis in journal articles is the tightness of the space they have available to elaborate their arguments and ideas. Once the abstract, introduction, literature review and methodology are written – all of which are, of course, fundamental to setting up and contextualizing the analysis – there are very few words available for discussing the actual process of the analysis. This is particularly frustrating as the data can itself take up significant space. Researchers can try to minimize the impact of extracts from the data on the word count of an article by placing data in an appendix section or in textboxes, rather than as text. All journals have their own guidelines about such practices, however, and it is important to conform to these when preparing a manuscript.

Some journals specialize in publishing particular *types* of analysis, e.g. discourse analysis, multimodal analysis, thematic analysis or ethnographic work. As such, they may have particular conventions on transcription or modes of discussing data (e.g. using line numbers to refer to particular sections) that are worth using when writing up the analysis. Other journals are more eclectic, and will publish work from a variety of perspectives or analytic orientations. In such cases, there may well be more scope for presenting work in more creative, varied and less conventional ways.

While the submission of work to journals is ultimately motivated by the desire to have a piece of work published, the actual process of publication can itself be very useful. Most journals use a system of anonymous refereeing, where the identities of the author and the referees selected to comment on the work are not known to each other. Referees are usually chosen because their expertise fits more or less closely with the piece that has been submitted. The review process results in a detailed critique from an insider and is very much a unique opportunity to get nuanced feedback and insight. It can be difficult to remain as detached as this if you receive a scathing review, but it is important to remember that, by definition, such critique is not personal and is an opportunity for development.

Professional reports

Reports to funding bodies or to non-academic and non-research institutions need to take a very different structure from the more detailed reports that are given to members of research communities. Typically, professional reports are much more brief in their descriptions of the technicalities of the processes of research, and do not involve detailed reflection on methodological problems or issues. Reports of this kind are more pragmatic than other forms of writing as they involve 'getting to the heart of the matter' quite quickly and concentrating on the implications of the findings and analysis.

In their report, which was written as part of a study into pharmacy practice, Gibson et al. (2001) organized the presentation of data around the concepts under investigation: namely, the competencies of the pharmacists. The report used selected quotes from interviews with the participants to highlight particular features of the thematic analysis that was conducted. The bulk of the report, however, was concerned with the implications of this analysis, rather than with the analysis itself. The project funders made explicit that they wanted the report to focus on how their analysis may be used rather than on how their analysis was conducted. This approach to report writing is fairly typical and creates distinctive challenges for researchers as it restricts even further the opportunities for discussing the analysis. A good report will link the interests of the stakeholders very clearly with the findings of the analysis.

In many environments, particularly in policy circles, qualitative research is not a commonly used approach to investigation, so readers of reports may not be familiar with conventions of data presentation or with the methodological issues surrounding the genre. Common criticisms are that qualitative analysis is 'impressionistic' or 'subjective'. It can be tempting in such instances to dig out the big 'theoretical guns' and to engage in debate regarding the nature of research practice and knowledge. In our experience, such strategies are rarely good ways to deal with what are, at heart, matters of unfamiliarity. It is far better to concentrate on the effective ordering and presentation of data, and in trying to create as clear a picture as possible for the reader of the analysis that was conducted.

Academic theses

Probably the most freedom that any researcher has to explore and present their analysis in detail is in the context of academic theses. The conventions of theses production nearly always require their authors to outline all four of the analytic areas described above in detail, including the ways in which they actually conducted their analysis. Thus, while the production of a thesis is usually, and understandably, seen as a rather daunting task, the frequently uttered advice 'Enjoy the opportunity' couldn't be more apt – the level of discursive freedom open to researchers in theses, i.e. the extent to which they can describe and reflexively interrogate their analysis, is distinctive to postgraduate work. The research reports, journal papers and even books produced by researchers rarely offer quite the same opportunity for a comprehensive analytic account of the research process.

The way in which the data analysis sections of a thesis are organized is contingent on the nature of the analysis undertaken. Any of the approaches outlined above may be used as strategies to organize data. It is highly advisable to work in close dialogue with one's supervisor or mentor when designing an outline for the presentation of analysis. In all forms of writing associated with qualitative research, the process is very much cyclical, with many drafts being produced before anything approaching a 'final version' is created. As we said at the beginning of this chapter, writing and analysis are so intimately intertwined that, in many respects, the writing *is* the analysis. This can be frustrating for postgraduate researchers who are, very often, as interested in finishing their thesis as they are in conducting the research, but the sooner this basic characteristic of analysis is realized, the easier it is likely to be.

One important strategy for avoiding the high pressure to *write quickly* that so many postgraduate researchers face when producing a thesis is to allow enough time for analysis, and to use this period to actually write about the data. As we suggested earlier, writing has a formative role to play in all stages of the research. Again, this is a very common suggestion that is much harder to realize than it is to state. Precisely because analysis is very much a journey with no defined end point (apart from a rather vague sense of wanting to 'answer the question' or, more nebulously still, 'say something interesting'), it is very difficult to judge how long might be needed to work on a given set of data. While for some researchers deadlines can be more paralyzing than motivating, the restriction of having to finish something by a given time does provide the most tangible end point in qualitative research.

Some simple rules of thumb about analysis and writing

Simple rules of thumb that may be useful when developing a plan for writing and analysis include:

- Think in terms of months, rather than weeks. Analysis *always* takes longer than you think it will.
- Remember that analysis is a *process* and not a *stage*. You need to plan the analysis so that it can actually inform the other aspects of research, such as data collection, design and question formulation. Do not treat data work as beginning *after* data 'collection'; analysis starts as soon as you have something to analyze.
- Your analysis may lead you to want to read some more published research. You may well generate new ideas through the analysis that require further literature research. This can be a lengthy process so build in time for it.
- Assume that you will have some false starts in your analysis. Some of your ideas will lead down blind alleys but you won't know that until you try them out. Create space for these eventualities and don't regard them as 'mistakes' but as simply *part of the process.*
- If you are doing collaborative work, make sure that you have a clear understanding of who is going to do what, and when. Effective collaboration requires effective communication.
- Write and present your work at every stage in the process, both to formulate and develop your ideas and to get feedback, and support, from others.

Concluding remarks

Throughout this chapter we have emphasized that working through analysis in the form of writing is an integral aspect of qualitative work. Because of this, the most successful strategies involve integrating writing into the research process. It can be particularly useful to get regular feedback on writing from colleagues and friends as a means of maintaining a critical development of one's work. Like writing, other forms of presentation, such as conference or seminar papers, should not be regarded simply as a means of dissemination but as opportunities to involve others in the process of analysis. In this way, researchers can move beyond analysis as a solitary process, and gain insights and input from people from broad and diverse fields.

Recommended further reading

Thody, A. (2006) *Writing and Presenting Research*. London: Sage. A thorough and accessible guide to writing and presenting social research.

13 Concluding remarks

This chapter discusses the following issues:

- Analysis as a contextualized practice
- Approaches to data analysis
- Theory and data analysis
- Data work

Introduction

In the introduction to this book we outlined a number of aims that we hoped to achieve. Centrally, we wanted to provide an account of the relationship between data analysis and other components of social research work. Related to this, we suggested that in order to clarify and thoroughly explore the notion of analysis in qualitative work, it would be useful to discuss a range of particular approaches to analysis; to look at some of the more common data forms in qualitative research; and to review some of the key strategies and concerns used to surround them. In these concluding pages we would like to revisit the central arguments that we provided in Chapter 1 and to briefly think about the relationship between them and the topics we have been discussing.

Revisiting 'analysis as situated practice'

Let's just briefly recap our argument:

- We said that researchers often have difficulty in understanding what qualitative data analysis is all about.

- We suggested that a part of the problem here is that it is very difficult to come up with a meaningful definition of qualitative data analysis that covers the very broad range of work that gets done in qualitative approaches.
- One of the reasons why producing definitions is so difficult is that the specific research context and research problem are *constituent aspects* of any given example of analysis.
- Given this, we wondered how we can usefully talk about analysis in a way that has general value to researchers.
- Our answer to this was to suggest that thinking about the relationship between data work and other types of research work may help to *situate* analysis.
- Our definition of 'contextualized analysis' was the ways in which researchers think through the relationship between a research problem and the data needed throughout the research process.

So, the basic idea is quite straightforward: by thinking about the alignment of data and research topic as a feature of social research practice we may be able to see a little more clearly the relationship between data analysis and other types of social research work. In this way, it should be possible to give a little more definition to the roles of analysis and the types of activity that constitute it. Here is a quick overview of what we have said about the relationship between data and research practice:

Research questions and research problems – Empirical research is directed to 'saying something' with data. It is important to put the matter in such vague terms because, as we have seen, the aims of research are many and varied – solving a problem, answering questions, investigating hypotheses, pursuing a general concern, contributing to understanding and developing theory being just a few examples. However the central research issue is formulated, the purpose of empirical research is to generate data in order to 'deal with' that issue. Again, 'deal with' is equally ambiguous as the precise nature of the work that the data will be made to do is also very varied and entirely contextual – e.g. to develop a theory, to contrast cases, to present or evaluate opinions, to display normative practice, to define categories or ideal types, to specify interventions, or to describe contexts. Research problems (or questions, topics, issues, concepts, foci, etc.) are iteratively developed through research. They are figured out through an orientation to literature, the specification of design, the working out of that design in the generation of data, through data work, and through writing. Data analysis is as much directed towards working out the problematic as it is to answering a question. In this respect, data work is about giving definition to the research issues, and to the contribution that the research will provide.

Literature – The role that literature plays in the formulation of a research focus is key. Literature helps to frame research interests in relation to existing knowledge, opinion and forms of work, and to develop concepts and theoretical spaces that are, in turn, used to conceptualize, organize and manipulate data. However, this is not just a one-way orientation, as through data work researchers can feed back on the conceptual turns and resources created through engagement with literature, producing critiques, amendments, alternatives and redirections to them. Further, data work can itself raise questions and issues that require further literary engagement, and open up new theoretical genres that need to be explored.

Research design and research practice – We described research design as the development of a strategy for generating data in order to deal with a particular research concern. In this view, data is the central referent in all considerations of how the research should proceed. We distinguished between *preliminary designs* and *working designs*, with the former referring to the idealized plans to action, and the latter to the process of working through those plans in real contexts. This 'working through' involves reflecting on the emerging data and how it relates to the original plan and the research interests. The implementation of a research design is a key component of data work, in which the researcher manages the generation of appropriate data. When conducting interviews, observing behaviour or examining documents, researchers work by asking the questions 'what is going on here?' and 'why is that relevant/interesting?', and use their responses to these questions to decide how to proceed. This can only be accomplished effectively if the researcher has an active engagement with the actual data. Data work is a component of the working through of a research design and not an afterthought to it, and it has relevance to every aspect of that work, including the formulation of sampling strategies, thinking about appropriate research methods and approaches to implementing them, ethical issues, and so on. Indeed, to speak of 'analysis' away from the context of the generation of data, and the specific issues that are worked through there, is to remove the very problems to which the data is relevant.

So what does this mean for researchers trying to get a better grip on the ways in which they can approach their data work? Well, to restate the point we outlined in Chapter 1, most researchers' concern with qualitative data analysis is not with how to get data, but with what to do with it once they have it. The above arguments show quite clearly that if you already have some data, then your analysis has already begun because you will have been making key decisions about your research interest, your conceptual focus, the types of data you need in order to address it, the appropriateness of your original design and the moves needed to enact or modify it, and so on. So, the question 'what now?' is better phrased as 'how do I continue what I have started?', and conducting some detailed reflection on the research process is a good way to begin answering that question. For researchers who are very much at the beginning of their research, or who are new to qualitative work, what we have said here should illustrate the importance of adopting an analytic attitude throughout the research process, and the payoffs of detailed interrogation of the relationship between data and research problems.

Another component to what we have been trying to achieve in this text is to offer a guide to specific approaches to data analysis and some of the key components of data work. We will deal with each of these in turn.

Approaches to data analysis

In addition to the fact that analysis is always contextually specific, we suggested at the beginning of this book that one of the reasons why researchers new to qualitative analysis find it difficult to understand is because of the broad range of perspectives and approaches in the field. These approaches are diverse in their aims and character, and come from many perspectives and disciplinary orientations. Our aim has been to provide some examples of these approaches in order to demonstrate the ways that they direct enquiry. For example, in Chapter 2 we looked at some of the theoretical aims and conceptual schemas of critical discourse analysis and how they can lead to an interest in a particular kind of data for particular kinds of reasons. In Chapter 6 we saw how narrative analysis emerged from a concern for making sense of the ways in which people presented and constructed accounts. This general concern, and the many variations of its method, also steers researchers in particular directions when thinking about the types of data they might require and how they should organize it.

But this last sentence is key: no matter how well formulated or detailed these various approaches may be, they are, in the end, formulated as general interests and general approaches. If they are to become useful to researchers, they need to be worked through in the particular contexts of their empirical work and in relation to the specific issues or interests that drive that work. Researchers who orientate to one or other defined approach will still have to undertake the kind of situated reflection on their analysis that we have been describing in this book. While they often have 'analysis' in their title, these approaches do not offer a ready-made way of working through data. At best, they provide some theoretical commitments and specializations that can be used to think through a research design and the particular context of analysis to which it relates. They do not *constitute* analysis; they are one component of the 'working through' of a particular problem in relation to data. It is not necessary for researchers to orientate themselves to one or other of these domains of work in order for them to be seen as doing qualitative data analysis. This is not in any sense intended to be disparaging about such specialized approaches, but is merely an attempt to try to characterize their role in the process of analyzing data.

One of the things that researchers often say they are looking for in approaches to analysis is *theory*. Given the fact that it is so often such an important concern, it is perhaps useful in these concluding pages to specifically address the relationship between theory and data analysis.

Analysis and theory

As we stated in the introduction, not all research involves the explicit use or production of theory, and the relevance of theory is very much dependent on the context within which one is operating. Some research work is directed to what are often described as 'pragmatic' concerns, and explicit theory is often regarded as unnecessary in these contexts. Where theoretical resources are used – or perhaps, where they are *appropriate* – the conceptual development that they offer does usually give rise to a more coherent, interesting and nuanced analysis.

Theory can be both a *resource for* and a *product of* analysis. All research is situated in the context of existing research and other literature, and in all but the most 'puritanical' form of grounded theory, ideas and concepts drawn from this work exert some influence on the research in all its phases. The 'orientation' to existing conceptual frameworks or theories can be explicit (which would be our preference, in order to make the processes of research and analysis as transparent and accessible to the reader as possible) or implicit (which carries the risk that decisions made in the research are guided by the invisible hand of unstated assumptions, or that a number of inconsistent ideas or concepts are at work behind the scenes, leading to incoherence). 'Orientation' can involve a number of things, of course:

- Testing theoretical concepts
- Applying or adapting existing theory to the examination of new empirical domains
- Critiquing established theoretical positions
- Creating alternative conceptual resources
- Developing additions to particular theories
- Clearing a space for a contribution

...and even, in the case of the more 'pragmatic' genres we eluded to...

- Ignoring theory all together (because this is an orientation too).

While some might argue that theory is not necessary, or that it can act as a distraction from or bias to the open and creative process of analysis, we would wish to signal the potential of an engagement with or an orientation to theory in helping data to speak and assisting the researcher in producing a coherent analysis.

Every discipline has its exalted analysis – the products of its esteemed practitioners that are held up as paradigmatic exemplars of theory work. Where researchers operate in a defined and bounded discipline, they are likely to use, in one way or another, the theories and concepts from that discipline. Where researchers do not see themselves as occupying a particular disciplinary space, it can be much harder to find a way into the discourses of social theory.

In this book, where we have spoken about theory we have done so in relation to general perspectives, to more specific positions, to individual authors, and to particular concepts. This shows that there really is nothing defined about the ways that people refer to or orientate to theory in social research or in terms of their uses of it in the analysis of data. The point we would emphasize, of course, is that the *uses* of theory are worked out in context. Just as a general approach to analysis must be worked through in relation to a particular problem, so any theoretical or conceptual components needs be given specification through the detailed consideration of data and problem in the ways we have been describing.

Components of data work

Ultimately, of course, when researchers end up with data, they have to do something with it, and we have dealt with some of the key components of the work that gets done with data. There are some very complicated and far from obvious issues here, and we certainly hope that these discussions have provided some practical help in giving people tangible ideas about how they may approach these aspects of data work:

how they might produce a transcript, use a computer program, think about different forms of data like audio-visual or photographic modes; or simply *how they might write*. In the end, though, such discussions and considerations are always contextualized – worked through in relation to this or that problem or empirical context.

Transcription – Our discussion of transcription drew attention to the fact that transcription is a key component of analysis and by no means just a precursor to it, which is how it is often regarded. Through transcripts, researchers are able to give sense to their data, to focus on particular issues or data features rather than others, to analytically filter their data, to impose and explore structures. In this respect, while there are technical issues related to transcription, there is, in the end, nothing technical about the aims of transcription.

Image, text and audio/video data – Different data forms have different 'affordances' – distinctive ways of helping researchers to achieve particular ends. We looked at the ways that all of these types of data can be used in research, and at some of the forms of work that they are often implicated in. Our discussions of these matters were centred around conceptual issues by showing how semiotic forms of analysis may be used to examine photographs, and how conversation analysis may be used to produce and explore detailed transcriptions of audio and video data forms. The purpose of this was not to suggest that researchers should necessarily use these approaches when examining such data, but to show that data work is always centred around motivated concerns, and that these motivations will drive the relevance of a given data form as well as decisions about how it is to be organized and used.

Computers – Computers are fantastically useful tools to help researchers to organize, store, explore and share their data. There is no doubt that computer programs have taken much of the mundane labour out of qualitative data work, and that in many forms of qualitative work there are real payoffs for using them. It is increasingly common to associate computer programs like NVivo or Atlas.ti with qualitative data analysis, and to assume that computers are a necessary component of data work. But the relevance or otherwise of a given program depends entirely on the type of work being undertaken. Figuring out whether or not there is a role for computers and, if so, what role that might be, is a part of working through the now familiar issue of 'the relationship between data and problem'.

Writing and presenting – We have discussed a range of ways in which researchers write as a feature of their data work, about the value of writing in thinking through problems, and the various textual forms that researchers produce and use as a routine feature of their work. We described the ways in which different presentation forms, such as conferences, articles, theses, and so on, offer opportunities to open up analysis to others – to make analysis collaborative or at least publically available for input. There are practical issues in all of these features, but none of them is an exclusively pragmatic concern.

The nexus of data and topic

This book has been directed towards demonstrating and exploring the relationship between qualitative data analysis and the other features of social research practice. The purpose has been to show in detail the ways in which data analysis both comes from and impacts on these other aspects of work. Our hope is that this may have helped to give definition to this very fuzzy term 'qualitative data analysis', or at least to show why it is fuzzy and to stop that being a cause for concern. We hope to have shown, too, that while there are procedures within analytic work, data analysis is not a procedural issue; it is a conceptual and contextual one that involves working through the puzzle of 'the nexus of data and topic'. The exploration of this nexus is implicated in every aspect of research work and researchers therefore live their analysis throughout their research project. Once 'finished' a researcher's analysis is not *static*. Most research projects are finite, and they need to result in something concrete, like a research report, a thesis, an answer to a question, or a set of recommendations. But these 'end points' are other people's beginnings: the things that we produce through research go into the bank of resources that form key reference points for new research and new analyses. Analysis has a life beyond the confines of a given research project and may take on new forms as it is reapplied and recontextualized by other researchers dealing with other issues. The products of research are also the seeds of new research ideas, and the continual development of analysis through distinct research frames is what makes social research such an exciting and vibrant enterprise.

References

Adler, P.A. and Adler, P. (1987) *Membership Roles in Field Research*. London: Sage.

Alford, R.A. (1998) *The Craft of Inquiry: Theories, Methods, Evidence*. Oxford: Oxford University Press.

Anderson, R.E. (1989) 'Computing in sociology: promise and practice'. *Social Science Computer Review* 7(4): 487–502.

Barthes, R. (1993) *Mythologies*. London: Vintage.

Becker, H. (1974) 'Art as collective action'. *American Sociological Review* 39: 767–77.

Becker, H. (1984a) 'Fieldwork with the computer'. *Qualitative Sociology* 7: 16–33.

Becker, H. (1984b) 'Becoming a Marihuana User', *The American Journal of Sociology* 59(3): 235–42.

Becker, H. (1998) *Tricks of the Trade: How to Think about Your Research while You're Doing It*. Chicago: University of Chicago Press.

Becker, H. (2000) 'The etiquette of improvisation'. *Mind, Culture and Activity* 7: 171–6.

Becker, H. (2002) 'Visual evidence: a seventh man, the specified generalization, and the work of the reader'. *Visual Studies* 17: 3–11.

Becker, H., Geer, B., Hughes, E.C., Elliot, H. and Strauss, A. (1977) *Boys in White: Student Culture in Medical School*. New Brunswick, NJ: Transaction.

Belcher, D. and Braine, G. (1995) *Academic Writing in a Second Language: Essays on Research and Pedagogy*. Norwood, NJ: Ablex.

Berelson, B. (1952) *Content Analysis in Communication Research*. Glencoe, IL: Free Press.

Berg, A.M. and Eikeland, O. (2008) *Labor, Education and Society: Action Research and Organization Theory*. Frankfurt: Peter Lang.

Berliner, P. (1994) *Thinking in Jazz: The Infinite Art of Improvisation*. Chicago: University of Chicago Press.

Bitner, E. (1973) 'Objectivity and realism in sociology', in G. Psathas (ed.), *Phenomenological Sociology: Issues and Applications*. London: John Wiley & Sons Ltd.

Bitner, E. (1983) 'Realism in field research', in R.E. Emerson (ed.), *Contemporary Field Research: A Collection of Readings*. Boston: Little, Brown & Co.

Bloom, L. (1996) '"I write for myself and strangers": private diaries as public documents', in S.L. Bunkers and C.A. Huff (eds), *Inscribing the Daily: Critical Essays on Women's Diaries*. Boston, MA: University of Massachusetts Press.

Bloor, M.J. (1983) 'Notes on member validation', in R.E. Emerson (ed.), *Contemporary Field Research: A Collection of Readings*. Boston: Little, Brown & Co.

Blumer, H. (1969) *Symbolic Interactionism: Perspective and Method*. Englewood Cliffs, NJ: Prentice-Hall.

Boyatzis, R.E. (2008) *Transforming Qualitative Information: Thematic Analysis and Code Development*. Thousand Oaks, CA: Sage.

Brent, E. (1984) 'Qualitative computing: approaches and issues'. *Qualitative Sociology* 7: 34–60.

Brown, A. (1999) 'Parental participation, position and pedagogy: a sociological study of the IMPACT primary school mathematics project'. *Collected Original Resources in Education* 24(3)/A02–11/CO9.

Brown, A. and Dowling, P. (1998) *Doing Research/Reading Research: A Mode of Interrogation for Education*. London: Routledge/Falmer.

Brown, T. and England, J. (2004) 'Revisiting emancipatory teacher research: a psychoanalytic perspective'. *British Journal of Sociology of Education*, 25(1): 67–73.

Bucholtz, M. (2000) 'The politics of transcription'. *Journal of Pragmatics* 32: 1439–65.

Burke, C. and Ribeiro de Castro, H. (2007) 'The school photograph: portraiture and the art of assembling the body of the school child'. *History of Education* 36(2): 213–26.

Button, G. and Casey, N. (1984) 'Generating topic: the use of topic initiation elicitors', in M. Atkinson (ed.), *Structures of Social Action*. Cambridge: Cambridge University Press.

Charmaz, K. (2000) 'Grounded theory: objectivist and constructivist methods', in N.K. Denzin and Y.S. Lincoln (eds) *Handbook of Qualitative Research*. Thousand Oaks, CA: Sage.

Charmaz, K. (2006) *Constructing Grounded Theory: A Practical Guide through Qualitative Analysis*. London: Sage.

Cleaves, A. (2003) 'Forming post-compulsory subject choices in school: a longitudinal study of changes in secondary school students' ideas, with particular reference to choice about science', unpublished PhD thesis, Institute of Education, University of London.

Cleaves, A. (2005) 'The formation of science choices in secondary school'. *International Journal of Science Education* 27(4): 471–86.

Clifford, J. and Marcus, W. (1986) *Writing Culture: The Poetics and Politics of Ethnography*. Berkeley, CA: University of California Press.

Coffey, A., Holbrook, B. and Atkinson, P. (1996) 'Qualitative data analysis: technologies and representations'. *Sociological Research Online* 1.

Cresswell, J. (2007) *Qualitative Inquiry and Research Design: Choosing among Five Approaches*. London: Sage.

Cruickshank, J. (2003) *Realism and Sociology: Anti-foundationalism, Ontology and Social Research*. London: Routledge.

Cuff, E.C., Sharrock, W.W. and Francis, D. (1990) *Perspectives in Sociology* (3rd edn). London: Unwin Hyman.

Davies, B., Browne, J., Gannon, S., Honan, E., Laws, C., Mueller-Rockstroh, B. and Petersen, E.B. (2004) 'The ambivalent practices of reflexivity'. *Qualitative Inquiry* 10: 360–89.

Denzin, N. (1989) *The Research Act: A Theoretical Introduction to Sociological Method*. Englewood Cliffs, NJ: Prentice-Hall.

Desmond, M. (2006) 'Becoming a firefighter'. *Ethnography* 7: 387–421.

DeWalt, K.M. and DeWalt, B.R. (2001) *Participant Observation: A Guide for Fieldworkers*. Palo Alto, CA: AltaMira Press.

Dicks, B. and Mason, B. (1998) 'Hypermedia and ethnography: reflections on the construction of a research approach'. *Sociological Research Online* 3.

Dicks, B., Mason, B. and Coffey, A.J. (2005) *Qualitative Research and Hypermedia: Ethnography for the Digital Age*. London: Sage.

Dicks, B., Soyinka, B. and Coffey, A. (2006) 'Multimodal ethnography'. *Qualitative Research* 6: 77–96.

Dixon-Woods, M., Bonas, S., Booth, A., Jones, D.R., Miller, T., Sutton, A.J., Shaw, R.L., Smith, J.A. and Young, B. (2006) 'How can systematic reviews incorporate qualitative research? A critical perspective'. *Qualitative Research* 6: 27–44.

Dressler, R. and Kreuz, R. (2000) 'Transcribing oral discourse: a survey and a model system'. *Discourse Processes* 29: 25–36.

Elliot, H. (1997) 'The use of diaries in sociological research on health experience'. *Sociological Research Online* 2.

Elliot, J. (1991) *Action Research for Educational Change*. Milton Keynes: Open University Press.

Emerson, R.E. (ed.) (1983) *Contemporary Field Research: A Collection of Readings*. Boston: Little, Brown & Co.

Emerson, P. and Frosh, S. (2004) *Critical Narrative Analysis in Psychology: A Guide to Practice*. New York: Palgrave Macmillan.

Fairclough, N. (1995) *Critical Discourse Analysis: The Critical Study of Language*. London: Longman.

Fielding, N. (2003) *Interviewing*. London: Sage.

Fielding, N. and Lee, R.M. (1995) 'The Hypertext facility in qualitative analysis software'. *ESRC Data Archive Bulletin*. Available online at http://caqdas.soc.surrey.ac.uk/fieldinglee hypertext.pdf

Fielding, N. and Lee, R.M. (1998) *Computer Analysis and Qualitative Research*. London: Sage.

Fish, S. (1978) 'Normal circumstances, literal language, direct speech acts, the ordinary, the everyday, the obvious, what goes without saying, and other special cases', *Critical Inquiry* 4(4): 625–44.

Flick, U. (2004) 'Design and process in qualitative research', in U. Flick, E. von Kardorff and I. Steinke (eds), *A Companion to Qualitative Research*. London: Sage.

Flick, U., von Kardorff, E. and Steinke, I. (eds) (2004) *A Companion to Qualitative Research*. London: Sage.

Frake, C. (1964) 'Notes on queries in ethnography'. *American Anthropologist* 66: 132–45.

Garfinkel, H. (1967) *Studies in Ethnomethodology*. Englewood Cliffs, NJ: Prentice-Hall.

Gee, J. (1999) *An Introduction to Discourse Analysis: Theory and Method*. London: Routledge.

Geertz, C. (1973) *The Interpretation of Cultures*. New York: Basic Books.

Geertz, C. (1990) *Work and Lives: The Anthropologist as Author*. Stanford, CA: Stanford University Press.

Gibson, W. (2006) 'Material culture and embodied action: sociological notes on the examination of musical instruments'. *Sociological Review* 54(1): 171–87.

Gibson, W., Campbell, M., Hall, A., Richards, D. and Callery, P. (2005) 'The digital revolution in qualitative research: working with digital audio data through Atlas.ti.', *Sociological Research Online:* 10(1).

Gibson, W., Picton, C., Cantrill, J. and Wilson, P. (2001) 'Assessing the competencies of MPharm graduates', Professional Report: preceedings of the Health Service Research and Competency Practice Conference. Leeds, UK.

Glaser, B. (1978) *Theoretical Sensitivity: Advances in the Methodology of Grounded Theory*. Mill Valley, CA: Sociology Press.

Glaser, B. (1992) *Basics of Qualitative Research: Emergence vx. Forcing*. Mill Valley, CA: Sociology Press.

Glaser, B. and Strauss, A. (1999 [1967]) *The Discovery of Grounded Theory: Strategies for Qualitative Research*. New York: Aldine de Gruyter.

Goffman, E. (1959) *The Presentation of Self in Everyday Life*. Garden City, NY: Doubleday.

Goodwin, C. (2000) 'Action and embodiment within situated human interaction'. *Journal of Pragmatics* 32: 1489–522.

Goodwin, C. (2001) 'Practices of seeing visual analysis: an ethnomethodological approach', in T. van Leeuwen and C. Jewitt (eds), *Handbook of Visual Analysis*. London: Sage.

Goulding, C. (2002) *Grounded Theory: A Practical Guide for Management, Business and Market Researchers*. London: Sage.

Grbich, C. (2007) *Qualitative Data Analysis: An Introduction*. London: Sage.

Guba, E. and Lincoln, Y. (1982) 'Epistemological and methodological bases of naturalistic inquiry'. *Educational Communication and Technology Journal* 30: 233–52.

Gubrium, J. and Holstein, J. (2001) *Handbook of Interview Research: Context and Method*. London: Sage.

Hakim, C. (1983) 'Research based on administrative recards', *Sociological Review* 31(3): 489–551.

Hammersley, M. (2001) 'On "systematic" reviews of research literatures: a "narrative" response to Evans and Benfield'. *British Educational Research Journal* 27: 453–4.

Hammersley, M. and Atkinson, P. (1994) *Ethnography: Principles in Practice*, 2nd edn. London: Routledge.

Hart, C. (1998) *Doing a Literature Review: Releasing the Social Science Research Imagination*. London: Sage.

Hart, E. (1995) *Action Research for Health and Social Care: A Guide to Practice*. Buckingham: Open University Press.

Heath, C. and Hindmarsh, J. (2002) 'Analysing interaction: video, ethnography and situated conduct', in T. May (ed.), *Qualitative Research in Action*. London: Sage.

Heath, C., Hindmarsh, J. and Luff, P. (1999) 'Interaction in isolation: the dislocated world of the London underground train driver'. *Sociology* 33(3): 555–75.

Heaton, J. (2000) *Wittgenstein and Psychoanalysis*. Cambridge: Icon Books.

Henn, M., Weinstein, M. and Foard, N. (2006) *A Short Introduction to Social Research*. London: Sage.

Hester, S. and Eglin, P. (1997) *Culture in Action: Studies in Membership Categorization Analysis*. Washington, DC: University Press of America.

Hitzler, R. (2005) 'The reconstruction of meaning: notes on German interpretive sociology'. *Forum: Qualitative Social Research* 6(3) Art. 45 http://nbn-resolving.de/urn:nbn:de:0114-Fqs 0503450.

Holstein, J. and Gubrium, J. (1995) *The Creative Interview*. London: Sage.

Hughes, E.C. (1993) *The Sociological Eye: Selected Papers*. London: Transaction.

Humphreys, L. (1970) *Tearoom Trade: A Study of Homosexual Encounters in Public Places*. Chicago: Aldine de Gruyter.

Hyland, K. (2005) *Metadiscourse: Exploring Interaction in Writing*. London: Continuum.

Israel, M. and Hay, I. (2006) *Research Ethics for Social Scientists*. London: Sage.

Jefferson, G. (2002) 'Is "no" an acknowledgment token? Comparing American and British uses of (+)/(−) tokens'. *Journal of Pragmatics* 34(10/11): 1345–83.

Jewitt, C. and Oyama, R. (2001) 'Visual meaning: a semiotic approach', in T. van Leeuwen and C. Jewitt (eds), *Handbook of Visual Analysis*. London: Sage.

Jordan, B. and Henderson, A. (1995) 'Interaction analysis: foundations and practice'. *Journal of the Learning Sciences* 4: 39–103.

Katz, J. (1983) 'A theory of qualitative methodology: the social system of analytic fieldwork', in R.E. Emerson (ed.), *Contemporary Field Research: A Collection of Readings*, Boston: Little, Brown & Co.

Kelly, P. (2005) 'Awkward intimacies: prostitution, politics, and fieldwork in urban Mexico', in L. Hume and J. Mulcock (eds), *Anthropologists in the Field: Cases in Participant Observation*. New York: Columbia University Press.

Knoblauch, H. and Luckmann, T. (2004) 'Genre analysis', in U. Flick, E. von Kardorff and I. Steinke (eds), *A Companion to Qualitative Research*. London: Sage.

Kress, G., Jewitt, C., Bourne, J., Franks, A., Hardcastle, J., Jones, K. and Reid, E. (2005) *English in Urban Classrooms: A Multimodal Perspective on Teaching and Learning*. London: Routledge Falmer.

Krippendorf, K. (2003) *Content Analysis: An Introduction to Its Methodology*. London: Sage.

Kurotani, S. (2005) *Home Away from Home: Japanese Corporate Wives in the United States*. Durham, NC: Duke University Press.

Leach, J. (2000) 'Rhetorical analysis', in M. Bauer and G. Gaskell (eds), *Qualitative Researching with Text, Image and Sound: A Practical Handbook*. London: Sage.

LeCompte, M. and Goetz, J.P. (1982) 'Problems of reliability and validity in ethnographic research'. *Review of Educational Research* 52: 31–60.

Lee, R. and Fielding, N. (1996) 'Qualitative data analysis: representations of technology. A comment on Coffey, Holbrook and Atkinson'. *Sociological Research Online* 1.

Lemke, J.L. (2002) 'Travels in hypermodality'. *Visual Communication* 1: 299–325.

Lewins, A. and Silver, C. (2007) *Using Software in Qualitative Data Analysis: A Step-by-Step Guide*. London: Sage.

Lincoln, Y. and Guba, E. (1985) *Naturalistic Inquiry*. London: Sage.

Livingston, E. (2008) 'Context and Detail in studies of the witnessable Social Order', *Journal of Pragmatics* 40: 840–62.

Lloyd Jones, M. (2004) 'Application of systematic review methods to qualitative research: practical issues'. *Journal of Advanced Nursing Studies* 48: 271–8.

Loehr, D. and Harper, L. (2003) 'Commonplace tools for studying commonplace interactions: notes on entry-level video analysis'. *Visual Communication* 2(2): 225–33.

Lonikila, M. (1995) 'Grounded theory as an emerging paradigm for computer-assisted qualitative data analysis', in U. Kelle (ed.), *Computer-Aided Qualitative Data Analysis*. London: Sage.

MacWhinney, B. (1996) 'The CHILDES System'. *American Journal of Speech–Language Pathology* 5: 5–14.

Maiwald, K.O. (2005) 'Competence and praxis: sequential analysis in German sociology'. *Forum: Qualitative Social Research* 6(3). Art 31, http://nbn-resolving.de/urn:nbn:de014fqs 0503310

Marshall, C. and Rossman, G.B. (2006) *Designing Qualitative Research*. London: Sage.

Mavers, D., Somekh, B. and Restorick, J. (2002) 'Interpreting the externalised images of pupils conceptions of ICT: methods for the analysis of concept maps'. *Computers and Education* 38: 187–207.

McCulloch, G. (2004) *Documentary Research in Education, History and the Social Sciences*. London: Routledge Falmer.

McCulloch, G. (2007) *Cyril Norwood and the Ideal of Secondary Education*. Basingstoke: Palgrave Macmillan.

Mead, M. (2001) *Growing Up in New Guinea*. London: HarperCollins.

Meinefeld, W. (2004) 'Hypotheses and prior knowledge in qualitative research', in U. Flick, E. von Kardarff and I. steinke (eds) *A Companion to Qualitative Research*. London: Sage.

Merrett, F. and Wheldall, K. (1986) 'Observing pupils and teachers in classrooms (OPTIC: a behavioural observation schedule for use in schools'. *Educational Psychologist* 6(1): 57–79.

Miles, M. and Huberman, A. (1994) *Qualitative Data Analysis: An Expanded Sourcebook*. Thousand Oaks, CA: Sage.

Mills, C. Wright (1959) *The Sociological Imagination*. Oxford: Oxford University Press.

Mishler, E. (1990) 'Validation in inquiry-guided research: the role of exemplars in narrative research'. *Harvard Educational Review* 60(4): 415–42.

Mishler, E. (1991) *Research Interviewing: Context and Narrative*. Cambridge, MA: Harvard University Press.

Mishler, E. (1999) *Storylines: Craftartists' Narratives of Identity*. Cambridge, MA: Harvard University Press.

Monson, I. (1996) *Saying Something: Jazz Improvisation and Interaction*. Chicago: University of Chicago.

Nässla, H. and Carr, D.A. (2003) 'Investigating Intra-Family communication using photo diaries', Proceedings of HCI International 10th International Conference on Human-Computer Interaction, Crete, Greece. 22–27 June, 2003.

Newbold, C. (1996) 'Narrative analysis for moving image research'. *Leicester University Discussion Papers in Mass Communication*. Leicester: Leicester University.

Norris, S. (2002) 'The implication of visual research for discourse analysis: transcription beyond language'. *Visual Communication* 1(1): 97–121.

Petersen, E.B. (2007) 'A day at the office at the University of Borderville: an ethnographic short story'. *International Journal of Qualitative Studies in Education* 20(2): 173–89.

Pink, S. (2001) *Doing Visual Ethnography: Images, Media and Representations in Research*. London: Sage.

Podolefsky, A. and McCarty, C. (1983) 'Topical sorting: a technique for computer assisted qualitative analysis'. *American Anthropologist* 84: 866–71.

Pollard, A. (1996) *The Social World of Children's Learning: Case Studies of Pupils from Four to Seven*. London: Cassell.

Polsky, N. (1971) *Hustlers, Beats and Others*. Harmondsworth: Penguin.

Popper, K. (1959) *The Logic of Scientific Discovery*. London: Hutchinson.

Reichertz, J. (2004) 'Abduction, deduction and induction in qualitative research', in U. Flick, E. von Kardorff and I. Steinke (eds), *A Companion to Qualitative Research*. London: Sage.

Richards, L. and Richards, T. (1991) 'The transformation of qualitative method: computational paradigms and research processes', in N. Fielding and R.M. Lee (eds), *Using Computers in Qualitative Research*. London: Sage.

Richards, T. and Richards, L. (1995) 'Using computers in qualitative research', in N.K. Denzin and Y.S. Lincoln (eds), *Handbook of Qualitative Research*. London: Sage.

Riessman, C.K. (1993) *Narrative Analysis*. London: Sage.

Ritzer, G. (1990) 'Metatheorizing in sociology'. *Sociological Forum* 5: 3–15.

Robben, A.C.G.M. and Sluka, J.A. (2007) *Ethnographic Fieldwork: An Anthropological Reader*. Oxford: Blackwell.

Roberts, K.A. and Wilson, R.W. (2002) 'ICT and the research process: issues around the compatibility of technology with qualitative data analysis'. *Qualitative Social Research* 3.

Robinson, J. (1998) 'Getting down to business: talk, gaze and body orientation during openings of doctor–patient consultations'. *Human Communication Research* 25(1): 97–123.

Robinson, J. (2001) 'Closing medical encounters: two physician practices and their implications for the expression of patients' unstated concerns'. *Social Science and Medicine* 53: 639–56.

Rumsey, S. (2004) *How To Find Information: A Guide for Researchers*. Maidenhead: Open University Press.

Sacks, H. (1995) *Lectures in Conversation* (vols 1 & 2). London: Blackwell.

Sacks, H., Schegloff, E. and Jefferson, G. (1974) 'A simplest systematic for the organization of turn-taking for conversation'. *Language* 50: 696–735.

Sanjek, R. (1990) *Fieldnotes: Making of Anthropology*. New York: Cornell University Press.

Schegloff, E. (1968) 'Sequencing in conversational openings', *American Anthropologist* 70(6): 1075–1095.

Schegloff, E. (2007) *Sequence Organization in Interaction: A Primer in Conversation Analysis*. Cambridge: Cambridge University Press.

Schegloff, E. and Sacks, H. (1973) 'Opening up closings'. *Semiotica* 8: 289–327.

Scott, D. (1990) *A Matter of Record: Documentary Sources in Social Research*. Cambridge: Polity Press.

Sharrock, W.W. and Anderson, B. (1986) *The Ethnomethodologists*. Andover: Tavistock.

Silverman, D. (1998) *Harvey Sacks: Social Science and Conversation Analysis*. New York: Oxford University Press.

Silverman, D. (2005) *Doing Qualitative Research: A Practical Handbook* (2nd edn). London: Sage.

Sixsmith, J. and Murray, C.D. (2001) 'Ethical issues in the documentary data analysis of internet posts and archives'. *Qualitative Health Research* 11: 423–32.

Snape, D. and Spencer, L. (2003) 'The foundations of qualitative research', in J. Ritchie and J. Lewis (eds), *Qualitative Research Practice: A Guide for Social Science Students and Researchers*. London: Sage.

Sproull, L.S. and Sproull, R.F. (1982) 'Managing and analyzing behavioral records: explorations in nonnumeric data analysis'. *Human Organization* 41(4): 283–90.

Strauss, A. (1987) *Qualitative Analysis for Social Scientists*. Cambridge: Cambridge University Press.

Strauss, A. and Corbin, J. (1990) *Basics of Qualitative Research: Grounded Theory Procedures and Techniques*. London: Sage.

Tannen, D. (2007) *Talking Voices: Repetition, Dialogue, and Imagery in Conversational Discourse*. (2nd edn). Cambridge: Cambridge University Press.

ten Have, P. (1999) *Doing Conversation Analysis: A Practical Guide*. London: Sage.

Tesch, R. (1990) *Qualitative Research: Analysis Types and Software Tools*. London: Falmer.

Thiel, D. (2007) 'Class in construction: London building workers: dirty work and physical cultures'. *The British Journal of Sociology* 58: 227–51.

Thody, A. (2006) *Writing and Presenting Research*. London: Sage.

Tizard, B. and Hughes, M. (1984) *Young Children Learning: Talking and Thinking at Home and at School*. London: Fontana Press.

Tomal, D.R. (1993) *Action Research for Educators*. Oxford: Scarecrow Press.

van Leeuwen, T. (2005) *Introducing Social Semiotics*. London: Routledge.

van Leeuwen, T. and Jewitt, C. (2001) *Handbook of Visual Analysis*. London: Sage.

van Manen, M. (1998) *Researching Lived Experience: Human Science for an Action Sensitive Pedagogy* (2nd edn). Ontario: The Althouse Press.

Van Maanen, J. (1983) 'The moral fix: on the ethics of fieldwork', in R.E. Emerson (ed.), *Contemporary Field Research: A Collection of Readings*. Boston: Little, Brown & Co.

Venuti, L. (2000) *The Translation Studies Reader*. London: Routledge.

Vigouroux, C.B. (2007) 'Transcription as a social activity: an ethnographic approach'. *Ethnography* 8(1): 61–97.

Walker, T.C. (2007) 'Leading primary schools through and beyond special measures: a study of headteachers leading cultural transformation within primary schools', unpublished EdD thesis, Institute of Education, University of London.

Walkerdine, V. and Lucey, H. (1989) *Democracy in the Kitchen*. London: Virago.

Wang, C.C. and Burris, M.A. (1994) 'Empowerment through photovoice: portraits of participation'. *Health Education Quarterly* 21: 171–86.

Wang, C.C. and Burris, M.A. (1997) 'Photovoice: concept, methodology and use for participatory needs assessment'. *Health Education and Behaviour* 24: 369–87.

Wang, C.C., Burris, M.A. and Xiang, Y. (1996) 'Chinese village women as visual anthropologists: a participatory approach to reaching policymaking'. *Social Science and Medicine* 42: 1391–400.

Weber, R.P. (1985) *Basic Content Analysis*. Beverly Hills, CA: Sage.

Weider, L. (1983) 'Telling the convict code', in R.E. Emerson (ed.), *Contemporary Field Research: A Collection of Readings*. Boston: Little, Brown & Co.

Weiner, J. (1995) *The Lost Drum: The Myth of Sexuality in Papua New Guinea and Beyond*. Madison, WI: University of Wisconsin Press.

Weitzman, E. and Miles, M. (1995) *A Software Source Book: Computer Programs for Qualitative Data Analysis*. London: Sage.

Whiteman, N. (2007) 'The establishment, maintenance and destabilisation of fandom: a study of two online communities and an exploration of issues pertaining to internet research', unpublished PhD thesis, Institute of Education, University of London.

Whyte, W.F. (1955) *Street Corner Society: The Social Structure of an Italian Slum*. Chicago: University of Chicago Press.

Wittgenstein, L. (1961) *Philosophical Investigations: The English Text of the Third Edition*. Englewood Cliffs, New Jersey: Prentice Hall.

Wolcott, H. (1994) *Transforming Qualitative Data: Descriptions, Analysis and Interpretation*. London: Sage.

Yin, R.K. (2003) *Case Study Research: Design and Methods*. Thousand Oaks, CA: Sage.

Index

Note: page numbers in *italics* refer to tables.

A level choice study 34
academic theses 202–3
action research *49*
analysis
    contextual character of 6–7, 11, 32, 205–6, 208
    described and defined 2–6
    iterative nature of 25
    observation as 106–7
    and relationship with theory 11–13,
        31–2, 208–9
analysis sheets 95–6
analytically filtered/focused methods 66, 77
anonymity 61–2, 161–2
apriori codes 130, 132–3
Atlas.ti software 177, 178, 179, 188, 190
audio and video techniques 160–75
    advantages and disadvantages 160–2
    data analysis 162–3, 210
        gesture and contextualization 170–3
        practicalities 173–5
        see also conversation analysis
    diaries 78
    hyperlinking data types 185
    recording technology 122–3, *124*, 174
    transcription 114, 161–2, 173
authorship
    internet postings 79
    written documents 71–2
automated coding 189

Barthes, R. 146–7
Becker, H. 19–20, 130
Berliner, P. 37–8
bibliographic databases 44–6
blogs 79, 80, 183, 186
boosters 153–4
bottom-up theory 15, 16, 26–7
brainstorming 68
broad transcription 114
brothel study 102
Brown, A. 68–9, 70
Bush, George W. 154
business-at-hand 169

CAQDAS 123, 176–90, 210
    automated coding 189–90
    code and retrieve functions 178–80
    collaborative analysis 181–3
    concerns and debate about 187–90
    hypermedia/hyperlinking 184–7
    theory building functions 180–1
    websites/online resources 190–1
case studies *49*, 197

categorization 11
    of data 4
    and grounded theory 27, 28–9
    of methods 54–5
cause and causality 140–1
CHAT software 178
chat-room 79, *94*
CHILDES system 120
CLAN software 178
Cleaves, A. 34
codes and coding 4, 130–43
    apriori and empirical codes 130, 132–3
    creating codes
        code definitions 135–6
        code logs 137
        code properties 137
        deleting/discontinuing codes 137
        reasons for 133–5
        splitting and merging codes 136
    and grounded theory 27
    relational analysis
        code families 138–9
        hypotheses 139–42
        sub-codes and parent codes 142
        supercodes 143
    and structured interviews 87
    see also CAQDAS
collaborative analysis 173, 181–3
colloquialisms 117
commonality 128, 130
comparative coding 178–9
computer assisted analysis *see* CAQDAS
concepts
    combining in literature searches 43–4
    concept mapping 186
    defined 17–19
    developing from keywords 50–1
    development through literature 35–6
    formulating as questions 51–3
    and grounded theory 27
    structuring analysis around 196–7
conferences 200–1
confidentiality 61–3, 161–2
connotations 147–50
consistency 182
constant comparative method 27, 28
content analysis 179
context
    and interviewing 97–8
    and meaning of images 150–1
    removal of in CAQDAS 188–9
    of talk/conversation 171–2
    and thematic analysis 129–30

contextualized analysis 6–7, 11, 32, 205–6, 208
contradictions 141–2
conversation analysis 7, 151, 163–75
    context of talk 171–2
    and ethnomethodology 163–5
    exemplar of 165–7, 178–9
        topics/conversational issues 168–9
        turns and preferences 167–8
    key concepts 169–70
    phases in 169
    practicalities 173–5
Corbin, J. 26, 28, 29–30, 35
costs 58
covert observation 104
craftworker study 99
credibility 182
critical discourse analysis 21–4, 157–8, 162, 208
critical incident analysis 7
cross case analysis 7
cultural context 150–1
cultural memory/assumptions 156

Darwin, C. 154
data
    choosing relevant 54–5
    contradictions and inconsistencies 141–2
    data saturation 27
    fieldnotes 104–6
    and hyperlinking 185, 186–7
    observation as analysis 106–7
    plans/strategy for collecting 31, 55–8, 63–4
    primary and secondary sources 66–7, 76
    role of transcription 110–11
    storage and protection 62–3
    validation of 28, 38, 58–60, 70, 182
    see also documents
data analysis see analysis
databases 44–5
deduction 27, 28
denotations 147–8
Desmond, M. 198
diaries 66, 69
    advantages and limitations 78–9
    research 195
    structured and unstructured 76–8
digital diskette/recorder 123, 124
discourse analysis 7, 98, 178
  presentation/write up 198–9
discourse marker 166
doctor–patient study 119
documents and documentary research
    analytically focused/filtered methods 65–83
    categories/classification of documents 72–3
    combining other sources with 69–70
    forms of data 74
        diaries 76–9
        digital/electronic/ online 74
        newspapers 74–6
        photographs and images 66, 78, 81–3
    interrogating and examining documents 70–2, 112
    primary and secondary data 66–7
    sources of documents 67–9
Dressler, R. 120–1

email 74, 79–80
    and interviews 94, 95
empirical codes 130, 132–3, 137
Endnote software 44
ERIC database 42
ethics 60–1
    anonymity and data protection 61–3, 161–2
    and building trust 69
    covert studies 104
    email and online communication 80
    and hyperlinking of data 187
ethnography 19, 37–8
    defining characteristics 49
    and photographs 81–2
    presentation/write up 198
    and reliability 182
    social anthropology 103
ethnomethodology 151, 158
    and conversation analysis 163–5
ethos 153–4
exigence 152–3
exploratory reviews 38, 39–41

Fairclough, N. 21–2
falsification 140
fans (internet) study 79–80
fieldnotes 104–6
    thematic organization/coding 131–2
financial constraints 58
firefighters study 198
focus groups 54, 58, 98

Garfinkel, H. 163–4
gender equality study 22–4
genre 155–6
gesture 171–3
Gibson, W. 37–8, 97, 141, 180–1
Glaser, B. 26–7, 28, 29–30, 139, 188
grand theory 16
grounded theory 7, 12–13, 26–7, 137
    and CAQDAS software 179–80, 187–8
    criticism of 29–30
    key features 27–9
Guba, E. 59

Hyland, K. 153–4
hedges 153–4
historical research 70–1
homosexual activity study 104
Humphreys, L. 104
hyperlinking/hypermedia 184–5
    alternative narrative routes 186
    data and ideas linking/sharing 185–7
    write-up and presentation 186
HyperRESEARCH software 177, 188, 190
hypotheses 28, 139–40
    cause and causality 140–1
    contradictions and inconsistencies 141–2
    and grounded theory 27

images, analysis of see semiotic analysis
inconsistencies 141–2
induction 27, 28

internal reliability 182
internet 74
    ethical issues 80
    resources 177, 190–1
    social networks 79–80, *94*, 163, 183, 184, 186
interviews and interviewing 54, 69, 86–100
    analysis sheets 95–6
    contextualizing issues for participants 97–8
    defined types
        semi-structured 86–7, 88–9
        structured 86, 87–8
        unstructured 87, 89–90
    diversity of the data set 92–3
    examples of practice 90–2, 93, 95
    interview setting 97
    modes of interview 93–5
    narrative analysis 98–100
    reflexive questions about 89, *91*
ISI Web of Science 42
Italian community study 103

jazz improvisation study 37–8, 40, 57, 105–6, 138
journal articles 201

Kelly, P. 103
keywords 45
    in design concepts 51–3
Kruez, R. 120–1

language, use of 21–2
letters 79–80
Lincoln, Y. 59
linear/non-linear research models 9–11
literature reviews and searches 31, 33–46, 206
    bibliographic databases 44–6
    reviewing 38
        exploratory and systematic 38–41
        focused 38–42
    search tools/sources 42–3
        strategies 43–4
    uses of literature 33–6
        alternative analyses 37
        concept development 35–6
        directing theoretical sampling 37–8
        as secondary sources of data 37
        validating theory 38
logos 155

McCulloch, G. 79
Maiwald, K. 169
Manus tribe 20–1, 101
MAXQDA software 177, 190
Mead, M. 20–1, 101
memos 27, 178, 186
metadata 15
metatag 45
metatheory 16
Mills, C. W. 16
mindmapping 186
mini-disks 123, *124*
Mishler, E. 99
multimodal analysis 151
myths 146–7

narrative analysis 98–100, 127–8, 158
    and fictional storytelling 198
narrow transcription 114
naturalism 8
newspapers 74–5, 153, 156
    limitations 75–6
Norwood, Sir Cyril 79
NUD*IST software 188
NVivo software 177, 179, 188, 190

observational research 54, 100–7
    analysis and recording 104–7
    covert studies 104
    participant and non-participant 102–3
    structured and unstructured 100–2
ophthalmology study 178–9

Papua New Guinea study 20–1, 101
parental participation study 68–9, 70
participatory research 102–3
pathos 154–5
Peterson, E. B. 198
pharmacy practice study 97, 141, 180–1, 189
photographs 66, 78, 81–3
    transcription 112, *113*, 114
Photovoice project 82
Piaget, J. 20–1
Pierce, C. 146–7
pilot study 55
Pledger's Group 22–4
polar opposition 141
Popper, K. 140
preliminary matter 168
preliminary research design 49–50
presentations 192–204, 210
    academic theses 202–3
    conferences 200–1
    and hyperlinking 186
    journal articles 201
    key features of presentation 199–200
        discourse analysis 198–9
        ethnographic analysis 198
        thematic analysis 196–8
    professional reports 201–2
    research diaries 195
    useful rules of thumb 203–4
primary data 66–7, 76
professional reports 201–2
pseudonyms 61
punctuation 117–18
purposive sampling 56

qualitative *vs* quantitative research 7–9
Qualrus software 188, 190
questionnaires 54
questions
    for interrogating observations 102
    and interviews *see* interviews
    see also research questions

re-presentation 110, 111
record sheets 72
recording technology 122–3, *124*, 174–5

reflexivity 8
RefMan database 44
relational analysis 138–43
reliability 182
representativity 57
research
    iterative nature of 25
    linear and non-linear processes 9–11
    quantitative *vs* qualitative 7–9
research design 31, 47–64, 207
    data choice and collection 54–8
        triangulation 58–60
    developing a plan 50–4
    ethics 60–4
    key specifications and strategies *49*, 63–4
    versus design process 47–8
research methods, choice of 55–6
research models 9–11
research questions 206
    as focus for research design 53–4
    formulating 31, 51–3
    organizing analysis around 197–8
response token 169
reviews *see* literature
rhetorical analysis 7, 163
    alternative approaches to 157–8
    key concepts 151–7
Ritzer, G. 15, 16

Sacks, H. 164–5, 167, 169, 170
sampling 56–8
    and thematic analysis 129–30
    theoretical 27, 37–8, 56
sampling frame 56
saturation
    data 27
    theory 29
Saussure, Ferdinand de 146–7
Scott, J. 73
searching literature *see under* literature
secondary data 37, 66–7, 76
semiotic analysis 7, 145–7, 162, 163, 210
    alternative analytic approaches 157–8
    key concepts 147–50
    meaning related to context 150–1
    of texts *see* rhetorical analysis
signs/signifying systems 146–7
social networking 79–80, *84*, 163,
        183, 184, 186
Sociological Abstracts 42
software 123, 128, 176–7, 183, 210
    see also CAQDAS
Strauss, A. 26–7, 28, 29–30, 35, 139, 188
subject disciplines 16–17
super code 143
survey *49*
symbol systems 120–2
systematic reviews 38–9

tape recording 122, *124*
teacher evaluation study 115, 165–8
textual analysis *see* rhetorical analysis

thematic analysis 4, 7, 158, 162
    codes *see* codes and coding
    described and critiqued 127–30
    key features *131*
    presentations/write-up 196–8
theoretical sampling 27, 56
    directed by literature 37–8
theory
    bottom-up 15, 16, 26–7
    common areas of concern about 12–13
    concepts defined and described 17–19
    contextual character of 11, 32, 208–9
    general terms and definitions 15–17
    generalized good practice 30–2
    and methodological framework 25
    relationship with analysis 11–13, 19–20
    selecting a theoretical perspective 36
    theory saturation 29
    theory-building software 180–1
    top-down 15, 20–5
theses 202–3
thick descriptions 8, 57, 81
timeline transcription 114–16
timescales 58
top-down theory 15, 20–5
topical sequence 166
transcription 100, 109–25, 210
    aims and role of 110–11
    audio and video data 169–70, 173
    conventions and symbol systems 120–2
    and epistemology 123–5
    forms of
        focused 113–14, 119, 120–2
        indexical/timeline 113–14, 114–16
        unfocused 113–14, 116–18, 119
    and gesture 172–3
    misrepresentation of data 118–20
    recording technology 122–3
triangulation 27–8, 58–60, 70
tricks, theory as 19–20
truncation symbols 43
trust, building 69

validation of data 28, 38, 58–60, 70, 182
Van Maanen, J. 62–3
variation theory 16
video data *see* audio and video
visual mapping 186

Walker, T. 197
web and web pages *see* internet
Whiteman, N. 79–80
Whyte, W. F. 103
wikis 79, 80, 163, 183, 184, 186
Wittgenstein, L. 18
Wolcott, H. 5–6, 7
working research design 50
writing-up 29, 192–4, 210
    collaborative writing 195–6
    and hyperlinking 186
    see also presentations
written texts, analysis of *see* rhetorical analysis